THE DRUMS OF TONKIN

To Bevery,
with Love

By *Helen and Frank Schreider*

THE DRUMS OF TONKIN
20,000 MILES SOUTH

Betty Lou

This is my country!
Given by God and
ruled by Satan!!

Helen and Frank Schreider

THE DRUMS OF TONKIN

An Adventure in Indonesia   DRAWINGS BY

HELEN SCHREIDER   PHOTOGRAPHS BY FRANK SCHREIDER

Coward-McCann, Inc.   New York

Photographs follow pages 96 and 224

We wish to thank the National Geographic Society and in particular Dr. Melville B. Grosvenor, President and Editor of National Geographic, for so generously allowing us to use some of the material and colored plates which appeared earlier in the Magazine. We wish to emphasize, however, that the opinions expressed in this book are our own and in no way reflect the opinions or policy of the Society or the Magazine.

TO DINAH. . . . a companion without peer
> whether traveling by Jeep or elephant back,
>> by dog team or dugout,
>> by bush plane or jet,
>> by freighter or luxury liner,
> whether in maharajas' palaces or chieftains' huts,
>> as ambassadors' guests or on a tiger hunt,
>> in the wastes of Patagonia or the temple of Borobudur,
>> with a hatcheck girl at Luchow's or at a literary tea,
>> in an Alaskan trapper's cabin or a Florinese convent,
>> among Inca ruins or in the gardens of Versailles.
> a companion whose vigilance when we camped in wild
>> lands gave us many a peaceful night's sleep,
> whose unfailing good humor made many friends for us
>> during her fourteen years of travel in twenty-eight
>> countries,
> whose enthusiasm for seeing new places never waned
>> right up to the last great journey into death.
> May she be reincarnated as the dog of someone
>> who will love her as much as we do.

IT seems that every book about a journey through remote areas begins with some such statement: "We would like to express our grateful appreciation to the following persons without whose help this expedition could not have been made." This book is no exception and while we hesitate to apply so lofty a term as "expedition" to our little foursome—two people, a dog and an amphibious Jeep—we feel that we may have set some kind of a record in the number of people to whom we owe thanks.

From the moment we arrived in Djakarta and found that, despite our reservations, there was no hotel space, to those last days on Sumatra when we were crating our equipment for the ship home, we were beholden to someone. Even when we were the sole inhabitants of an island a thousand miles from anywhere we were reminded that the charts we navigated by and the gasoline we poured into Tortuga's tanks were made available to us through the efficiency or extra effort of someone who wished us well, for it is a common expression that "Nothing is easy in Indonesia" and the logistics of getting about—or merely vegetating for that matter—are formidable.

Most of the people who were kind to us—and a few who were not so kind—are mentioned in the story. There are some, however, along with others who are not mentioned, to whom we would like to express our special thanks and affection:

Bob and Thalia Brougham, who dug up the Hydrographic Charts and Sailing Directions without which we could not have found our way to Timor and whose spare room in Djakarta was the nest in which part of this book was hatched.

Jean and Jim Burrill, who gave heart and hearth room to Dinah during the weeks we had to leave her in Palembang.

Dr. and Mrs. John Churchward of P and T Lands on Java, who introduced us to life on a tea estate.

Colonel Ray Cole, who shared his home with us and without whose help we might still be in Djakarta.

Dr. Franz Dumoulin, for thirty years a doctor in Indonesia, and Hetty, who shared those years with all their joys during Dutch administration, their sufferings during Japanese internment, and their uncertainties during independence. Since our first meeting with the Dumoulins in Sumatra their friendship has been a constant inspiration, for nothing has dimmed their love of Indonesia and to them we owe much of our own sympathetic attitude toward the Indonesian people.

Tom and Mary Hague, whose art-filled home in Djakarta

was often a haven and whose interest in old Batavia led us down many an obscure and fascinating alley that we might otherwise have missed.

Dr. L. Hoorweg of Jogjakarta, whose understanding helped as much as his medication.

Consul Jack Lydman and Jody, who introduced us to the joys of jade and Chinese porcelain and who countered our hectic life in Tortuga with the pleasures of an elegant, ordered existence.

Bill Palmer, impeccable host in his mountain retreat where the cocktails were deadly, the steaks celestial, the movies uncensored and the guest list a Who's Who in Indonesia.

Harry and Jerry Showman, perennial befrienders of all roofless visitors to Jogjakarta and even of those whose roof is relative. After rescuing us from the abominable Hotel Garuda they moved us into their hearts as well as their guest room.

Rev. and Mrs. Shekatz and their associates on Nias, who sheltered us for almost a week.

Allen and Jenny Steffen, whose home in south Sumatra was port of call, headquarters and information center for our quests for wild game in the nearby jungles.

Dr. Van der Muellen of the Netherlands, author, scholar, and former Colonial Officer, who willingly shared with us his knowledge of Indonesia.

Dick and Norma Wexler, companions on Bali and intermediators in the battle to save Dinah from execution, thoughtful friends who foresaw that a few delicacies would brighten our Thanksgiving on a distant island.

There are others we can thank only in groups:

All the Indonesian officials who did what they could to help us.

The staff of the American Embassy and Consulates.

The personnel of Goodyear Tire and Rubber Company, both Java and Sumatra.

Standard Vacuum Oil Company to whom we are grateful for air transport to inaccessible oil fields and for their many personal favors.

There is another group, the Society of the Divine Word, that has a lasting place in our hearts for the havens of quiet they offered from Flores to Timor.

Thanks too to the Explorers Club of New York for permission to carry Flag Number 176.

And to the Director and staff of the Royal Tropical Institute in Amsterdam for their inestimable help while we were researching our material.

And finally, a special bouquet to Darlene Armstrong, our sister, whose skill as cryptographer and typist is excelled only by her patience with our last-minute changes.

HELEN AND FRANK SCHREIDER

Nairobi, Kenya
May, 1963

Prologue

THE long hall was a cool, air-conditioned passage to the new wing of the hotel, and the light that filtered through the pseudo-Arabic grilled windows lent a temple-like quality to the white walls. There was a peace, a stillness, a feeling of security to the place. And yet, suddenly, we felt that old chill strike through us again. As though controlled by a single reflex we both froze in fright and stared at the square opening in the wall at the end of the hall. We saw the black muzzle of a machine gun pointing at us.

We could not have stood there more than five seconds. I knew it couldn't have been more than five seconds because our room was just beyond the ell in the hall and the boy with our bags had just turned the corner when we saw the gun and it was the sound of the key turning in the lock that triggered the rage that boiled up inside me all over again. It wasn't a key turning in a lock that I heard. It was the sound of a Sten gun being cocked, and the thump of our bags on the floor was the dull thump of a rifle butt striking Helen's soft flesh. I saw again the face of the amok soldier and felt the Sten gun rammed into my stomach and the paralysis I felt there in the hall of the hotel in Singapore was as consuming as it had been in Java when I'd first heard the click and first felt the hard round muzzle of the gun. But anger is its own destroyer. It faded and I realized that we were no longer in Indonesia, that we no longer had to live with guns and fear, that we were no longer traveling in a country where police shoot at traffic violators, where men are killed for driving too fast past a military post, where only uncertainty is certain. I nudged Helen and we headed for our room. Like a small boy breaking a snatching branch that had frightened him in the dark I shoved the nozzle of the fire hose farther back into its niche in the wall and a drop of pale rusty water splattered to the floor.

Later, we sat on the terrace near the swimming pool, and the starched-white Malayan waiter smiled as he placed our drinks on the table, but I saw the face of the soldier again. How long, I wondered, would that fungus of fear live within us, ready to crop out at the most innocent sound or half-seen vision caught from the corner of an eye? How long would it blur all the other images, hazing the memories of a beautiful land, of a friendly and gracious people, of an adventure that had never before been attempted nor was likely to be again?

The air was that heavy air of the equatorial tropics. The glasses were beaded with little jewels of moisture like the leaves at morning in the mountains of Sumatra—or the salt-sprayed windshield of Tortuga on some unnamed, uninhabited island somewhere east of Bali. We had been almost a thousand miles from guns and revolution but we had known fear then too—a fifteen-foot amphibious Jeep plunging and wallowing through monsoon seas was not the safest way to travel. We had been as cut off from the world as the first migrants from Tonkin had been thousands of years before as they pioneered our route through the Lesser Sundas. But as I looked back on those five months of island-hopping, reef-scraping and shark-dodging, the primitive peoples we had lived with, the jungles we had cut through and the trails we had bounced over, it seemed that those months had been the most peaceful of our more than a year in Indonesia. In retrospect the headhunters out on Alor seemed less dangerous than some of the soldiers in Djakarta, Indonesia's capital. If only we could have bypassed Djakarta. If only we could have found from the start the Indonesia of the old Dutchman we had met in Callao.

How long ago that seemed, five years it was. At the time we were nearing the end of a journey by amphibious Jeep over the Pan American Highway. It was such a casual meeting; I can't even remember the old Dutchman's name, and intent on reaching Tierra del Fuego, the things he told us we soon forgot. But later we remembered our meeting with the old Dutchman.

It was at a little outdoor café near the water in Callao. It was August, winter in Peru; the sky was a dull slate and I remember that the sea gulls were like snowflakes in the air. All the tables were full and the old Dutchman asked us to join him. He asked about Tortuga, our amphibious Jeep, and we told him how she had carried us through storms and reefs in the Caribbean, the jungles of Mexico and the surf off Costa Rica to bridge the gaps in the Pan American Highway. A distant look came to his eyes.

"I would have given anything to have had a vehicle like yours when I was in the Indies," he said.

That started it and for the rest of the afternoon we sipped Pisco Sours and listened while he talked of his life in the Indies. I remember that it was always the Indies he spoke of, never Indonesia.

Before the war he had been a planter on Java. "Not a large planter, mind you, just a small one. A few hectares of tea, that's all." During off seasons he used to travel, and once he went to the Spice Islands. "You know," he said, "it was a shorter route to the Spice Islands that Columbus was looking for when he discovered your part of the world." He told us of the Dragon Lizards of Komodo and the colored lakes of Flores. On Sumatra he saw elephant and tiger and rhinoceros tramping unhindered through rich groves of pepper, and Lubu tribesmen who lived in trees and hunted with blowpipes within miles of modern oil installations. He knew the head-hunters of Borneo where longhouses were decorated with polished and yellowed skulls. He wandered through the terraces of the great Borobudur and watched the life of Buddha unfold before him in stone relief. On the green cool nights, with the rice fields silver in the moonlight, he used to sit under a banyan tree on Java and listen to the music of the gamelan or watch a shadow play. "And Bali," he sighed, "Bali is another world." He had gotten out of Java when the Japanese occupied the Indies in 1942 and he knew he would never return. "Just a few hectares of tea," he said again, "that's all. But it was all I ever needed or wanted. That was paradise on earth." And I remember that he looked down at his drink to hide the tears in his eyes.

At the time we had no idea that that meeting would launch us on a journey along a three-thousand-mile chain of islands, through seas that Magellan, Drake and Bligh had known. It

was only when our Pan-American venture was over and we
were back home in California and felt the emptiness that follows the realization of any long-anticipated journey that we
remembered the old Dutchman. Full of confidence in Tortuga that had carried us from island to island in the Caribbean
and across South America's Strait of Magellan, we saw in
Indonesia with her thousands of islands and hundreds of straits
a challenge at least equal to the Pan American Highway. We
converted another World War II surplus amphibious Jeep
into Tortuga II, a rolling, floating home, a redesigned and
improved model of the one that had carried us on our Pan-
American adventure. With the backing of *National Geographic* we gathered our equipment and booked passage to
Asia.

The Indonesia we found when we arrived was not the Indonesia of the old Dutchman. The country was in a state of
war and emergency. The Indonesians were blaming the
Dutch; the Dutch were blaming the Indonesians; the few foreign companies still operating in Indonesia blamed corruption
in the government, and the Indonesians claimed they were
being exploited. The country was on the verge of bankruptcy
—though before the war she had exported important per-
centages of the world's rubber, tin, petroleum, pepper,
cloves, nutmeg, quinine, coffee, tea, palm oil and copra. Whole
sections of the country were terrorized by bandits, and villages barricaded themselves behind bamboo enclosures.
Learned historians, economists and political scientists are still
devoting volumes to the reasons behind this situation, and we
are content to leave this subject in their capable hands. We
were looking for something else. We were sure that beneath
the debris of hate and economic chaos left by Indonesia's revolution against the Netherlands something still remained of
that other Indonesia, the Indies of the old Dutchman, the In-

donesia of laughter and music, of dancing, painting and sculpture, the Indonesia whose cultural heritage, both indigenous and imported, at one time made it the greatest country in Southeast Asia. This book is the result of that search.

But today, when the free world is vying with Russia for Indonesia's allegiance and potentially vast natural resources, when President Sukarno has made his country, as the largest Moslem nation, an important voice in the Afro-Asian bloc that represents over half the world's population and over half the votes in the United Nations, when Indonesia is a strategic stepping-stone between Asia and Australia, when nearly everywhere in Indonesia one is forced to live with conflict, we wanted to have at least a hint of what lay behind the tension and the shambles.

The Republic of Indonesia is a lacework of over 3,000 islands stretching along the equator from west to east for more than 3,000 miles, from north to south for some 1,300 miles, an area larger than the United States. It is a phantasmagoria of a dozen different ethnic groups ranging in culture from the megalithic to the jet age. Its 90,000,000 people speak more than 200 different dialects, many of which are in no way related to the national language of Bahasa Indonesia.

It is a nation in name only, held together by the fanatical nationalism of President Sukarno, by its national motto UNITY IN DIVERSITY, and by its national philosophy, Sukarno's own *Pantjasila* embodying the five principles: belief in God; nationalism; humanism; democracy; social justice.

Backed by his army, navy and air force, President Sukarno has kept his nation together, by force when necessary, since its Proclamation of Independence on August 17, 1945, two days after Japan's surrender ended World War II. Under Dutch rule for 350 years, under Japanese rule all during the war, Indonesia would accept nothing short of full independence. The

Netherlands had promised Indonesia independence, but not until the country had been properly prepared to handle its own affairs. This was too nebulous for the Indonesians. They resisted reoccupation by the Netherlands. Months of brutal, terrible fighting, with atrocities by both sides, followed until in March of 1947 the Linggajati Agreement was signed. By this agreement the United States of Indonesia was formed with the new Republic of Indonesia in control of Java and Sumatra, and the Netherlands in control of Borneo, Celebes, the Spice Islands and the Lesser Sunda Islands. But the Indonesians repeatedly trespassed the line of demarcation, harassing and sniping at the Dutch troops until, according to Dutch claims, there were more casualties after the cease-fire than during the fighting. For a few months the Dutch troops, under General Spoor, were restrained from fighting back. Then, with little or no preliminary negotiations, they launched an all-out military campaign aimed at crushing the Republic. The United Nations stepped in and in January of 1948 the Renville Agreement was signed whereby the Republic, under pressure by the United Nations, agreed that the Dutch might retain control over the territory they had just recaptured provided that a plebiscite be held within one year to determine whether the people in these areas wished to be part of the Dutch- or the Indonesian-controlled states. But the Indonesians again violated the lines and the Dutch established an effective blockade of the Indonesian-held territories. In December of 1948, shortly before the deadline for the plebiscite, the Dutch again launched a military offensive in which Sukarno and other nationalist leaders were taken prisoner. In the months that followed, world opinion swung to the side of the Indonesians who, though poorly equipped and deprived of food, medical supplies and textiles by the Dutch blockade, were putting up a gallant stand, often in the face of starvation. The United Nations, and particularly the United States, applied pressure to the Netherlands, and in August of 1949 a cease-fire was arranged. At the so-called Round Table Conference in The Hague in December of that year, the Dutch relinquished all claim to their former territory except for New Guinea, transfer of this area to be decided by further negotiations within one year. Indonesia agreed to take over a debt to the Netherlands amounting to $1,130,000,000. Shortly after August 17, 1950, the fifth anniversary of her Declaration of Independence, Indonesia became the sixtieth member of the United Nations.

But the new republic's problems were just beginning. Java assumed an overlordship of the outer islands; rebellious groups resented Java's own brand of colonialism. The Darul Islam, a group of politico-religious dissidents that demands an Islamic state with Koranic law, has terrorized whole sections of the country, burning, looting, murdering and torturing, robbing trains and buses, using every means to undermine the government. Insurrections and banditry have kept the country in a state of chaos right up to the present.

Through all this the cry of *merdeka*, freedom, the battle cry of the revolution, was still heard, but the people, intoxicated by their hard-won independence, took freedom to mean freedom from responsibility: the workday was shortened; all holidays, both Christian and Moslem—though Christians represent less than five percent of the population—were recognized. Production dropped and prices soared.

Squatters moved onto the export-crop estates and uprooted rubber and palm oil trees that had taken decades to grow. The government, claiming that the lands were needed for food crops, upheld the intruders, and the estate crop production, the country's principal source of revenue, fell even more.

The condition was aggravated still more when the Dutch, angered by Indonesia's failure to make payments on her debt to the Netherlands, kept procrastinating on negotiations for the transfer to Indonesia of disputed New Guinea as agreed at the Round Table Conference. In support of their delay the Dutch claimed that New Guinea was ethnically different from the rest of the islands, that they wished to retain it as a refuge for some 200,000 Eurasians who did not wish to remain in an independent Indonesia nor go to Holland, that they were preparing New Guinea for independence, or that they just did not wish to give up their last colony in Asia. The Indonesians, who were looking for an excuse, claimed that since New Guinea was a part of the Netherlands East Indies and as such was now a part of Indonesia, retaliated by repudiating the debt to the Netherlands, nationalized Dutch enterprises without indemnification and forced the repatriation of some 90,000 Dutch nationals—leaving the country with virtually no doctors, teachers, engineers, technicians or trained personnel of any kind.

And to climax Indonesia's troubles, army colonels in Sumatra, complaining that Java was siphoning off all their island's wealth, opened a full-scale civil war that further disrupted the nation's economy and security.

This then—ruinous inflation, banditry, civil war, martial law—was the state of affairs when we arrived in Indonesia. President Sukarno had just returned from another of his aid-raising and goodwill tours of the world—which he seems to take whenever the pressure in the political boiler threatens to pop the last rivets of stability—and his new cabinet, hand-picked for its willingness to comply with his wishes, had just ratified the reinstatement of the 1945 constitution, in force during the revolution, with its principle of "guided democracy," a euphemism for strict government control of every aspect of Indonesia's life and economy. Freedom of press, radio, speech, assembly and movement was curtailed. An air of xenophobia pervaded the government; foreigners could not leave Djakarta without special clearance and journalists were under special surveillance.

This was not the Indonesia we had come to see, but it is the political and economic climate in which we traveled for thirteen months. The Indonesia we had come to see was that of the old Dutchman in Callao.

"Paradise on earth." That's a potent lure.

Chapter One

IF Helen has one characteristic that can be said to have most often gotten us into trouble, I think it would be her idea of justice, or perhaps I should say her reaction to what she considers an injustice. Similarly, according to her, I have a trait which has been just as responsible for getting us into awkward and sometimes dangerous situations: "an optimism that borders on folly." Keeping this optimism within reasonable limits is a cross she bears cheerfully, which is what she was doing one morning as our ship, the S. S. *Drente*, approached the island of Java and Tandjung Priok, the port for Djakarta, Indonesia's capital. It was Sunday and Helen, never eager to face customs officials—whom she considers particularly unjust, especially on Sunday—was in favor of postponing the ordeal until Monday.

"I'll be very surprised if we clear customs today," she said. "You remember how long it took in India."

I was quite content to forget those three weeks of frustration in Calcutta as we tried to clear three hundred rolls of film, six cameras, a dog and an amphibious Jeep through Indian customs. And I was eager to start seeing Indonesia, even if it was only from the port to downtown Djakarta. I said I was sure that this time it would be different, but Helen just smiled in that way of hers that needs no words.

"But look," I argued, waving the telegram from our friend Sumarjo who was Spokesman for the Indonesian Ministry of Foreign Affairs, "it says right here that everything has been arranged."

Helen just smiled.

Sumarjo had been our introduction to the quiet easygoing charm of the Indonesian people. We had met in Washington, D.C., where he was Press Attaché at the Indonesian Embassy and we were free-lance writers with an assignment from *National Geographic* Magazine and a yen to island-hop the Indonesian Archipelago. But then the flare-up of the Indonesian-Dutch crisis over New Guinea brought on the nationalization of Dutch enterprises and the repatriation of Dutch nationals. The civil war in Sumatra broke out, and we went to India instead. We had almost finished our assignment there when the telegram from Sumarjo confirmed our hopes that we might now travel in his country.

It had been a fast trip from Calcutta to Djakarta, seven days with no ports of call. We had hoped for a more leisurely voyage with time to continue our study of Bahasa Indonesia, the new national language, a sophisticated form of Malay, for centuries the *lingua franca* of the coastal regions of Southeast Asia. Instead we spent the days servicing Tortuga, which, as she was both slow and amphibious, we had named for the Spanish word for turtle.

Helen and I went on deck as the *Drente* entered the break-water. The water was an oil-green, in the still air smooth as syrup. Near shore a wreck, a casualty of World War II, lay bottom up; I thought of a great dead whale. Some small boys were fishing from its sides and their bamboo poles made yellow streaks against the rust.

On the main deck Tortuga was ready to be unloaded. Dinah, our German shepherd, who had the run of the ship, was lying in the shade of Tortuga's overhanging bow. She had watched us packing, and the last few days had stayed close to the Jeep. She had spent most of her eleven years in one Jeep or another, and she seemed to know that something was about to happen. She watched a sea gull circle low over the ship. She sniffed toward land.

Beyond the long low warehouses, salt-white in the sun, and the row of tall cranes leaning over the water like praying mantises, we could see the harbor master's tower at the old port where many years ago sailing ships from all over the world set up shop on their decks and traded for pepper and nutmeg and clove. Only it was Batavia then, a trading post that was also a fort, founded by the Dutch in the early 1600's. The plan of its founder, Jan Pieterszoon Coen, was to make Batavia (named after a Germanic tribe that once occupied the lowlands of what is now Holland and Belgium) a clearing-house for products from Persia, India and Ceylon, the Spice Islands and Japan. These products in turn would be exported to Europe. The Netherlands East India Company was formed with Batavia as its headquarters. Adventurers and East India Company employees came to make their fortunes. But few lived long enough to enjoy their successes, for the Batavia of those days, surrounded by fever-infested swamp, justly deserved its reputation as a place of death.

Those settlers who lived had their own formula for survival: a glass of straight gin taken early in the morning on an empty stomach was deemed a sure preventative of fever—if the remedy was repeated often enough during the day and at night before retiring. In 1619 Coen wrote, "Our nation must drink or die," and Captain James Cook offered proof positive of the efficacy of alcohol. The only member of his crew who did not become ill during a stopover in Batavia was a seventy-year-old seaman who was drunk the entire time.

Today the old harbor is silted in, the fort is gone, and where noble square-riggers were careened in what Captain Cook wrote was the best marine yard in the world, small sailing *prahus* cluster in an abstraction of masts and ropes and gaudy hulls. Where the silks of Persia met the nutmeg of Ambon, the porcelain of China the pepper of Sumatra, and the glass of Venice the sandalwood of Timor, now fish in a hundred colors and varieties are hawked from bamboo stalls. Now bales of rubber, ingots of tin, boxes of tea and bags of coffee are traded for cement and steel and automobiles, and Batavia is Djakarta.

The *Drente* was alongside the concrete pier; her hawsers and rat guards were secured and the gangway lowered. It would be some time before Tortuga could be swung over the side; nothing moved fast in the sultry heat, least of all the longshoremen. With the easy informality that makes freighter travel so enjoyable the captain invited us into the wardroom for a farewell drink.

"A glass of Genever before you leave us?" he asked, pronouncing the name of the Dutch gin so it sounded like "you never" and then pouring it as if one never refused, even at so early an hour. Apparently one custom had survived.

The captain and all the officers were Dutch, old Indonesian hands, and all the way from India they had filled us with tales of how it was in the old days. Things were not the same since independence, they reminisced sadly; not the same at all. They spoke with an air of wonderment as if they could not understand what had happened to their paradise on earth.

"Why, before the war," one of them told us, "when we made port in Batavia, we'd all go to the Des Indes for a *rijsttafel*. We'd have some beer, Heineken's, as good as we make in Holland, and then the food would come." His eyes took on a misty look. "Can you imagine," he continued, "a whole line of boys, each with a different dish, twenty or more, boiled, fried, steamed, baked, or curried, meats and vegetables, and a great big mound of rice and hot pepper sauces that sharpen your tongue and make you want more. And there was always a boy there to fill your glass with more cold beer." He leaned back and cradled his stomach. "That was food.

"Now we don't go ashore much when we're in port. 'Incidents,' I think your papers call them, sometimes happen, even in downtown Djakarta. A while ago a KLM pilot was killed, shot while he was driving along the street. Of course for you, not being Dutch, it may be different."

We were to learn that not being Dutch was no insurance when a white skin is your only identification.

Always, sprinkled among the officers' memories of cool weekends at the fine resorts in Java's mountains, of dancing girls on Bali or parties at the exclusive Harmony Club, there were stories of official delays and irritations—and these only increased Helen's pessimism about clearing customs that day. The captain repeated his invitation to spend the night aboard ship, but about that time the question was decided for us when a slightly built Indonesian entered. He wore horn-rimmed glasses, his hair was oiled straight back and his sport shirt, open at the neck, hung loosely around his waist. He gave a polite but cool nod to the Dutch officers and addressed himself to me.

"Mr. Schreider," he breathed in slow, careful English, so softly that I could hardly make out the words, "I am Mohasson of the Ministry of Information. Your friend Sumarjo is out of the country for the present."

From the corner of my eye I caught Helen's "I told you so" look.

Mohasson's lips curled slightly at the corners in what we later learned he really meant to be a bright smile. "Since you are journalists you would come under my department anyway. I have come to bid you 'Selamat datang,' Welcome, and to expedite your entry to my country."

As we cleared customs in minutes and loaded case after case of equipment and supplies into Mohasson's station wagon without having one of them opened, I could not suppress a smile of satisfaction.

There was only one moment of anxiety—when the customs officer saw Dinah.

"I don't know what to do about your dog," he said, and I saw Helen start to bristle. Where Dinah is concerned, Helen is more protective than a Spanish dueña. Once when we had an overnight plane stop in Mexico City the customs officer insisted that Dinah stay in her crate at the airport though she had all her papers. Helen replied, "All right, I'll stay too." Defeated, the customs officer had stamped in Helen's passport *mujer y perra* (woman and dog) and Dinah spent the night with us in our hotel.

Before Helen had time to do more than bristle, Mohasson pulled out the permit for Dinah he had already acquired from the Ministry of Agriculture.

"No, it's not that," the customs officer said, "it's just that I'm afraid I'll have to charge you duty on the dog—unless," and he examined his tariff book again, "unless we could call her a circus dog. Circus animals don't have to pay duty." He thought a moment. "Does she do tricks?"

"Well," I replied weakly, "she shakes hands. But I don't imagine that would qualify her as a circus animal."

"And why not?" he retorted with a smile, and wrote on our declaration *one trained dog.*

"*Selamat djalan,*" he called after us, "a pleasant journey," and as we followed in Tortuga behind Mohasson toward downtown Djakarta, Helen was all smiles too.

For a Sunday afternoon, traffic was heavy as we drove along Djakarta's miles-long main street. The ban on making personal use of official vehicles was not yet being enforced, and everywhere were cars, Jeeps, and trucks filled with government gas and happy families. Bicycles, the new status sym-

bol, rolled two or three abreast, extra passengers hanging on fenders or crossbars, looking neat and crisp in white Western-style shirts and trousers and black velvet *pitjis*, like overseas caps, Indonesia's symbol of nationalism. *Betjaks*, the three-wheeled pedicabs, of which there are 70,000 in Djakarta alone, exuberant in raw reds, blues, oranges, purples and yellows, zipped in and out of side streets without regard for other traffic, blithely commandeering the right of way with their clanging bells. Here and there groups of them waited for passengers, their drivers sprawled on the red plastic-covered seats, their bare feet dangling as if warming them over the smoking volcanoes or washing them in the placid lakes cartooned on the sides. Each betjak was named, usually after an island in Indonesia, the new names of Kalimantan for Borneo, Sulawesi for Celebes, Moluccas for the Spice Islands, or Nusa Tenggara for the Lesser Sundas. Other names were more familiar; Bali is still Bali, and Sumatra and Java are still recognizable though spelled differently now that Indonesian is the official language of the country.

We moved slowly, driving on the left and separated from the oncoming traffic by a vertical-banked canal. Djakarta seemed a double city with gabled houses along the edge of the canal mirrored upside down, their white walls and red tiled roofs reflecting amber and rust in the brown water. Under the bright sky the canal was a ribbon of warm gold flecked with a myriad of colors where clothes had been laid out to dry. At intervals, where steps led down to the water, women gathered to bathe, to brush their teeth, to wash more clothes, their black hair streaming down their backs, their wet sarongs clinging to delicate figures, their smiles flashing at the antics of a small splashing child, their eyes turned away from the line of men defecating over the edge.

An average Sunday in Djakarta, Mohasson told us later,

but for us, direct from the grimness of Calcutta, the city danced with an air of carnival. Buses, trolleys and jitneys bulged with a gaiety that was infectious. And when we waited for the white-putteed policemen to give the go signal, all the drivers inspected Tortuga. They shouted questions, *"Ada kapal djuga, tuan* [Is it a boat too, sir]?" At my affirmative, they exclaimed *"Bagus, tuan,"* their thumbs went up in that gesture that means the same in any language, their brown faces were suddenly creased with white and I remember thinking how easily Indonesians smile.

Vendors were everywhere among the swelling masses of people—squeaking, clicking, and ringing their distinctive announcements of their wares: shoelaces and cigarette lighters, razor blades and wallets and sunglasses. Walking restaurants with glowing charcoal braziers and glasses of poisonous-looking drinks, all jiggling from a pole on the shoulder of the chef. Customers squatted on the curb and the chef barbecued tidbits of chicken or beef, and served it skewered on a sliver of bamboo, along with a banana leaf heaped with cold cooked rice and green vegetables. From the middle of a group of sarong-clad men came the singsong patter of a *dukun,* casting horoscopes, telling fortunes, prestidigitating with eggs pulled from ears and selling pastes and powders and poultices for everything from impotence to impetigo. Down the street came a mountain of pastel balloons bristling with whirring pinwheels that seemed to be self-propelled until we saw the pair of feet padding along beneath. Cigarettes were carried on trays like those of a night-club hostess, anything from clove-spiced *kreteks* wrapped in corn husks to contraband American and European brands. Signs showing ghastly cutaway drawings of human heads with veins outlined in red and nerves in black and prominent chalky teeth proclaimed the shop of a *tukang gigi,* a tooth artisan who with Inquisitional instruments will pull or fill bad teeth or cap with gold the perfectly good front ones.

The neon lights that outline its modern façade were just blazing into life when we arrived at Djakarta's premier hotel. But despite our reservations there were no rooms, and the clerk was noncommittal as to when we could savor the delights of the famous Hotel Des Indes, Pearl of the Orient, now renamed the Duta Indonesia.

As calmly as if such things happened every day, which as we learned later they did, Mohasson telephoned each of the hotels on his recommended list and many that were not recommended. All were full. Each ministry of the government has its guest house, but they were full too. Gratefully we accepted Mohasson's invitation to spend the night with him. "That is, if you don't mind sharing the room with my two children," he added hesitantly.

Mohasson lived in the respectable old former Dutch residential district, an area of stuccoed, tile-roofed houses with leaded windows overlooking canals. He had the top floor of a small but neat two-story dwelling. Mrs. Mohasson was expecting us; dinner, she said, was almost ready. A petite woman with clear, almost luminous golden skin, she wore a fresh *kain*, a wraparound, ankle-length skirt of hand-blocked batik, which with the *kebaya*, a tight lace jacket, and a wide sash wound tightly around the waist, make up the Indonesian national dress. With gold flowers in her hair she embodied all the sensitive refinement we soon came to associate with Javanese women.

Mrs. Mohasson spoke less English than her husband, but she and Helen got along fine from the start. In a few minutes they were whispering, and Helen was led off toward the *mandi*, the bath. I expected to hear happy splashing immediately—when it comes to water Helen makes a duck look like an aquaphobe—but there was nothing but silence, then a plaintive "Frank." I found Helen standing like September Morn in the middle of the tiled floor puzzling over a massive concrete tub filled with cool water. It was too high to climb into and too deep to sit in even if you could. A large dipper at the side gave a clue and we had just discovered a drain in one corner of the floor when Mohasson's amused voice verified our deduction that it was a sort of do-it-yourself shower.

That night we were introduced to Indonesian food, an abbreviated rijsttafel: fragrant *sate*, like miniature kabob; flaky chips of *krupuk* made of ground shrimp dried in the sun and then fried crisp; *gado-gado*, vegetable curry covered with peanut sauce, and mounds of boiled white rice. We thought that Mexico and India had prepared us for spicy food, and we were liberal with the *sambal*, the fiery red pepper sauce that is as much a part of Indonesia as rice itself. We found that nothing had prepared us for sambal. When we could see again we murmured something appreciative and groped for the tea.

Later, sitting in rattan chairs, surrounded by planters of orchids and wall hangings of handloomed cloth from many parts of the Archipelago, we listened for a while to Radio Republic Indonesia's nightly broadcast of popular American music, a program that a few months later was discontinued as being detrimental to the development of Indonesia's national identity. Briefly we discussed our travel plans, and in his soft, emotionless voice Mohasson expressed doubt, despite our long correspondence with the government, that we would be able to leave Djakarta as planned at the end of ten days.

Mohasson's two children, a boy about six and a girl of eight, were already asleep when we said good night. The windows were tightly shuttered—night air is considered unhealthy—but the mosquito-netting-draped beds were bright with embroidered sheets. In the middle of ours was a long cylindrical pillow, "the Dutch wife" of the Indies, a prop for arms and legs on hot still nights. But three's a crowd on a single bed, and that night our Dutch wife slept on the floor. In deference to Mohasson's religion—Moslems consider dogs unclean— Dinah slept in Tortuga.

The next morning we were introduced to Mrs. Saleh, Public Relations Officer for the Ministry of Information. All foreign journalists had to obtain clearance from the Ministry of Information, and it was the responsibility of Mrs. Saleh to hear their requests. A slim, angular woman with her hair in a stern bun at the back, Mrs. Saleh carried this responsibility with an air of resolute and perpetual remorse which seemed to say before she was even asked, "I'm sorry, there is nothing I can do," an attitude that was reflected in the dejected expressions of several correspondents who were waiting in her office.

Mrs. Saleh's face was a study in gloom as she listened to our plans to visit the major areas of her country: Sumatra, Java, Borneo, Celebes, the Spice Islands, and the Lesser Sunda Islands. At my mention of the Lesser Sundas she said, "You mean Bali, of course."

Bali is the first in this chain of islands that stretches a thousand miles almost to the coast of Australia. I explained that while we were certainly looking forward to visiting Bali we wanted to take our amphibious Jeep all the way to Timor, near the end of the Lesser Sunda group.

"Well," she replied, handing us a number of multipage forms to be filled out in quadruplicate, "why not come back next week? I may have some news for you then."

Her gloom was catching. I made a feeble request that since housing was such a problem perhaps she could expedite matters.

"Now Mr. Schreider, we must be patient. There is much to do."

It seemed that not quite all had been arranged. We would need a permit to take photographs, a permit to leave the city, and, since Indonesia was still under martial law, a clearance from the Ministry of Information countersigned by the military.

"And don't forget to register with the police," she concluded.

As we left, Mrs. Saleh was assuming her most resolute and sorrowful expression to deal with the Hong Kong correspondent of an American news magazine who was politely complaining that his editors could not understand why for ten days he had seen nothing but the inside of her office. We began to suspect that whatever Indonesia was, it was certainly not a paradise for journalists.

Our most immediate problem—after registering with the police—was finding a place to stay. Another round of the hotels produced nothing, not even a promise, and though Mohasson had graciously extended his invitation for as long as we were in Djakarta, we knew that we were overpopulating his small home.

At the new glass-fronted American Embassy—later it was stoned by a Communist-led mob of students—we learned that our problem was not at all uncommon. Many a stranded tourist with reservations at some hotel or another had slept on the couches in the foyer, and the guest rooms of State Department personnel were rarely vacant. Bob Lindquist, then Second Secretary of the Embassy, was the first to come to our rescue.

"My guest room is empty until Friday," he offered. "After that we'll see what we can do. By the way, how long do you expect to be in Djakarta?"

"Not over ten days," I replied.

Bob grinned. "My, you have just arrived, haven't you?"

By this time I was becoming accustomed to such allusions to my optimism.

Bob and Carol Lindquist lived in one of the newer residential areas not too far from Mohasson. Their home was bright and modern, one of their few concessions to that propensity of Britons and Americans to take their countries with them overseas. In contrast to those Foreign Service officers and their wives so deplored in *The Ugly American*, both Bob and Carol spoke Indonesian, had Indonesian friends, and participated in Indonesian affairs. By the time our reprieve ended on Friday we were good friends, Dinah and their Siamese cat had progressed from wary circling to an uneasy tolerance, and Bob had introduced us to a United States Information Service Officer, Walter Wein, who was leaving town for ten days and was happy to have someone watch his house.

Our housing problem thus solved, at least temporarily, we could concentrate on seeing Djakarta, a city that had come a long way from the old Dutch trading post. Today, little is left of those early days. The Dutch are gone, and their street names, store fronts, buildings and social clubs have been purged of the Dutch language. Only in the few historical remains—the Portuguese church dating from 1695, an old palace of the Governors General that is now the National Archives, and the countinghouse of the Netherlands East India Company—could we still imagine the dark paneled and heavy gilt elegance of Batavia's age of greatness.

The Djakarta of today is a sprawling metropolis swollen to over three million people by a fivefold increase in civil servants and military personnel and by thousands of refugees from bandit terrorism in the surrounding mountains. It is a city gripped by a chronic power shortage, water shortage and housing shortage. When the Dutch were repatriated their homes were occupied before they were vacated. New construction is rampant, with government-built offices, banks, apartments, and houses sprouting everywhere. But construction lags far behind demand, and hotels are filled with permanent residents, a situation that would plague us everywhere we traveled in Indonesia.

Chronic too is the tension. It is a tension we learned to live with but never adjusted to. We could feel it in the swarming warrens of the Chinese Glodok section and in the new residential area of Kebajoran. We could feel it in the dark tunnels of the markets where the price of rice had tripled and where cloth was at times unobtainable. We could feel it in the daytime at the sidewalk sate stalls and at night in the *kampongs*, the cane-and-thatch villages squeezed into every vacant area in the city. Here, in these jerry-built shacks of paper and flattened oil tins, with no water, electricity, or sanitary facilities, throbbing masses of discontent are jammed ten to a room —the betjak drivers, the prostitutes, the servants, and the jobless. Here, where laughter and the music of the gamelan echo through the night, the natural gaiety and complacency of the Indonesian people cloak but do not conceal the tension.

The following Monday Mrs. Saleh's expression was even more resolute than before. Our permits were still not forthcoming, and her only advice was that we must be patient.

"I really doubt that we can do anything until after Independence Day," she explained.

"But Independence Day is three weeks away," Helen and I chorused.

By this time we were moved by more than impatience. We were beginning to be concerned about the weather. In Indonesia there is no summer, no winter, only the monsoons, the wet and the dry. Now was the best time to travel along the

f the neighborhood we lived and I was born!

Lesser Sundas to Timor, now when the dry southeast monsoon was moving from the deserts of Australia west along the equator, across the Timor Sea, the Flores Sea, and the Java Sea, leaving them lake-calm, picking up moisture from the eastern islands, leaving the roads dry. But come December the northwest monsoon would blow down from central Asia bringing with it whipping gusty winds and squalls, avalanches of rain, a fretfulness that would churn the waters and lash the coasts, and after we left Java, between us and Timor lay five hundred miles of sea and five hundred miles of dirt roads that become mires at only a hint of rain. Our experience in the Caribbean had taught us what it was like to be out of step with the seasons. We had only until December to reach Timor; we could not afford to waste more time in Djakarta. But when we explained this to Mrs. Saleh, she merely shrugged. We decided to see what we could do by ourselves toward getting those permits. Exhibiting as much patience as we could muster—to do otherwise is in poor taste in Indonesia—we made the rounds of the various ministries whose stamp of approval we needed. We sat at the low tables that are fixtures in every office, sipped the sweet lukewarm tea, made small talk about the weather or the traffic, alluded to the subject of our visit, and finally got around to the details. Without exception the officials were courteous, sympathetic and full of helpful suggestions, and when Independence Day rolled around we were— That's right—we were still in Djakarta.

At Merdeka, or Freedom, Square the burning sun glinted from the rifles of hundreds of soldiers as the flag that proclaimed Indonesia's independence a decade and a half ago was raised again.

The trade unions, the schoolchildren and the military units had all passed in review, their banners demanding the return of West Irian, the Indonesian name for New Guinea. Sukarno mounted the small red and white buntinged grandstand. A Communist banner with its white hammer and sickle on a red background fluttered prominently in the crowds. There was a scuffle, the banner was furled and its bearer quieted by a squad of police. This Independence Day was dedicated to regaining West Irian, and partisan politics must be sublimated toward that end—by order of the Army.

For an hour President Sukarno railed against imperialism and colonialism and capitalism, terms he seemed to use synonymously, against the rebels in Sumatra and Sulawesi, the secessionists in the Moluccas, and the Western influences he claimed were undermining his nation's progress toward recovery. With his beige uniform, his gold swagger stick and black velvet pitji, he was a dynamic figure and though we understood only some of his words we felt ourselves drawn into his oratorical spell. And yet the crowds were strangely apathetic. We had the feeling that what they really wanted to hear was that rice would be cheaper and cloth once again available at a price they could afford.

That evening at the great white Presidential Palace, strung with lights like a Christmas tree, all the dignitaries in Djakarta and the representatives of the press were invited to the annual exhibition of folk dances from all over the Archipelago. Here we saw the other Sukarno, the patron of the arts, the promoter of Indonesia's culture, the genial host who greeted warmly the ambassadors and businessmen of those countries and companies whose influence he had harangued that afternoon.

When the banners and streamers came down we resumed our peregrinations of government offices. On one of these daily quests for permits our morning started with a bang—a .30-caliber bang. Our ears were still throbbing as a cordon of soldiers herded us into the Military Commandant's office.

"But all I did was make a wrong turn," I protested. "Your sentry could have blown his whistle. He didn't have to shoot at us."

The officer smiled apologetically and then, as if it explained everything, said, "But you know, Indonesia is in a state of war and emergency."

"Well," Helen commented as we climbed back into Tortuga and drove gingerly away, "if this happens in downtown Djakarta at ten o'clock in the morning, what can we expect in the rest of the country?"

Though we could find no holes in Tortuga, we were still unnerved, and that evening we discussed the pressing matter of permits with our latest host, Colonel Ray Cole, United States Army Attaché. A big rugged man who speaks little but smiles easily, Colonel Cole was of the opinion that he was a guest in Indonesia, and as such he should do things the Indonesian way, a philosophy that made him very popular with the Indonesian officers with whom he associated.

When we had brought him up to date he smiled, and in his casual way, said, "Well now, that shouldn't be too difficult. Let's see what we can do at a party or two."

With that our "business" hours changed from daytime to night as we accompanied Colonel Cole on a round of official receptions. Each night we met a different dignitary, and by the end of a week we had all of our permits plus a dozen introductory letters. But most important we had a letter from Colonel Soenarjo of Military Intelligence, next to the Ministry of Defense the most powerful agency in the country, requesting all authorities to assist us.

As we picked up the last permit, a smiling Indonesian official said, "What a pity we did not meet five weeks ago. In Indonesia you must always do things through friends."

Chapter Two

A FEW miles from Djakarta I pulled Tortuga to the side of the road. For the first time we were away from the capital and the change needed a moment to penetrate. Gone were the strident cries of the *tukangs*, the vendors who bring everything to your door from tropical fish to rare old Chinese porcelain. Gone was the persistent clamor of betjak bells, the piercing siren of the police, the unexplained shot in the night.

Instead of the mustiness of masonry there was the fragrance of frangipangi. The southeast monsoon, that heavy breeze that brings little rain, sighed through clumps of coconut palms. Instead of the brown sluggish canals clogged with refuse, briskly flowing streams flashed with prismatic hues of sarongs and golden skins where Javanese women bathed modestly, covering their small breasts as we passed.

Helen and I leaned back and breathed deeply. Dinah sat between us, her long nose raised, her nostrils vibrating, sampling the scent-laden air from a nearby village, the tang of chili cooking in coconut oil, the sweet-sour pungence of copra drying in the sun, the wet fragrance of earth freshly turned by the plow, the pale dankness of creepers and ferns long sheltered from the sun by the overgrowth of tall canarium and bamboo, the hundred other smells that mix and become the one dominant aroma from a village.

Away from the suffocation of Djakarta's delicately balanced protocol and red tape, its tensions and superficial gaiety, its restrictions and registrations, we felt a new lightness and freedom. Our pockets were full of permits: from the Army—Tortuga would travel by land; from the Navy—Tortuga would cross hundreds of miles of sea; from the Air Force—no, Tortuga couldn't fly, but her compass had been calibrated at the airport. Even Dinah had a travel permit. Our eventual goal: Timor, near the end of the chain of islands known as the Lesser Sundas, fifteen hundred crow-flight miles to the east.

But first, there was a little fishing village some friends had told us about. "Pelabuhan Ratu—it's on the south coast of Java, only two hours out of your way," they said, "a wonderful spot to relax and recover from Djakarta."

We came upon Pelabuhan Ratu suddenly, almost startlingly. The road turned, the forest opened, and there it was: one paved street dead-ending at the sea, still marked with a starting and finish line for the footraces held on Independence Day, two rows of frame houses with blistered paint, windows framed with plants in margarine tins, a jumble of kampongs to the sides, the whole flanked with flooded rice fields that lay like gleaming panes of scarlet glass in the afternoon light. The sea was a Monet lake stippled by the sun, the sky a canvas of bold brushstrokes in crimson, the beach peopled by Gauguin. Nets were stretched to dry where an armada of high-peaked prahus was drawn up on the sand to await the tide. It was one of those scenes that is too beautiful, too like a travel poster. I reminded myself that those puddles between the houses that picked up every bit of color from the sky were open sewers, pools of fecundity for mosquitoes.

We looked for the inn, followed by a growing parade of wobbling bicycles, pairs of youths hand in hand, and young children, the girls in loose cotton print dresses, the boys in nothing, everyone kicking at the yapping bony dogs whose sleep on the warm black asphalt we had disturbed.

We were the only guests at the blue, one-story frame inn. It was clean, with little cells for rooms, and there was a large room open to the air from the sea, with a long bare table for dining. There was no food, but the innkeeper, a young man in his twenties, sent for some from the Chinese shop down the street: *nasi goreng*, rice fried in coconut oil and flecked with bits of dried fish, red chili and hard-boiled egg. And there was coffee, thick and sweet with the rich flavor of the fire-roasted bean.

Two soldiers came bringing forms to fill: passport numbers, names, dates of arrival and departure and next destination. The forms were a good excuse to visit; their bronze faces, so mobile at times and yet so unrevealing at others, reflected a deep loneliness, and there is nothing so alone as an Indonesian away from his family. Their wives were in Djakarta, but they seldom went. Three hours away by bus but it might as well have been another island.

They inspected Tortuga. "*Bagus, tuan,*" and the thumbs went up. Why not go fishing in it? The fishing is good here.

Many foreigners came here to fish. How many? Maybe two, maybe three a month. Not so many now that the Darul Islam are acting up again. The roads are too insecure. But why not try Tortuga? I had an answer, not the real one, that sand and salt cause bearing wear, that we were saving Tortuga for her journey through the Lesser Sundas. Conservation is just a word, an incomprehensible concept to most Indonesians. What you have you use. Food should be eaten, money should be spent, for who knows about tomorrow.

I told them the propeller was disconnected temporarily. Ah, *rusak*, broken. This they understood. They shooed away the throng of children around us and bid us good night: *"Selamat malam, tuan, selamat malam, njonja."* The children returned, staring, tittering, but never touching anything. They followed us as we walked toward the beach, diminished echoes of our own shadows, moving and stopping in concert.

Near the water, pressure lamps glittered with a hard steely light, like spear points. The tide was right now; the fishermen were putting to sea, their sails hanging in limp arabesques, the lamps guiding them over reefs, attracting the fish, but even more important, their umbilica to the mother comfort of land. To the Javanese the sea is not a friendly place.

In our room the kapok pad was firm over the wooden slats. Through the haze of mosquito netting the lamps of the fishermen, far out on the water, were scattered into a thousand eight-pointed stars. A giant shadow from our own oil lamp wavered and danced on the whitewashed wall, a monstrous saurian shape from when the earth was young. It was a tiny house lizard, pale, translucent, its ribs and vertebrae revealed as if fluoroscoped when he darted near the lamp for an insect. His name—and his sound, a roar from such a minim creature

—is *tjetjak*, a timid, ubiquitous, welcome guest in every house, a prodigious killer of mosquitoes.

A shriek and a tinny clatter spilled me from my bed. In the mandi I found Helen scooting on her knees across the floor, grabbing, clutching at a wriggling something in the corner.

"I just went fishing," she explained wryly, and tossed a four-inch goldfish back into the mandi where it had lived and procreated until Helen, in the dark, had poured it squirming over her back.

There was no hint of impending crisis when we arrived in Bogor to interview President Sukarno. Soldiers with fixed bayonets guarded all the entrances to the presidential palace, but this was normal. Always heavily guarded, precautions had been increased since the last attempt on the President's life. His many close escapes from assassination had added credence to the people's belief, carefully nurtured by his followers, that Sukarno is protected by divine intervention. But that day all was quiet at the colonnaded white mansion, the four-winged Parthenon with dome and mansard roof that was formerly the official residence of the Dutch Governors General, now the President's summer palace.

Hundreds of spotted deer, fawns, does and imperious stags, their antlers in velvet, grazed serenely under mimosa trees and tall, sparsely needled pines. A large aquatic lizard slipped into a kidney-shaped pool near a Japanese bridge, barely rippling the yard-across lily pads and silvery plum-colored lotus blossoms. The top of one tall tree was dark with bats of the flying fox variety. We rapped sharply on the hollow trunk, but the bats only rustled and lapsed into sleep again.

Near the palace a great blue-gray stone Buddha meditated under an immense banyan tree, the trunk of closely entwined creepers a forest unto itself. But inside the palace meditation of another sort was taking place: Sukarno was meeting with some of his ministers.

It was several hours before our appointment, set up just before leaving Djakarta, and we spent the time wandering the graveled paths of the adjacent 145-year-old Botanical Gardens where over half a million varieties of tropical trees, plants and orchids are assembled. For a while we were joined by Jackie, a young orangutan who enjoyed trustee status in the Gardens' small zoo. His brown eyes wise and ancient, he solemnly took our hands in his, and like a child in a furry red snowsuit he ambled between us on his short thick legs—a quaint family on a Sunday stroll. We parted company when he dislodged the horn button in Tortuga, bared his teeth at Dinah, and masticated, tinfoil and all, my last package of American cigarettes.

We were on our way to the palace when we heard the President's helicopter warming up. A message reached us: *Due to pressing matters of state I regret I will be unable to see you today.* A few minutes later the helicopter took off for Djakarta amid the frightened scurrying of the deer and a vague stirring of the bats in the tall tree. That afternoon it was announced officially that thereafter all 1,000- and 500-rupiah notes would be worth ten percent of their face value, and that all bank accounts were frozen. The official rate of exchange was raised from 30 rupiahs to the dollar to 45. The result: an overall currency devaluation amounting to seventy-five percent.

The immediate result of the devaluation was chaos; the cut reached far beyond its three main targets: the country's runaway inflation, the rebels in Sumatra, and the Chinese who controlled most of the businesses. Hard hit was Indonesia's small middle class, who, since the rash of bank failures some months earlier, preferred to keep what little money they could save in cash. Small shops closed their doors; staples were unobtainable for a while; the suicide rate jumped sharply. In Bogor, Goodyear Tire and Rubber Company, unable to meet its payroll, closed its factory temporarily, throwing thousands out of work.

But any benefit that might have been realized was as permanent as that of the last devaluation. The government printed more money, the rebels continued to honor the devalued currency, the Chinese resorted to barter, and the black market exchange rate rose from 80 rupiahs to more than 600 rupiahs to the dollar.

Reaction of the people we spoke to was varied. One service station owner remarked bitterly as we paid for our gas in almost worthless 500-rupiah bills, "I see that you too have contributed to Indonesia." But the majority of the people, like the bats in the tall tree, merely fluttered a bit and lapsed back into complacency. *"Insh'Allah,"* they said. "It is God's will."

Beyond Bogor the road climbed steeply into the mountains, part of the chain of over four hundred volcanoes that stretches the length of the Archipelago. Motorized traffic was light as we drove on, but hundreds of bicycles thronged the roads. Women pedaled leisurely, somehow unencumbered by their tight kains, easily balancing on their heads heavy baskets of mango or papaya or dried fish; soldiers, Sten guns slung from their shoulders, rolled in squads; children, their faces scrubbed, their hair combed, their shirts and shorts neat, hurried to the schools that almost every village now has.

Of all the programs Indonesia has started, perhaps none has achieved such success as her drive for education. Since World War II she has nearly doubled the number of schools, tripled the number of teachers and quadrupled the number of stu-

dents. With her adult education courses she has raised her lit-
eracy rate in a few years from seven percent to more than
fifty percent. We visited many of these schools, and the eager
look of a child as he solved a problem in arithmetic on the
blackboard, the proud smile of his teacher, often only a high
school student himself, the wonder on the seamed face of an
old man the first time he wrote his name, these are images I'll
carry a long while.

The air grew perceptibly cooler as we wound higher into
the mountains through tea estates and rice fields, casuarinas
and giant ferns, toward the resorts of 4,800-foot Puntjak Pass,
a weekend target for enervated Djakartans, Indonesian and
European alike. Gaudy bungalows in primary colors, interspersed with Swiss-style chalets and restaurants, clung to the
steep hillsides, while here and there a spot of turquoise from
a swimming pool broke the smooth green of a golf course. At
the top of the pass we dug sweaters from Tortuga's cabinets.
After the heavy heat of the lowlands, the cold wet mist that
rolled in white puffs over the vast panorama of green seemed
to wash away the haze on our spirits. We stood there a long
time—until a military convoy bound for Bandung stopped
and advised us to go on. This was Darul Islam country, they
warned, not a pleasant place to be after dark.

Bandung, with its hermaphrodite ferro-concrete architecture, by Indonesian standards the country's handsomest city,
lies on a broad, undulating 3,000-foot-high plateau. Flooded
rice fields stretch everywhere, intruding on the city limits
where new buildings cast their shadow across heaving buffalo
plowing hock-deep in mud that is as dark as melted chocolate.
But away from town, rice follows its ageless pattern, spreading across the valleys a patchwork of multihued green, and
ascending the hills in stepped terraces. Wherever there is wa-

ter, rice is a year-round occupation, and in places we saw the whole cycle at a glance: the women transplanting the spring-green rice seedlings; in adjacent fields the maturing crop, that rich green that only rice can achieve; and the dry fields, golden and heavy with bursting kernels, clamorous with the bright confetti of rainbow-clothed harvesting girls. Deftly they palm their *ani-ani*, the crescent-shaped rice knives, concealing them so as not to offend the Rice Goddess, whose blessing is needed for the rice to germinate. Swiftly they cut the stalks; laughing they carry them to the village cooperative. Harvest is a happy time, for rice is life to Java.

For thousands of years the Javanese have known irrigated rice culture; for as many years the rich volcanic soil, carried by abundant rain from the mountainsides, has supplied their needs. But now Java's population has reached the critical point —sixty million people in an area the size of Pennsylvania; in places a density of over a thousand per square mile. Divided between sons according to village law, the fields become smaller each year, and each year Java imports hundreds of thousands of tons of rice, using millions of dollars of foreign exchange. To alleviate this condition the government is opening new land in Sumatra and Borneo and starting large irrigation schemes. The most important of these is Djatilahur Dam in west Java, aimed at irrigating 600,000 acres of land, relieving the sanitation and power problems of Djakarta, providing a freshwater fishery and recreation area. But projects such as this are hampered by a lack of experienced engineers. The second assistant to the director of Djatilahur had graduated only three years earlier from Bandung's Technical Institute. Here, the country's first engineering college, founded by the Dutch in 1920 and where President Sukarno received his degree in architecture, a team of Americans from the University of Kentucky is trying to streamline the curriculum, which, based originally on Dutch, is being converted to English, now the new nation's second language.

Bandung lies in the heart of Java's most troubled area; the Darul Islam were making raids right to the suburbs of the city. Much of the road from Bandung to Jogjakarta in central Java was classified as insecure; villages were barricaded and the few trucks and buses that risked the drive were often burned. On the advice of the military we detoured north toward the Java Sea.

Near the high hill that dominates Bandung's northern limits there was ample evidence of the depredations of the Darul Islam: burned army barracks, shattered windows, yellowed masonry pocked with bullet holes. Armored cars waited beside the twisting road, shaded under dun-dry canopies of palm fronds. Like jack-in-the-boxes their turrets popped open as Tortuga passed, and helmeted soldiers of Indonesia's crack Siliwangi division answered our waves with thumbs up and cries of *"Bagus, tuan."* Being shot at once was enough and near the military posts we observed strictly the speed limit— six miles per hour—and then hurried on, trying to make the safety of the coast before dusk.

Beyond the pass the road sloped off toward the sea, the varying elevations providing the range of climates needed by miles upon miles of estates: deep green tea crowning the hilltops, each low bush separate in the distance, like clumps of dichondra in a newly planted lawn; rubber trees, arching away in stately cathedrals until the rows converged in shadow-gloomed naves. Here too grow coffee, sisal, tapioca, kapok, cinchona, teak, cocoa, and pepper. The list of crops reminded us of the old Spanish proverb: "He who would bring home the wealth of the Indies must carry the wealth of the Indies with him." For though it was the spices of Indonesia that first brought the Europeans, it was the Europeans that first brought the estate crops that today give Indonesia her wealth, among them tea from Assam, rubber from Brazil, cinchona from Bolivia, and coffee from the Congo, a fact often overlooked by most Indonesians.

Java's north coast, with the shallow sea fading from brown to green to hazy blue, was the scene of the first Japanese landings on the island. Rusted hulks of landing craft still littered the shore, but in the coastal town of Tjirebon the anti-litter campaign was in full swing, part of the Army's attempt to teach merdeka-conscious Indonesians some civic responsibility. The streets were patrolled by rifle-toting soldiers, all traffic was stopped for an hour while the employees of the British American Tobacco Company, at full pay by the company, of course, swept the streets clean. In other cities in Indonesia the same thing was tried, and in Djakarta when sirens sounded all cars on the street were required to stop, and their passengers and drivers to get out and clean the area around them. The system was changed somewhat when a diplomat objected to being straw-bossed by a private with a Sten gun.

At the Grand Hotel Tjirebon, an immaculate hotel on the main street, we were relaxing over a bottle of still-excellent Heineken's when a group of teen-agers approached. With their white shirts and polished black shoes, their tight trousers low on their lean hips and supported by nothing more obvious than faith, they were as alike as club members—which they were. Would we address their youth association that evening? They had been mightily impressed by four youngsters sent to Indonesia by the American Field Service on an exchange visit of high school students. All were anxious to practice their English, hoping for a chance at the next exchange.

But the assembly of more than five persons without special clearance was still prohibited by the military; permission was refused, and that evening we all sat on the lawn in front of the hotel. More youngsters, including a few girls in crisp, Western-cut batik dresses, their long hair tufted in glossy black pony tails, drifted in until there were a score or more, and Helen and I expected any moment to see a squad of police come to disperse us. But though soldiers passed they looked the other way, and we talked until curfew, answering questions about public schools in America, the cost of living for students, about Little Rock, Hollywood and Elvis. Bright, serious students, they were shy at first, but as they relaxed and spoke more freely I found myself thinking how much better it would be for Indonesia—and for the United States—if much more of the hundreds of millions of dollars of American aid that now dribbles down through the sieve of Indonesian bureaucracy until its effect on the people is invisible were spent instead on direct educational grants or exchanges of young people such as these.

From Tjirebon to central Java's capital of Jogjakarta is an easy one day's drive, but Tortuga's lumbering ways, abetted by the wealth of archaeological remains in the area, lengthened the journey considerably. As the miles rolled by we tried to piece together the complexity of Indonesia's past. And yet, how little is known of the centuries before the Christian era, of the time when migrants from central Asia brought the use of bronze, irrigated rice culture, domestication of the ox, the ritual sacrifice of the buffalo, and the religion of animism, the belief that all things, inanimate as well as living, have souls. Could it be that these are the "isles of the gentiles" spoken of in the Bible from whence came gold, bright iron, silver, ivory, apes, peacocks, tin, lead, and spices? Was it to Indonesia that Hiram of Tyre ventured? Chinese mariners sailed to the islands 2,000 years ago, an ancient text records, in quest of pearls and other precious gems. And in the first century A.D., a Chinese emperor sent a delegation to Sumatra to procure a rhinoceros for the imperial zoo.

Only with the fifth century does Indonesia's written history begin: the early chapters of Hindu, Buddhist, and Islamic kingdoms; the sequels of Portuguese, Spanish, British and Dutch colonization; and finally the Japanese occupation and the postwar struggle for independence.

During those days in central Java we stopped at ruin after ruin, remnants of the once-great cultures that thrived here. Once we climbed a jolting trail, past lines of aloof, stocky women carrying to market blue-green cabbages big as basketballs, past stone houses with trays of ocher tobacco drying in the thin sun, up through layers of mist, as though leaving the gay world of Java, to the chill of the 6,000-foot Dieng Plateau. Here fourteen hundred years ago, stone ditches drained the basin of what was once a lake, stone stairs climbed to temples where Hindu priests worshiped the god Shiva, imported from India by traders. Today a scattering of small, rectangular temples remain, pathetic in their aloneness, inspiring in their simple, classic lines. A few badly defaced sculptures are inside, and a herd of goats graze around the plinths.

A drab village of gray, weathered boards and rusted corrugated roofs stood on a rise a few hundred yards from the temples. The people had heard Tortuga whining up the steep grade, small, ragged, stocky people with scraggly beards and mustaches, and swarthy complexions as if the blood of the golden-skinned Malays of the coastal regions had not been able to flow so high up to Dieng to dilute the darker strains of the Indians who built the temples, or those people who were there before them.

They had horses already saddled for us, but the horses looked as if we could carry them easier than they could carry us. We hired them anyway, but led them across the spongy, boglike ground, avoiding the rudimentary road that had been started recently. It seemed sacrilege to walk on it; many of its stones were beautifully carved slabs that had once adorned the temples, each mud-scabbed piece an ignored treasure.

It was a gray world, as if the sun never touched it; even the grass seemed gray. Somehow, with sulphurous fumes steaming in the cold air, with volcanic pools bubbling with some force from the other, the black, world below, with drab human forms hovering eternally over Dante's brimstone, digging and carrying the dull yellow sulphur to the crude crusher for a few cents a load, it seemed more a place to worship the Black One. But perhaps to the Hindus of old it was this very quality that prompted them to build Dieng in honor of Shiva, the Creator—and the Destroyer.

Sometimes on those side trips we stayed in *pasangrahans,* government rest houses for official travelers built when Indonesia was a colony but today often roosting places for bats. Sometimes we stayed in *losmens,* small inns where we could generally follow our noses to the "sanitary" facilities and slept in airless cubicles under tattered gray mosquito netting. Once, in a town in west Java, the only room available was an eight-foot-square shaft with a tiny barred opening near the ceiling. Stained whitewash peeled from the barren walls, and phalanxes of cockroaches advanced on us when we entered.

Helen took one look and declared like Papa Bear, "Somebody's been sleeping in my bed." We would have been happier in Tortuga, but this was Darul Islam country and there was nowhere else to stay. Exhausted by a hard drive, energy sapped by the humid heat, I told Helen it was her imagination, to go to sleep. But she doggedly examined the bed by candlelight and I called the slovenly clerk away from his card game outside our room.

"This bed has been slept in," she told him, indignantly.

A surprised expression sheathed his face. "*Tetapi, tuan, satu orang sadja* [But, sir, only one man]."

"Well, that's one man too many," Helen retorted, and the clerk grudgingly changed the one sheet, muttering all the while. For the rest of the night we tossed, fanning the still air to drive away the mosquitoes attacking from above and slapping the bedbugs boring from below.

But more often, once we were in the secure areas of central Java where the Darul Islam had not penetrated, we preferred Tortuga's facilities to anything the losmens had to offer. We would duck into a stand of teak, a clump of palms, or higher in the mountains a grove of casuarinas overhung with Spanish moss and alive with all the squeals and whistles so abundant in a tropical forest.

Satisfied that we were unobserved, we would select tinned food from Tortuga's cabinets, uncover the sink and alcohol stove built into the dash, pump our teakettle full of water piped from the tank in the bow, and while Dinah explored or relished her supper of kibble and tinned horsemeat, we relaxed and read until it was dark. We would extend our foam-padded bunks from behind the seats, and protected by the screens over the windows, we would sleep easily until dawn.

But sometimes, soon after we thought we were unseen, Dinah would growl. A face would peer from the bamboo, and a child, drawn by that unexplainable aura that exudes from anything or anyone strange to the countryside, would go running to his village, crying, "*Orang putih, orang putih, kapal dharat* [White people, land ship]," and the elders would come to investigate, no matter how far.

Speaking through the schoolchildren—the elders knew little Bahasa Indonesia—we would explain our presence and our nationality. "No, we are not Dutch. We are Americans; yes, our kapal dharat goes on the sea and the land."

Astounded they would walk around the Jeep; smiles would replace scowls, and the thumbs would go up. *"Bagus, tuan, selamat datang,"* and they often invited us to their village.

Perhaps there would be a Moslem circumcision ceremony in the village that night, or a marriage with the groom and bride dressed as prince and princess of the royal families that are still revered though deprived of temporal power in the new republic. Or perhaps there was a *selamatan*, the ceremonial feast of rice cakes in all shapes and colors, of syrupy sweets, and curried buffalo meat from an animal sacrificed in the traditional one-stroke decapitation that is to appease the spirits on the opening of any festivity, for even devout Indonesian Moslems still carry in their hearts the beliefs of their animist forefathers.

But even if there was nothing special we were usually invited for tea. Once we walked along the narrow dikes between flooded rice fields, joining the good-natured laughter when we slipped off the edge into knee-deep mud, past flocks of brown dappled ducks trained to stay near the little white flags in their midst, to a palm-hidden village of rectangular cane-and-thatch houses. The mosque, open-sided with a two-tiered roof, was the most prominent structure, but the huge wooden drum for calling the people to prayer was silent and only one man knelt on the bare wooden floor inside.

The village chief, a diminutive ancient whose bones jutted beneath parchment skin, waved us into chairs in the hut's front room. His wife, equally ancient, but arrow-straight from a lifetime of carrying heavy loads on her head, brought tea, each glass capped with an embossed aluminum cover to keep out the flies that droned around us.

As we waited for the invitation to drink, our eyes wandered from the inevitable picture of President Sukarno on the thatched wall to the rolled sleeping mats in the corner, the string of dull red chili peppers hanging from the rafters, the charcoal brazier glowing through the door to the cooking room where the number two wife, a smear of green paste on her brow to cure headache, prepared the supper of sago, rice, fried bananas and dried fish.

The door and the unglazed windows were dark with children, the young ones healthily clad in nothing, all eager for a look at the strangers, the orang putih. Beyond them an old man, a neat, scanty turban of blue and brown batik on his head, his age-corrugated chest bare and his sarong pulled to his knees, hunkered on the ground and fondled his fighting rooster, probably ruminating on its former conquests, for cockfighting and its accompanying gambling, once so popular as to be almost a vice, has been banned on Java, and is permitted only on holidays on the neighboring island of Bali.

Finally, when the tea was cold, the old chief said, *"Selakan"*; we drank, and our glasses were immediately refilled. We ate the rice cakes he offered, and, anxious to show him we enjoyed it, we finished our tea. Again the glasses were refilled, despite our protests. These were not demitasses. They were large tumblers, and I could see the distress in Helen's eyes saying plainly, "I just can't drink any more." It was months and gallons of tea later before we learned that a sip and a nibble are all that etiquette requires. To consume all is considered rude, an indication that you are not satisfied, that your host has not been generous.

One evening we camped at the base of the Borobudur. The night was clear, the stars seemed closer, and the stupas and terraces of this colossal monument to Buddha made jagged silhouettes against the surrounding mountains. Clouds paraded across the sky, and when the blue light of the moon burst through spasmodically, life seemed to come to Boro-budur's hundreds of carved reliefs depicting Buddha's rise to Nirvana through the trials of earthly existence.

Early the next morning we traced the path of pilgrims, a path worn smooth by monks from India and Ceylon and China as far back as the ninth century when the Borobudur is said to have been built in a single night by the gods. Con-structed around a natural mound of earth, the Borobudur dwarfs the cathedrals of Europe; its delicate yet strong reliefs, if placed end to end, would run almost three miles. Here craftsmen trained in the finest traditions of Indian sculpture lavished their attention on the most minute detail of bird and flower and animal, of scenes of battle and dance, of tender love and deep thought, of perplexity and enlight-enment, hands and expressions and postures all frozen in stone. And yet so fluid and graceful are the reliefs that we had the feeling that this was not hard stone chiseled by some sharp instrument, but a soft pliable substance caressed into shape by a loving hand, and it was easy to believe that the Borobudur really was created by the gods.

In the manner of pilgrims we read in this open book of stone, with its patina of yellow and green lichen, the story of Buddha's search for the answer to the mysteries of life. We climbed from rectangular terrace to rectangular terrace: the base, now covered with earth, but which when excavated dis-played the torments of hell and the passions that bind man to mortality; the first terrace where Buddha's life is depicted from his conception, when an elephant appears to his mother, Maya, in a dream; the miracles and healings attending his birth; his demonstrations of the skill and knowledge with which he was born; his life of pleasure as a young prince; his marriage, and the eventful days when he first saw the blind, the sick and the dead. Stricken by these sights, he leaves his

wife and child and goes in search of truth, of the reasons for
man's suffering. We followed his trials, his austerities and
his temptations, his enlightenment under the Bodhi Tree, and
his evolvement of the Eightfold Path, a code for living which
in a subjective way is as all-encompassing and compassionate
as the Sermon on the Mount, as simple as the Golden Rule, a
personal philosophy which if followed faithfully will lead
man to Nirvana, a condition of mind in which suffering cannot touch him.

We ascended to the upper terraces where Buddha's disciples
search also for Nirvana; along open walkways where stone
images of the Buddha gaze serene and all-seeing, their hands
in the traditional *mudras,* the classic postures of teaching,
meditating, benediction, and touching the earth as witness
against the accusations of Mara, the temptress. We passed
through arches crested with *kalas,* the lion-faced temple
guardians; up sandal-worn steps to the circular terraces, so
devoid of ornamentation, in their simplicity symbolizing the
circle of life, the beginning and the end as one, when man
rises above the physical and enters the world of the spiritual.
Here, surrounded by seated Buddhas enclosed in latticed bells
of stone, with the massive center stupa towering above us representing the attainment of Nirvana, we allowed the torpor
of Java's midday to absorb us, just as Indonesia has absorbed
the teachings of Buddhism, Hinduism and Islam, alloying them
with her own prehistoric animism to form a religion in which
all four live as one.

After a week of camping, even the most seasoned traveler
longs for a bath—and other facilities—and when Helen was
flushed from a bamboo grove by a twelve-foot python we
headed for central Java's cultural capital of Jogjakarta.

On the outskirts of town, called Jogja for short, Tortuga
passed bullock-drawn carts shaped like the Conestoga wagons

of America's pioneer days. They moved quietly along the roads, the hoofs of the animals muffled with shoes fashioned from pieces of automobile tires. But in the city, the main street of Malioboro was a bedlam. Jazz blared from radio shops, the bells of thousands of bicycles—one person in four in this city of over a quarter of a million has a bicycle—mingled in awful discord, and from the main square came the sound of a merry-go-round and the squeaking cries of vendors. It was the beginning of Sekaten, a festival with so many elements of animism, Hinduism and Islam that its meaning and origin are completely obscured.

Jogja is famed all over Indonesia for its hand-tooled silver products and its batik kains, the latter produced by a patient process of designing in wax on cotton cloth, followed by successive dippings in dye, the wax applied by hand and removed for each different color. But more important, it is the capital of the Special District of Jogjakarta, the only active sultanate retaining any temporal power in Indonesia.

Near the *kraton*, or sultan's palace, we could hear the royal gamelan echoing somberly through the courtyards by the mosque. We were two among hundreds of entranced listeners as bronze gongs as large as cartwheels, as small as cups, xylophones of dully gleaming brass, barrel-sized drums and delicate two-stringed rebabs resonated from the dark ceilings of the pavilion in rhythms and melodies as old as gamelan itself. For centuries before the Hindus came, Indonesia had gamelan, and when Islamic traders converted the rulers of the already well-established Hindu kingdoms, the gamelans were placed in the mosques. The people came to listen, and stayed and were converted.

At the main gate of the kraton we were met by the Chief Guard, who holds a hereditary post of great dignity. An old man, he wore the traditional court costume, the royal batik kain of indigo and brown, the close-fitting, high-necked jacket of tightly woven striped cotton, and the neat Javanese turban with a bun at the back. In his wide sash was a long kris, the wavy-bladed dagger commonly credited with magical powers. Every element of the Guard's dress was dictated by centuries of custom that at one time reserved even the pattern of the batik for the exclusive use of members of the court; it was an offense punishable by death for anyone else to wear it.

Intrigued by the workmanship of the Guard's kris, I asked to see the blade. For a moment I thought I had offended the old man, but he pulled it slowly from its scabbard of polished, grained wood, and touched it to his forehead, his lips moving in a silent prayer, beseeching forgiveness for disturbing its spirit. With pride he pointed out the *pamor* of the blade, the whorls and lines where the light color of the meteoric iron accented the blue-black of the common iron with which it is amalgamed. I was careful not to touch it for to a Javanese the magic of a kris is strong. Many were the tales we had heard of these weapons, how the forges where they are made are sanctified as the smith re-enacts the ritual when the gods gave weapons to man, how a kris made for a particular person will protect him from all harm but will bring death or misfortune to all others who acquire it. But a sultan's kris is the most powerful of all, so much so that it was once common for the kris to substitute for the sultan at his own marriage.

But the Sultan of Jogjakarta is bound by no such tradition. A progressive man who drives his own car, dresses casually, served as Minister of Defense and is now Director of the Council of Tourism, Sultan Hamenku Buwono IX is an ardent republican. During the revolution he turned part of his palace and official buildings over to the new government; Jogja became Indonesia's capital from 1946 until 1950, and Indonesians claim proudly that the struggle for Independence was

directed, fought and won from here. As a reward for the
Sultan's help the Special District of Jogjakarta was formed
with the Sultan retaining his title and his power. But it is said
that the Sultan believes that such a title is an anachronism in a
republic. Thus far he has not designated any of his wives as
the Sultana, and consequently none of his sons has a legitimate
claim to the title.

It became evident immediately, however, that the Sultan's
officials were considerably more conservative than he. Steeped
in the tradition of the Sultan's divinity, so powerful that until
recent times his bath water, fingernail clippings and hair trim-
mings were saved for medicinal use—or at the very least were
disposed of in secret to prevent an enemy from obtaining and
using them to work a curse on him—the old Guard indicated
where we could step, where we could look, and where we
could photograph. We became more and more frustrated as
we passed the sacred weapons room, the bridal chamber, the
throne platform, and the Golden Pavilion with its high, gold-
embossed ceiling, all without getting a single photograph.

We were almost at the end of our tour of the kraton
when a procession of women crossed the courtyard. Servants
of the Sultan's wives, they wore the kraton dress, the long,
wraparound kain, with their shoulders bare and their breasts
bound tightly with bands of the royal yellow cloth. One carried a teapot shaded by the royal umbrella. Against the backdrop of the pavilion, with the sun filtering through the trees,
it was a vision from the past. I raised my camera. The Guard
leaped forward.

"No, no," he exclaimed excitedly, "no photographs!"

I groaned. "If only that progressive sultan were here now
instead of in Djakarta."

In the days preceding Sekaten, we tried to learn what time
the festivities would start. But though this celebration had

been held since beyond memory, we received answers that varied anywhere between 7 A.M. and noon. Not wishing to take a chance of missing anything, we arrived at the kraton courtyard at six. It was still dark within the walls, and we were among the first there, but the Rice Mountains were already in place on their red palanquins in the shade of the pavilion. The largest stood almost eight feet tall, a slender conical frame of bamboo dripping with long green beans and red chili peppers and crowned with oranges with a tuft of paper packets of rice on top. Called the male or the Bridegroom Rice Mountain, it was obviously phallic. On a separate palanquin stood the smaller Bride Rice Mountain, a squat inverted conical basket filled with little cornucopias of sanctified rice. And there were still smaller Rice Mountains scattered about, some similar to the Bride, others mere piles of white paper packages filled with rice. How far back this custom goes no one could tell us, but there is no doubt it is related to the animistic rice fertility rites still practiced by the country people throughout Indonesia, rites which are climaxed by husbands and wives going at night to their fields when the rice is about to germinate and engaging in sexual intercourse. And when the harvest is in, in many places the first cuttings are tied in two bundles, one representing the male and the other the female, which are never eaten but are left in the rice barns to insure the propagation of future crops. But to the people of Jogjakarta the symbolism was lost in the gaiety of the affair and the prospect of acquiring a packet of rice or even a piece of the Rice Mountains, which coming from the sacred precincts of the kraton would bring them good fortune.

For a while Helen and I wandered around, removing our shoes when we approached the Rice Mountains, and asking questions which no one could answer, but at the rate the courtyard was filling with people it was obvious that by the time the Rice Mountains were ready to be carried to the mosque we would be lucky to see, let alone photograph, the procession. A low portico, long disused from the look of the door with its rusty lock beneath it, extended from one wall of the courtyard. Amid the good-natured smiles of some bystanders who told me no one would mind, I clambered onto the flat surface of the portico and settled contentedly on my "box seat" to wait.

From my perch I had a clear view. Beside the large gate to the kraton proper, spear-bearing guardsmen, carbon copies of the old Chief Guard, stood watch. Above their heads I could faintly see in the shadows two entwined serpents carved on the wooden lintel. To a Javanese versed in ancient numerology and literature the cabalism is clear: the number assigned to snakes is eight; to entwining is six; therefore, two snakes entwining as one reads 2861. Read backwards this becomes 1682, the year in the Javanese calendar corresponding to our year 1757, the year when the kraton was built. Somehow, this esoteric approach reminded me of our cryptic five weeks in Djakarta.

By eight o'clock I could feel central Java's heat begin to weigh on me. Helen was waiting near the gate to the kraton to give me a signal when the procession was about to start, but in the pulsing crowd I couldn't see her. The portico was too small to move around on and my legs were falling asleep. Surely the procession would start soon?

There was a stirring in the crowd, and the gates opened. But it was only a contingent of the female kraton guards. Bulky women with formidable krisses in their sashes, whose duty it is to guard the women's quarters, they made last-minute—I hoped—adjustments to the flowers and tinsel decorations on the Rice Mountains. Vendors of sweets, balloons, pinwheels, cigarettes, ice cream and vile-colored soft drinks circulated among the spectators, screeching their wares. A vendor of *sirih* stopped beneath my portico, smeared lime on the bright green betel leaves, and folded them around a piece of red betel nut. His customer handed over a few coins and popped the green bundle in his mouth, chewing happily and expectorating the blood-red spittle with great satisfaction. Dust from thousands of feet clouded the air, and everyone was hawking and spitting and blowing his nose on the ground, aided by a finger pressed to a nostril, a good old Asian custom, one which any Indonesian will tell you is far more sanitary than carrying around a soiled handkerchief.

Another hour passed; then another. Several policemen strolled by, grinning up at me as I tried to stretch my cramped legs. The gates opened again, and the kraton officials, wearing the white turbans and flowing white robes reserved for *Hadjis*, those who have made the pilgrimage to Mecca, paraded out. In formation they seated themselves comfortably on thick cushions, and I squirmed on my hard portico.

About that time a policeman approached. He was one of the same policemen who only a short while before had waved and smiled up at me.

"Come down," he ordered.

For a moment I wasn't sure I had heard him rightly. The gamelan was marching in. The procession *was* about to start.

"But why?" I asked foolishly. "I'm not in anyone's way, and you know I've been up here for four hours. Why must I come down now just when the procession is going to start?"

The policeman shrugged off my question. "Come down," he ordered again.

In desperation I showed him my press card. I showed him all my permits. By this time I was the main attraction, and a satellite crowd was surging around my perch watching the drama. My German stubbornness was beginning to show. I wanted a reason for coming down or I would stay, and somehow I felt that the crowd—hilarious by this time, either at my Indonesian or my defiance of the policeman—was on my side. With relief I saw the policeman turn without a word and walk away.

Then a young lady broke through the crowd.

"I'm the teacher in the kraton school," she said in good English. "I'm sorry, but you really must come down. You're sitting higher than the Sultan's head."

"But the Sultan isn't here. He's in Djakarta," I protested.

"I know, but you're sitting higher than the heads of the Sultan's representatives. It is considered impolite."

Defeated by both her explanation and her friendly, sympathetic manner, I jumped down. The gamelan was ready, and the men who were to carry the Rice Mountains to the mosque had the palanquins on their shoulders. I couldn't help grumbling over my lost picture.

"I'll speak to the officials. Perhaps there's another vantage point you can use," the teacher said, and disappeared. In a minute she was back, breathless. "Over there, quickly," and she indicated a sheer fifteen-foot wall a monkey could not have scaled. Divining my dismay, she said, "Come, I've already sent for a ladder."

The bearers had started their rhythmic march, the gamelan was striking up a fast pace, and the crowd was milling toward the gate. With two of her students running interference, we pushed through the tight pack. The procession was crossing the courtyard. It was nearing the gate when the ladder arrived. In a performance that would have done credit to a fireman I scampered up the ladder, hung over the wall and between panting breaths squeezed the shutter just before the procession passed out of sight. As I thanked the teacher and her cohorts, I thought to myself that Indonesian education was in good hands if all the teachers were as resourceful as this one.

Jogjakarta, in addition to being Java's principal stronghold of traditional culture, is also the site of the country's first completely Indonesian-inaugurated university, Gadjah Mada University, named after the prime minister of the last Madjapahit Kingdom, under whom in the fourteenth century Indonesia reached her greatest heights of influence and power in Southeast Asia. At Gadjah Mada, although the buildings were still under construction, more than 10,000 students were already enrolled in thirteen departments ranging from engineering to philosophy. Here, in a program similar to that at the Technical Institute at Bandung, a team of American professors from the University of California at Los Angeles, our own alma mater, was doing a tremendous job of assistance in the teaching and organization of the curriculum.

One evening, with a newfound friend, a student from the university named Humardani whose hobby was the study of Javanese dance and drama, we watched a *wayang-kulit* shadow play. It was in an old section of Jogja, away from the noise of Malioboro, down a dim street where the lamplit stalls of vendors were little islands in the dusk. Humardani led us through a great carved gate in the wall of what was once an old palace and across a courtyard to a pavilion. A single oil lamp flickered overhead, casting a hemisphere of yellow light that drew little darting reflections from the gongs and the lacquer-and-gilt stands of a gamelan orchestra. The face of each musician was a half mask, the other side lost in the darkness. Other faces, bodiless in the gloom, ringed the pavilion waiting for the drama to begin.

Beyond the gamelan, at the base of a white screen, the *dalang*—master storyteller, philosopher, puppeteer, whose magic brought shadows to life—sat cross-legged on the stone floor. To either side of him was an array of lacy, buffalo-parchment puppets, like paper dolls with arms that moved. The dalang selected a figure, the Tree of Life; the oil wick of the lamp was turned up, the gamelan struck a thunderous chord and a shadow pulsed on the screen. The performance had begun, a performance whose origin goes back in time to when shadows were believed to be the souls of the dead and the dalang the medium between these souls and the living.

From the screen the shadow of the Tree of Life quaked as if in a wind and the voice of the dalang floated through the thin muslin, narrating the introduction to the Mahabharata, the great Hindu epic that for some sixteen hundred years in India and for almost as long in Indonesia has championed the victory of good over evil.

Perhaps, were it not for the many times we had heard the story in India, we could not have followed the dalang's interpretation of the Mahabharata, moved to a Javanese setting with Javanese characters. But as the dalang imparted life to the puppets, as they breathed with passion, fought with vigor, quivered in fear, we forgot that we were watching only shadows and the drama unfolded:

Long, long ago, when men and gods mingled, there were five young princes, noble and virtuous, the Pandava brothers. On the death of their father they are left in the care of their uncle who raises them as heirs to the throne; but by trickery their one hundred evil cousins, the Kauravas, usurp their position and force them to flee. For many years they wander the forests, befriending all creatures, acquiring strength and spiritual power through their privations. But when the lovely Princess Draupadi is offered in marriage to the man who can pull her father's bow, they leave the forests and compete with the Kauravas and other nobles from all over the land. Only Ardjuna, the third Pandava, can draw the heavy bow;

he shoots five arrows through a swinging ring so that all are
in the air at the same time, so that all hit the target. He wins
the contest; Draupadi becomes the bride of all the Pandavas,
and the kingdom is regained. But the Kauravas again trick the
Pandavas and a great battle takes place. Arjuna, torn with
doubt and perplexed, ponders the futility of life, and Krishna,
as an incarnation of the god Vishnu, appears to him on the bat-
tlefield. Their conversation is the basis of one of the most inspiring verses of all time: the *Bhagavad-Gita*, the Song of
God. Krishna becomes Ardjuna's charioteer, the battle is won,
and the Kauravas killed. After a long and beneficent reign
the Pandavas abdicate and become ascetics as was the custom
of men in the last phases of their lives. For many years the five
Pandavas and Queen Draupadi wander in search of truth. One
by one they die until only Judistira, the eldest, and his loyal
dog are left. Across mountains and deserts Judistira continues
his lonely search accompanied by his faithful dog. At last, in
the distance, they see the mountain of the gods. With the dog
feeble with age and panting beside him, Judistira joyfully
ascends the mountain. A light blazes across the sky and Lord
Indra appears to them. He beckons Judistira to enter the
golden chariot and ascend to heaven where his brothers and
Queen Draupadi await him. But he must leave the dog.
Judistira's hand falls to the head of his faithful friend and protector, his companion through all the hardships of the long
journey. He cannot forsake the animal. Lord Indra blazes
with anger that he should prefer a dog, lowest of all creatures,
to the joys of heaven. Judistira turns away sadly to go back
down the mountain, and then Lord Indra's smile is as the light
of a thousand suns. Judistira has passed the ultimate test. He
has put the least of creatures before himself. Indra beckons
again and Judistira, his old dog cradled in his arms, mounts
the chariot and is carried off to immortality.

During one of the many intermissions Humardani told us how the wayang-kulit had developed, how the migrating Hindus had adapted the indigenous shadow play to their own epics of adventure and war, the Ramayana and the Mahabharata; how when Islam overthrew the Hindu kingdoms, wayang was discouraged because the puppets violated the Moslem prohibition against portrayal of the human form; how the Javanese got around this by cleverly stylizing the puppets into caricatures of humans, into gilt and enamel symbols of good and evil: almond-eyed, slant-nosed heroes and bulging-eyed, bulbous-nosed villains; how wayang had grown in popularity and had developed offshoots like the *wayang-golek* where three-dimensional wooden puppets are used and the *wayang-wong* where humans enact the dramas dressed in the same stylized costumes and assuming the same stilted postures as the puppets; how the dalang is considered a seer, a harbinger of news to remote villages, a man whose political views are often heeded.

All during the performance the dalang interjected his own comments: to the elders he emphasized the blessings and rewards of right living; to the children he spoke of the hero's strength and virtue. Though the spectators followed each word of the story and philosophy with rapt attention, the dalang, master showman that he was, realized, like Shakespeare, the need for comic relief. About midnight the pace changed and three clowns palpitated across the screen, a purely Indonesian innovation: Semar and his sons, the grotesque, wise, cunning servants who with their asides and stage whispers, their tricks on their masters, and even their slurs and criticisms of government figures and policies threw the audience into convulsions of laughter.

But even with this, as the hours passed a few heads began to nod, ours among them. Humardani turned to Helen.

"Would you like some refreshments before the show really gets going?"

Amused at Helen's startled expression, he added, "Oh, didn't you know? This goes on until six in the morning."

"But how can you study if you stay awake all night?" Helen asked weakly.

"Ah, but one of the lessons of the Mahabharata is that by staying awake one acquires spiritual power," was his smiling reply.

I lived here 2½ year

The road east from Jogjakarta toward Surabaja runs through rich sugar country. Dozens of sugar mills lay in ruins along the way, still unrepaired after their destruction during the scorched earth days of the revolution. Much of the land had been converted to rice; sugar exports, meanwhile, have fallen below five percent of the prewar levels. The Communists have capitalized on this blow to the country's economy; the city of Madiun was the scene of the violent Communist uprisings so ably suppressed by Indonesia's present Chief of Staff and Minister of Defense, General Abdul Haris Nasution, now one of the country's most powerful men.

It is in this part of Java that the PKI, Indonesia's Communist Party, has its greatest concentration of strength. Everywhere, in the smallest villages, we saw the red and white PKI sign prominently displayed. In the last election in 1956 the Communists of this area won a majority of the seats in Parliament for the district, and it is believed that in the next election, thus far unscheduled, the Communists—who are already the fourth largest party after the Nationalist Party, Masjumi Moslem Party and N.U. Moslem Scholars Party—will emerge even stronger.

And yet few of the students and none of the peasants we

spoke to had any concept of the international character of Communism. In the hard-pressed areas where Communism is strong they know only that the Communists promise them more rice and cloth, and they will vote for whoever promises them the most. Few have ever heard of Marx, and those who have find nothing new or startling in the idea of "To each according to his needs and from each according to his ability." For this in essence is the basis of the age-old Indonesian motto being heavily stressed by the government today—*gotong rojong*, mutual help. Farmers combine their efforts to plow a neighbor's field or harvest a crop; prosperous members of a family help their less fortunate relatives. There are few orphanages or old people's homes. For centuries Indonesians have practiced a communal society. It would not be a long step to full communization.

As we drove through the countryside of central and east Java we thought of the remote villages where newspapers and magazines rarely reach, where radios are few and the Communist organizer on his bicycle is a frequent visitor. If, instead of glowing accounts of communes in China and high-production quotas in Russia, the people could be told that land —private ownership of which to an Indonesian is his most prized heritage—would be taken from them; that religion— to Indonesian Moslems a vital force—would be suppressed; that forced labor—the most hated aspect of Dutch colonialism and what they fought hardest against—would be imposed on them; if they could learn these things not from a stranger, but from someone they trusted and knew as well as they know the local Communist organizer who is always from their own village—someone like the dalang—the Indonesians' natural love of freedom, their hard-won merdeka, would sway them far more than any promises of the Communists.

And, we thought, what better instrument to impart this information than the wayang where the struggle between good and evil has been the basis of all dramas, where parables—a most effective device, as Christ well knew—are used to get points across in an innocent manner, where the dalang is a man respected and trusted—even revered—wherever he goes, who sooner or later reaches the most remote village? And in addition the wayang would be an invaluable aid in improving the hygiene, sanitation, and farming techniques that today are still bound by centuries-old traditions. The Communists do not work through the government; they reach directly the hearts and minds of the people. The Free World, by sponsoring wayang, could do the the same thing.

In contrast to the formality of Jogjakarta, there was an air of businesslike activity about Indonesia's chief port of Surabaja. Freighters, tankers, warships and the Naval Academy training ship lay at anchor at the modern docks. The lower part of the Kali Mas, the city's main canal, was gay with sailing prahus, a vital part of the country's interisland shipping. The high-pooped prahus from the Celebes, from Sumatra, from Madura, were jumbled together in a tangle of masts and booms, of elaborately decorated sterns, of patched sails and bows with painted eyes that substituted for navigational instruments. Most Indonesian sailing prahus gross under 20 tons today, but in the proud days centuries ago when Indonesia was a great maritime nation, prahus of 300-ton capacity made the long *haj* to Mecca each year carrying thousands of pilgrims.

But for us these prahus of the Kali Mas were of special importance. They would carry our gasoline for our journey through the Lesser Sunda Islands. Though Indonesia supplies almost two percent of the world's petroleum, outside the main cities of Java, Bali, Sumatra, and Borneo, gasoline was unobtainable. And even on Java it had taken special arrangements with Standard Vacuum Oil Company, a subsidiary of Socony Mobil's familiar Flying Red Horse, to keep Tortuga's 60-gallon tanks filled. But once we left Bali there would be no gasoline, and even 60 gallons would not go very far when over half of the thousand miles to Timor would be by sea. At Standard Vacuum's Surabaja office we arranged for an additional 300 gallons of gasoline and motor oil to be delivered by prahu to the main islands along our route. It was an uncommon request, but with the same willing cooperation that marked all our dealings with this company, it was done—on condition that we supply fire extinguishers for the wooden-hulled prahus.

Across the narrow channel from Surabaja lies Madura, an island to which we had been looking forward ever since one of those nightly parties in Djakarta when a Madurese had said, "You must see the bull races of Madura. You'll never forget them."

He had backed his statement with a letter of introduction and we had timed our arrival in the area to correspond with the bull race season. But at the American Consulate in Surabaja where we called for our mail—the first since leaving Djakarta—the Consul, Jack Lydman, suggested that Dinah might not be welcome on Madura.

"The Madurese are ardent Moslems," he warned. "They are not fond of dogs. Why not leave Dinah with me?"

We accepted his generous invitation—and another letter of introduction to the Resident, the chief administrative officer of Madura whom Jack knew well—and after a twenty-minute ferry ride across the mile-wide channel we headed for Pamekasan, the capital of the island. We were barely away from the ferry landing when a child ran in front of Tortuga. We skidded to a stop on the dusty street and the child, waving a scrap of paper at us, shrilled *"Dimana andjing, dimana Dinah* [Where's Dinah]?" The USIS Indonesian-language magazine in Djakarta had run a picture of Tortuga and Dinah, and the look of disappointment on that child's face when we told him we had left Dinah in Surabaja was like a mask in a Greek tragedy.

But the look of the older Madurese was reason enough to be happy we had followed Jack's advice. Wild arrogant men, *proud* so different from the gentle Javanese, they wore black, knee-length trousers, loose black blouses, red scarves on their heads and wide leather belts. They could have been pirates—which at one time they were.

Dry, brambly and infertile, Madura used to be the chief source of labor for the estates of other islands, and Madurese became the main language of east Java. Today, Madura is still considered a deficit area though the island has Indonesia's only salt factory, a government monopoly where in hundreds of acres of evaporation ponds the sun-crackled salt from the sea appears like a checkerboard of Celadon. It has also a fishing fleet that totals over 6,000 prahus, and an untapped reservoir of natural gas that is so close to the surface that blue-burning seepage makes the countryside look as if St. Elmo is there. But the principal industry is still the raising of cattle, small sturdy animals descended from the wild banteng that once roamed all of western Indonesia, and the bull races are encouraged as a stimulus to improving the strains.

At Pamekasan we presented our letters of introduction to Soenarto Hadiwidjojo, the Resident, only to learn that the bull races had been canceled because of the currency devaluation.

"However," he added, looking again at the letters, "wait until tomorrow. I'll see what I can do."

Then followed some remarkable organization. The call

went out to neighboring villages, and the next morning we were awakened in our losmen by a piercing medley of flutes, drums and gongs from the direction of the Pamekasan stadium. Overnight Soenarto had gathered seven pairs of champion bulls, each with its festive trappings, its gamelan and its troupe of cheering supporters.

With half of Madura, it seemed, behind us, we ran to the stadium. The teams were parading around the grassy turf, each bull a dazzling display of gilt-and-tinsel leather bibs, flower-tasseled horn sheaths, and silver-studded head harnesses that crossed the faces of the animals like double Sam Browne belts. Jangling bells hung from the high enameled yoke that united the two bulls of each team, and over each pair was a tasseled parasol. Behind each team rode its jockey, balancing on a skid like a plow without the plowshare, controlling his wild-eyed, eager-to-race bulls with a short wooden prod.

The teams paired off, just as they had for generations. Long before bull racing became an island-wide sport, the spice of competition had already been added to gotong rojong plowing of a neighbor's field. The man whose team could plow the fastest was honored in his village, and even today the honor of winning a race is considered sufficient reward.

The gamelan around each team began an insistent, discordant beat that drove the already pawing and snorting animals into a frenzy. Shorn of their gay trappings, they stood in the sun, magnificent animals with coats like burnished copper. Helen remarked to Soenarto how healthy they looked.

"They should be," he answered. "Champion bulls get as many as fifty raw eggs a day."

Before the race each bull received an additional stimulus—a king-size bamboo tube full of rum. Then two teams at a time they headed for the starting line. The starter dropped his flag, and with a speed we could almost hear they blurred into motion. Heat after heat followed; it was a full-scale event. Each jockey was proud of his team and anxious to win. Soenarto was as excited as we were as he clocked the heats; the best was a little over nine seconds for a hundred meters, faster than the men's world track record. When the final heat was over there was a runoff of the heat winners. The winning team, the bulls seeming to prance and the jockey literally dancing on his skid, paraded around the stadium followed by his shouting entourage. Then, with a soft, soothing gamelan rhythm, the bulls were led back to their villages where they would be massaged until they were calm again, fed more raw eggs, and would become—their owners hoped—the sires of more champion racers.

The Surabaja area, until the fifteenth century, was the center of the Madjapahit Kingdom, the last and greatest of Java's Hindu dynasties, so powerful that it once repelled an invasion by the forces of the Mongol, Kublai Khan. Today little but legend remains of Madjapahit's splendor, but high in the Tengger Mountains of east Java still live the descendants of the Hindu priests of the Madjapahit era whose duty it was to appease the God of Fire residing in the volcano of Bromo. After returning to Surabaja from Madura to pick up Dinah—whom the Lydmans assured us had been a model guest and was welcome back when we returned from Timor —we headed for Tosari, in the heart of the Tengger country.

But the few physical remains of Madjapahit—the house-high stone ogres with gibbous eyes and malignant expression, the crumbled palace walls they guarded, the frangipangi trees so gnarled it seemed they could have witnessed the decay of the kingdom after Gadjah Mada's death—all held us too long, and we spent the night in the neighboring town of Malang.

When I met Kurt's dad! I worked as a saleswoman in "Whit Way laidlaw" biggest English store of the Orient.

An American film was playing, *Rally Round the Flag, Boys*, and we took in an early show, the first we had seen in months. But the busy scissors of the Indonesian censors had altered the story somewhat: a hand would reach for a cocktail and the glass would disappear—Moslems in theory are teetotalers; negligée-clad Angela approaches Harry for an enticing embrace and miraculously she is fully clothed in suit and hat and is shaking hands with him instead—display of affection in public is taboo. And to add to our confusion the middle reel was run last and the last reel first, and all the way back to the hotel we were trying to piece together the plot. I had just paired the characters into what I considered a reasonable relationship when I discovered I was talking to myself.

The streets of Malang that night had the usual carnival atmosphere; clumps of people surrounded the usual vendors, and in the middle of the largest and loudest group I found Helen. She was surveying a blue and white wooden hobby horse that would have looked big on a merry-go-round.

"I think this one is a little too big for Mark, don't you?"

I agreed. Mark is our three-year-old nephew in California. I also declared the idea was impossible.

"Be reasonable, Helen. What are you going to do with it—carry it all the way to Timor? Why, it's bigger than Dinah."

But Helen just selected another horse from the dozens on the sidewalk, a red and brown one that was only slightly smaller, and persuaded a boy about Mark's age to try it for size. The crowd had grown considerably, everyone offering suggestions as Helen and the little boy—trailed by four or five other eager subjects—tried horse after horse. By this time I was embarrassed. I had no intention of buying one and every time I raised an objection the price came down. I was still trying to convince Helen that it would be easier to ride the horse to Djakarta than to have it crated and shipped there to await

to Malang we always went danie

our return, when a young Indonesian in casual sports clothes stepped up. In excellent English he asked if he could be of any help.

"Not unless you can persuade my wife to be reasonable about this horse," I replied.

"You mentioned Djarkarta," he said, and with a conspiratorial grin at Helen, added, "Do you have a place to—ah—stable the horse there?"

"We have friends there, but . . ."

"I saw your Jeep at the hotel. I'm staying there too. When you've picked out the horse you like, have it sent to your room, and I'll be by to pick it up in the morning."

He smiled and extended his hand. "I'm Lieutenant Basarah, Indonesian Air Force. I trained two years in Bakersfield, California, and there isn't anything I wouldn't do to make some American kid happy. Your horse will be in Djakarta tomorrow night."

And it was.

It was late in the afternoon when we arrived at Tosari. The air was chill, and the fading sun was gilding the zinc roofs and dark wooden walls of the sturdy houses that terraced the hillsides. At the flower-bordered pasangrahan, the government rest house, we asked the mustachioed caretaker to make arrangements for us to climb Bromo.

"*Ja, tuan,*" he said, "I'll have horses and guides here at three in the morning."

That seemed a bit early, but the caretaker insisted that if we wished to see sunrise over Bromo, 3 A.M. it would have to be. The only way from Tosari to Bromo, he said, was by horse, and the trip was twelve miles.

It seemed we had slept but a few minutes when the caretaker brought coffee to our room. It was a cold, moonless night, and we could hardly see as we were introduced to our small but sturdy Javanese horses. Helen's mount, the guide vowed, was very gentle. Even his name testified to his character: Manis, meaning sweet. My horse was Selamat, an Indonesian greeting that can be roughly translated as "Blessings on you." It was soon apparent that they were both misnamed.

With flaming torches held high, the guides preceded us along a narrow trail, through dark villages, silent except when some dog, until he saw Dinah, ran snarling toward us, or the horses whinnied in terror when, in the quavering light, a drainage ditch crossed the path like some black serpent. Wind from the mountain crests whipped under our enshrouding blankets; the warming effect of the coffee soon dissipated and I could hardly believe that only a few degrees from the equator it could be so cold.

As long as the going was easy, Manis and Selamat performed ably, though begrudgingly. But as the trail narrowed, as it climbed steeply toward the ridge, Selamat left no doubt that he considered *me* no blessing on *him*. And Manis, his disposition soured apparently by the early hour, did everything from buck to bite to dislodge Helen.

"Stick with him," I encouraged Helen. "These horses have to know who's boss."

Once convinced who really *was* boss, Manis and Selamat had no more trouble with *us*. We joined Dinah and followed meekly afoot.

For several hours we climbed; in places where rain had eroded deep gullies we crawled, grabbing at knotted roots of fallen trees while the guides dragged the horses after them. All the while Helen was mumbling, "I can't understand it. They told me in Surabaja it was just a nice little walk from where you left the car." We reached the ridge, almost 8,000 feet above sea level, as the sun was erasing the shadows from the sea of sand around the caldera of Bromo.

With an exclamation of dismay, Helen pointed to a narrow line descending the opposite side of the ridge.

"Why yes, *tuan*," the guide said, "that's a road. You can drive all the way here from Probolinggo. But from Tosari, like the caretaker said, the only way to get here is by horse."

Later we returned to Bromo the easy way, maneuvering Tortuga down the steep gradient and through the white mist rising over the Sand Sea. There was a disturbing silence to the place. Not a blade of vegetation could be seen; it was as if the God of Fire himself had breathed over the terrain. It was no wonder that the ancient Hindus had felt the need to worship here, no wonder that even today once each year Tengger people by the thousands trek in an antlike stream from Tosari to throw their offerings of rice, sweets, chickens and goats into the seething caldron, no wonder that when sulphurous clouds rise and Bromo rumbles, the Tenggerese say, "The God of Fire is hungry."

The monsoon wind was frothing the Bali Strait when we arrived at Java's eastern shore. It was early evening and all afternoon we had been searching for a road or trail that led down to the sea, but every time we had followed a path that looked promising we had found ourselves in some village; we had been inundated with people, and we wanted quiet to inspect Tortuga and chart her course for her maiden voyage in Indonesia. Dusk had fallen with that sudden tropical swiftness when we found a faint trail that left the road and faded into a grove of banana palms, and then opened onto the sea. The area was deserted, the beach was fine gravel, the water a deep green close to shore with no patches of brown to indicate reef; it was an ideal place to launch Tortuga.

Across the Strait, at its narrowest barely a mile wide, we could see the green peaks of Bali's mountains. They seemed very close, but we knew that there we would find a world apart from Java. In a nation that is ninety percent Moslem, Bali remains a nucleus of modified Hinduism, the legacy of a Hindu prince of Madjapahit who refused to submit to Islam. With his priests, artisans, musicians and dancers, he fled to Bali and established a tradition that has become a way of life for the Balinese.

With the water white as phosphorus in the moonlight, Helen and I studied the Strait, said to have been formed by some mythical king who, wishing to banish his son, had drawn a line with his finger along the ground. The earth had parted and the waters of the Java Sea and the Indian Ocean had joined. A few hundred yards from shore we could see the tousled heads of whitecaps that marked the bands of currents in the Strait.

Stretching more than three thousand miles between the Asian mainland and the Indian Ocean, the Indonesian Archipelago forms a massive dike between two great bodies of water. Like floodgates the straits between the islands equalize the pressures as the seas rise and fall with the tides, and the resulting currents sweep from sea to sea and back at speeds sometimes exceeding ten knots. These currents, compounded with tide rips, whirlpools and coral reefs, would be our greatest hazard all the way to Timor.

In our favor, however, was the fact that the currents change direction, flowing south when the tide ebbs and north when it is in flood, and during the change there is little or no current at all. I was sure that by coordinating our crossings with the tides we could minimize to a great degree the effect of the currents. As we stood there the tide was coming in. We made up the bunks in Tortuga and fixed supper, and when the water had reached its high point we noted the hour and turned in.

But we did not sleep long. Dinah lunged at the window with a deep growl and a face leaped back. I sprayed my flashlight through the windows. Three soldiers with Sten guns asked what we were doing there. We showed them our papers; they said someone had seen us leave the road and notified their sergeant. They had come to guard us.

We never learned what they were guarding against, but there was little sleep for us that night. What appeared to be a whole village drifted by, building fires, sitting round them, chattering, waiting for dawn to see the kapal dharat take to the sea. When morning came we were bleary-eyed and not in the best of humor.

Dawn broke with the same swiftness as dusk, and while Helen plotted our course I inspected Tortuga, crawling beneath to check the rubber seals around the drive shafts that are all that keep the water out. And with Dinah dripping from an unauthorized swim, we slipped down the gravel shore toward the Strait, followed by the few dozen hardy souls who had lasted through the night.

Slowly I steered Tortuga into the water, watching her bow through the windshield. Her fuel and water tanks were full, and the beach fell off rapidly. The sea rose over the wheels, up the sides of the hull, over the bow. It seemed that the bow would never come up. The water was almost to the doors before I felt the bow lift and the wheels start to spin. Tortuga quivered a bit as if reluctant to become detached from land, and then the stern was afloat too. In one motion I shifted the wheels into neutral and engaged the propeller and bilge pump; a rumbling filled the cramped cabin as the propeller bit into the water, and suddenly, though five years had passed, it seemed like yesterday that we had navigated an amphibious Jeep along the coast of Panama in the Caribbean. I had that same feeling of wonder that this 5,000-pound mass of complex machinery that was neither car nor boat but a little of each could float. But there it was, a few yards from Java, a cream-white Jeep with protruding headlights and painted turtles on the sides, trailing a bright yellow rubber life raft, bobbing on the green waters of the Bali Strait, a 15-foot boat with spare tires, a monster that made even Bali's mythical demons of the sea seem real by comparison.

For a few minutes I steered Tortuga in large circles, listening to the engine, checking the bilge for leaks, moving the steering wheel from side to side to regain the feel of the rudder. The compass card followed slowly, and when it came around to northeast I advanced the hand throttle. The stern dipped a bit, the bow raised, and at four knots Tortuga headed for the broad band of steep whitecaps that indicated the tidal current that separated us from Bali.

It is strange, when traveling at four knots on the sea, only slightly faster than a brisk walk, with nothing stationary around you to judge by, how time and distance lose their relationship to each other. From the shore Bali had seemed so close, from the sea so far. And the tidal currents that swept through the narrows to the south of us, from the shore had seemed to dissipate where the Strait spread wide at the north. But in minutes we could feel their strength. Agitated by wind and current in opposition the waves had no pattern; they humped Tortuga from the stern, rocked her abeam, rolled over her bow in foaming cascades, but she took them all without faltering. To avoid the worst of the current we swung Tortuga north toward the Java Sea, farther from the narrows, and headed for a point fourteen miles away on Bali's north coast where our map showed a road touching the shore.

Once across the Strait and into the lee of Bali, the water

calmed, and we slowed our speed. We skirted the coast, steering a zigzag course through rust-colored reefs where orange and black tiger fish flashed among purple sea urchins and red branches of coral. From our chart we tried to identify some landmark to locate the road, but all we could see was a jagged line of low cliffs that dropped off straight into the water. Toward midafternoon the cliffs opened and a cluster of coconut palms fringed the shore. We rolled up a gently sloping beach, bumped across a hedge of tidal debris, through the coconut grove, onto a trail and right into a procession of goddesses.

Chapter Three

I'M not sure who was the more startled, the goddesses at seeing Tortuga rising from the sea, or we at finding ourselves among a score of regal, statuesque girls in gold brocade kains, each with golden flowers in her hair and each balancing on her head a yard-high temple offering of exotic fruit and frangipangi blossoms.

But then Bali was full of surprises. The golden-brown cows with their large ears and the white ovals on their rumps looked like deer; the elongated, saggy-bellied pigs looked like oversized dachshunds; and in the rice fields the ducks quacked in formation, upright like penguins, behind the flags of their herders.

In every village there were temples, near each house an altar for offerings to the multitudes of higher and lower spirits. Everywhere were processions, for it was the beginning of

Bali is picturesque but awful dirt

the long Galunggan festival that occurs every seven months on this island where time seems to be measured by the weeks between holidays.

The road was only a few hundred yards from the beach, a rocky pocked road that runs through west Bali's poorest, most sparsely populated region. It is said that tigers and wild cattle still roam the brambled forests of west Bali, but we saw only monkeys, dozens of gray or black monkeys that were only slightly less brazen than their sacred cousins in India.

As we headed east and south across the mountains toward Denpasar, the island's main city, the country took on that rich green aura we had expected of Bali. The road improved, and the fields changed from ill-tended dry rectangles to precisely curved patterns of flooded fields in an endless variety of greens and silvers that stepped up and down the hills as if laid out by an engineer who really wanted to be a painter.

Instead of the thatch-and-cane villages of Java strewn haphazardly among palm trees, the villages of Bali are walled compounds of reddish stone carved in a proliferation of gargoyles and rococo floral patterns. Each village was dominated by the pagoda-roofed temples with their open courtyards and altars for the various deities. From each thatch-roofed stone house, streamers of yellow palm leaf danced in the light breeze, and other, more intricately woven palm leaf banners fluttered from the temples where Bali Hindu priests sprinkled sanctified water on the offerings. Brought by the women and girls of the village, the offerings were tapering mosaic pillars of fruit and flowers arranged on wooden compotes: mangosteen, pineapple, rambutan, mangoes, durian, accented with pink rice cakes and fringed with green palm leaf. The offerings would remain at the temples overnight before being returned to the homes, for the beneficent gods take only the essence, leaving the substance for the people.

Crowds congregated everywhere, but unlike Java where Tortuga's passing was a signal for everything to stop, on Bali she received only a passing glance. The Balinese live in a world that was created for them; strangers are welcome, but the Balinese are never distracted for long from the affairs of the gods, and that day Tortuga moved through the celebrating villages as if she were invisible.

Our progress was slow, however, and darkness found us high in the mountains. We pulled to the side of the road near an ancient banyan tree to camp until morning.

It was an eerie night. As soon as the sun dropped behind the "Navel of the World," Gunung Agung, Bali's sacred mountain, the roads were suddenly deserted. A mist as white and thick as cotton drifted in widening layers from the rice terraces far below us, and from the hills above came a mournful, soul-wrenching roar that rose and fell like some guttural, bass-tuned siren. A white shirt floated toward us from the darkness down the road, whistling loudly and tunelessly. I stepped from behind the Jeep to ask what the noise was, and a young man jumped back with an exclamation as though burned. Without stopping he blurted out, "To frighten away the *leyaks*," and hurried on, never looking back. I checked the word in our Balinese glossary; a leyak is an evil spirit that haunts dark lonely places, roads at night and graveyards. It can assume any shape, eats the entrails of babies and corpses, casts spells, and like a vampire drinks the blood of sleeping people.

In the morning we could smell the fragrance of frangipani, the flower of the dead. It came from a graveyard down the road. But on the hilltops above us, the wind-driven propellers that were still whirring their awesome noise had done their work well; no leyaks had disturbed our rest.

We passed quickly through Denpasar, a typical, noisy,

concrete-and-tin Indonesian town cluttered with automobiles, trucks and bicycles; we headed for the Segara Beach
Hotel on the ocean at Sanur. From our cottage room we
could look across the Strait toward the distance-hidden island
of Lombok, our next destination after Bali.

Strangely, it was only here at the hotel, where the people
are accustomed to the weird sights of foreign tourists and
their activities, that Tortuga was any competition to the order
of life on Bali. I was lubricating the Jeep on the grounds of
the hotel. The road gang—young girls in kains and kebayas
with immense hats shading their full, sensuous faces—stopped
spreading gravel on the newly tarred road and leaned over the
wall to watch. Children from neighboring villages were un-
derfoot. The dancers who were to give a demonstration at the
hotel, even the cooks and waiters—dinner was late that night
—crowded in until there was no room to work. Dinah tried
to help out by growling a bit, but she was as big an attraction
as Tortuga. There are literally millions of dogs on Bali, but
they are scabrous, whimpering skeletons that to the Balinese
represent the lowest spirits, that are never fed but subsist
on the bits of rice dropped from the offerings. These pathetic
creatures seem to bear out Covarrubias' theory that dogs were
placed on Bali by the gods to keep the island from being perfect. But in comparison to these, Dinah with her sleek coat and
aggressive manner was as a lion. The people moved back a
bit, but then as Dinah, frustrated by sheer numbers, settled
down to pant, they eased in again and Tortuga and her crew
were smothered in the breathless air.

One morning at dawn, Njoman Oka, efficient and enterprising head of Balitour, pounded on the door of our cottage.
"Wake up, Mr. Frank!" he shouted. "There's a cremation."

"It's too early for jokes," I yawned. "You told us no cremations would be performed during the festivals."

"This is different. I'll explain later. Hurry up."

Helen and I tumbled out of bed, thinking how vigorous are these Balinese, how direct their approach to life. Their gods they visualize as super Balinese, their cremations a joyous time when families are privileged to release the souls of departed relatives to fly to the pleasures of heaven—which they see as merely a reflection of Bali with all the troubles removed.

In contrast to the somber Indian cremations where the only color is in the flames, the village where the event was to take place was riotous when we arrived. The cremation tower, a wooden structure covered with gold and silver foil streamers of colored paper and sprinkled with chips of mirror, was standing near the deceased's home, and the wooden coffin in the shape of a black cow with spangled head and silver-papered horns waited to receive the body. Lying in state on a shaded pavilion nearby, the body was surrounded with flowers, rice cakes, brass urns of holy water, and banners of gold-painted cloth and palm leaf. The corpse was a long sticklike bundle bound tightly in a white sheet. The body fluids had been drained to speed the burning, and the tower and coffin showed haste in their construction for it was imperative, Njoman told us, that the cremation be completed as quickly as possible.

Two men in sarongs and white shirts came from the house. They heaved the dripping head of a sacrificed buffalo onto its special palanquin. There was a great scurrying around the tower as friends and relatives scrambled for the privilege of carrying it. An *angklung* orchestra of bamboo rattles, flutes and xylophones played a happy melody and the body was raised to the tower. Accompanied by gongs and loud shouting the procession headed for an open field a half mile or so from the village. They took a devious route and ran in circles to confuse the evil spirits who might be following to steal the dead man's soul. They crossed a stream, for the spirits hate to get their feet wet.

At the field the body was slid from the tower down a white streamer of cloth into the coffin; a priest sprinkled it with holy water. I was near, and a man asked me for one of my paper film wrappers to kindle the fuel of chopped automobile tires. Wood would have been the traditional fuel, but the rubber would burn faster, and haste was all-important. A flame leaped from kindling to fuel to coffin; a vendor hawked colored ice; the angklung played a rousing beat. Black oily smoke rose in great clouds and the fire became a hissing, rumbling inferno of deep red whose heat drove the people to buy more and more colored ice from the vendor. The tower collapsed in a cascade of sparks; the coffin crumbled. A few relatives poked the corpse with long poles to hasten the burning, laughing and talking to it as they did. The head of the cow, its glass eyes peering from the flames and smoke, nodded as if overcome by the fumes; it sagged, then dropped into the flames. The eldest son raked the coals to be sure that all was consumed; the ashes were collected, and in another long procession they were carried to the sea and sprinkled on the waters and the soul was free at last.

Normally, we knew, months, sometimes years, went into the preparations for a cremation, the body being buried in the meantime. Then, on some auspicious date, determined by the priest after consulting a horoscope and set long in advance, the event would take place, often a mass cremation with many families sharing in the expenses. A cremation during the festivals was almost unheard of. We asked Njoman about it, and especially why all the haste.

"It's simple," Njoman explained. "This man was of high caste. By tradition he could not be buried. But as long as his body remained uncremated the village was considered impure and couldn't take part in the celebrations. So the people had a hurry-up cremation, and now the festivities can continue."

With Njoman Oka and art connoisseur Jim Pandy, a genial Indonesian Christian who had adopted the Bali Hindu religion, we saw many of these festivities. One night at the village of Paksebali, the War of the Gods took place. The invisible gods, carried on palanquins, had emerged from the temples, but pleased by the music, dancing and sweets offered by the people, they refused to return. A mighty battle like a tug-of-war ensued as youths in a state of self-induced trance tried to force the palanquins carrying the gods to re-enter the temples.

The night was black; a few oil lamps glanced from the spears and swords of the leaders of the battle. Time after time the palanquins reached the gates of the temple, but each time the force of the gods pushed them away again. Several young men lay twitching on the ground, their eyes rolled back in their heads, their mouths flecked with saliva, overcome by their entranced exertions. A joyful shout was raised as the palanquins at last entered the temples and the gates became blackened with people to keep them from emerging again.

"But why," we asked, "don't the gods want to return to heaven?"

"Because they are having such a good time here on Bali," Njoman answered.

"Then why can't they stay?"

"Because all this entertainment is too expensive for the people," Njoman said seriously. "And besides, they'll be invited back again next Galunggan."

Though the Balinese worship dozens of gods, they are not idolaters. There were no images on the palanquins, no statues in the temples or on the altars as are found in Hindu India. Separated from India by thousands of miles of ocean and isolated by Islam, which dominates nearly every other part of Indonesia, the caste system that was once such a powerful force has broken down, and Bali has developed a Hinduism that has a character all its own.

Balinese Hinduism is more of an animism with many of the spirits given Hindu names. The Balinese worship the forces that govern their lives: the sun, the earth, the sea, the seasons, and a hundred other spirits that inhabit every living and inanimate thing, but all these are merely the manifestations of a Supreme Being. The Balinese talk to their gods; they call them to earth to help them in adversity, to bless their crops, or to rid them of plagues or pests which they believe are caused by evil spirits who must also be propitiated. But sometimes these invisible spirits, both good and bad, are given form and battles ensue. One day at Kesiman, the Barong, the huge, shaggy, lionlike creature that personifies the guardian spirit of the village, did battle with Rangda, the pendulous-breasted, bloody-fanged witch of evil whose power is an ever-present danger.

In a temple courtyard a gamelan sat to one side shaded by a canopy of palm fronds. The musicians struck a shattering chord and the audience hushed. The Barong appeared at the gate at the top of the temple steps, its face echoing the fierce expression of the temple guardian carved in the stone arch over its head. For a moment the Barong stood there, its fanged jaws working, its white bushy mane and high arched tail shaking gently, the eyes in its gold and mirror-specked mask seeming to penetrate each member of the audience. Suddenly it was not a comical stage prop operated by two men. It was

the Barong who personifies good, whose magical power pro-
tects the village from Rangda.

But in a moment the illusion was shattered. The Barong
danced ridiculously; it rushed at the audience, throwing chil-

dren into gales of laughter, gamboling like a puppy enticing
its master to play, drawing back and staring with a foolish
clacking of its jaws.

There was another hush and Rangda entered. She too stood
a moment, allowing her frightful appearance to register, shaking her bulging, dangling, flour-sack breasts, clawing at the
air with her saberlike fingernails, her voice an evil mutter from
behind her long-haired demon's mask, her body a lumpy,
shapeless white form.

Instantly Barong was no longer the clown. He was the protector again. Rangda and Barong rushed at each other, scuffling, raising swirls of dust that obscured the combatants, and the audience sat tense, for no matter how often they witnessed the struggle nor how well they knew the outcome, this was a battle of supreme importance to them.

From the tangle on the ground Rangda rose in triumph and a score of youths rushed from the temple to Barong's aid. But Rangda waved her magic weapon, a white kerchief, and the youths became entranced by her spell. They turned the krisses on themselves; their faces contorted, their muscles convulsed as they pressed the sharp blades against their chests. Some rolled on the ground, moving the kris handles in violent circles as though trying to bore all the way to the heart. But the Barong's protective influence was too great; the krisses, though indenting deeply the flesh, did not penetrate. Rangda's spell was broken and she was put to flight; for good must always conquer evil on Bali.

Were the youths who waged the Battle of the Gods at Paksebali and those who aided the Barong really entranced? We could never be sure, but one thing is certain: the Balinese live with spirits and demons whose powers to protect and harm are as real to them as the Sign of the Cross and the danger of an automobile accident are to us. The ability to induce a state of self-hypnosis is an accepted fact, and on Bali this ability seems to run in families. It can be implemented by breathing the smoke from burning incense, by hunger or by prayers and concentration, but to the Balinese, one who is entranced is inhabited by the spirits. How else, they ask, can an untrained child perform while entranced the intricate movements of a dance that takes years to master? How else can a man eat live coals without harm or resist injury from a kris thrust fiercely against his flesh?

Though the Barong-Rangda battle is performed regularly for tourists, and there are nightly demonstrations of the dances at the hotels, the times we enjoyed most were those when Njoman Oka or Jim Pandy would lead us across dark fields to some obscure village. We would sit in a temple courtyard or under a sacred banyan tree while a priest burned incense and made offerings of rice and holy water to the gods. The gamelan would play with vibrant, pulsing life, so different from the stilted melancholy notes of Javanese music, and little girls would dance the *legong,* boys the warlike *baris,* and young men the *kebiyar.* The gamelan would crash and ripple, reach peaks of elation and depths of tragedy, and we would sit enraptured.

One night Jim Pandy took us to the village of Saba whose legong dancers are thought by many to be the finest on the island. A temple wall was the backdrop, pressure lamps the footlights, and the turbaned, saronged, bare-chested musicians of the gamelan, each with a red hibiscus blossom behind his ear, were the orchestra. And the audience? Groups like that of Saba have played in the capitals of the world to black ties and starched shirts and long gowns, but that night the dancers were performing for the Balinese. For hours the villagers from the surrounding area had been gathering; mothers sat nursing their babies, children barely able to walk waited expectantly, and the older people spoke in hushed voices, for to the Balinese a dance recital strikes at the very core of their lives.

The drummer, the leader of the orchestra, gave a signal, and the gongs, the two-stringed rebab, the xylophones and finger bells joined in a dynamic chord that silenced the audience. The figure of a child with the face of a woman appeared at the temple gate. No more than seven, she poised there, her arched brows, her dark eyes, the three white dots on her fore-

HT—Breakfast in Tor-
ja II, the amphibious
p in which the Schrei-
rs toured Indonesia's
ds and seas for thir-
n months. BELOW —
len and Dinah among
robudur's bell-shaped
ines, each enclosing
age of Buddha. Java.

Helen and Frank dine out in Djakarta.

Dinah, companion without peer.

LEFT—Ninth century Prambanan, where Javanese kings depicted themselves as gods. RIGHT—The royal gamelan echoes somberly through the courtyards of the sultan's palace in Jogjakarta, the cultural capital of central Java. BELOW—Spotted deer romp on the grounds of President Sukarno's summer palace at Bogor. Java.

olic rice mountains toward a mosque in Jogjakarta.

ABOVE—Backstage at the Javanese theater. BELOW—Batik making on Java: a patient process of designing in wax on cotton cloth followed by successive dippings in dye.

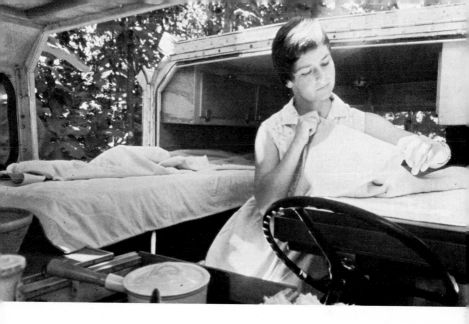

ABOVE—Helen "keeping house" in Tortuga. With its pullman bunks and alcohol stove, the Jeep has *almost* all the comforts of home. BELOW—Helen and Frank on a trip to Java's Mount Bromo.

ABOVE—Bull racing on Madura. Owners ply the animals with raw eggs and rum before the races. On plowlike sledges, jockeys prod the bulls with pointed sticks.

RIGHT—Java's Mount Bromo last erupted in 1930. To reach its 8,000-foot crest the authors struggled up a grueling 12-mile trail by night. Here, with the help of a guide, Helen explores the rim of the caldera where Javanese used to offer human sacrifices. Now they toss in chickens.

ABOVE—At Java's eastern shore, Helen gazes across the monsoon-tossed strait before Tortuga is launched for Bali. BELOW—The villages of Bali are dominated by pagoda-roofed temples.

UPPER LEFT—Bali: Their muscles convulse as they press the sharp blades against their chests. UPPER RIGHT—Offerings to the Balinese gods. LOWER LEFT—A Balinese who remembered the old days when only prostitutes covered their breasts.

LEFT—Balinese girls dance the *Legong*, enacting the drama of a princess kidnaped by a despised suitor. ABOVE—Balinese threshing rice in hollow tree trunks. RIGHT—President Sukarno (*photograph by N.G.S. photographer J. Baylor Roberts*).

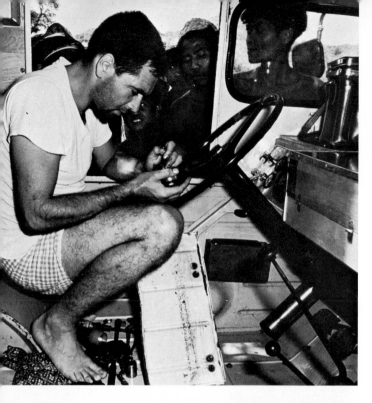

Tortuga II receives
overhaul from Fr.
after the rough pass
to Lombok. Onloo
stayed all day as Fr.
replaced the bearin

Circumcision ceremc
on Lombok: Boys a
girls are carried throu
the village atop carv
painted and gild
wooden lions.

ABOVE—The island of Sumbawa. Stopping at Bima only long enough to take on water and refuel. BELOW—Slowly Tortuga II moves across the bay, drawn by villagers spaced along 200 feet of nylon rope.

ABOVE—Tortuga II teeters above a 50-foot abyss after bumping onto a rotten bridge in Sumbawa. Frank levers vehicle back onto road.

RIGHT—Gold-and-enamel teeth of Sumbawa girl proclaim status of her rich farm family.

Courtesy National Geographic Magazine, © National Geographic Society

head, her red lips, all frozen in a mask that expressed only her own intensity, her only movement a slight quivering of the frangipangi blossoms in her golden crown. The gamelan blended in another chord; it rippled, and this animated doll, her body tortured in tight bands of cloth, her gold-painted bib of leather and cloth reaching almost to her waist, moved slowly down the steps, posturing on each one. At the bottom she stamped her small bare feet, her eyes darted from side to side, her fingers fluttered backwards, almost touching her wrists; she kneeled, and the legongs, two more dolls stamped from the same mold, appeared.

For an hour we watched as spellbound as the children, the nursing mothers and all the others as the legongs danced in their quick, abrupt movements, their gold fans fluttering until they were only blurs, their hands and heads and eyes moving as if controlled by the same string, enacting the story of a wicked prince who wanted to marry a princess of a neighboring kingdom. But the princess, though threatened by war against her father, resists his advances. The prince goes to attack her father's kingdom but encounters a crow, an evil omen. The crow, danced by one of the legongs, her arms wings of embossed leather, flutters violently around the prince, obstructing him, and he is killed.

The baris dance followed, as masculine as the legong is feminine, the embodiment in movement of all that is admired in a warrior. But the warrior is a boy, his armor a cape of ribbons, his helmet a dome of mother-of-pearl, his face and eyes expressing anger, ferocity, triumph.

And there was the kebiyar, a modern Balinese dance performed by a seated man, where only the upper body, arms, hands, head and eyes translate the tense music of the gamelan into movements of infinite grace and beauty.

There were other dances peopled by witches and demons.

Rangda made her appearance, and there were slapstick clowns, but the vision we carried away that night was of the little legongs who entered the makeup room as urchins and emerged as living golden dolls, precise little figures whose silent articulation bespeaks of splendors that still live in the minds of the Balinese.

In most of the Balinese dances sensuality is suppressed. Girls who have reached puberty are considered too old to dance the legong, and for other dances, performed by more mature girls, tight breast bands flatten the figure. But the Balinese are earthy people and far from prudish. In the village plays to which Jim or Njoman took us, where we were the only foreigners present, the jokes were bawdy, and a grab at the genitals of another player brought boisterous laughter from the audience.

One night Njoman took us to a *djoged* dance, village style. Here were no shy glances, no demure gestures. Surrounded by admiring males of all ages, a golden-crowned girl in her late teens danced voluptuously, moving her gold brocade-covered hips to the provocative beat of drums and gongs. She selected a youth from the audience; he feigned shyness. Then, charmed by her advances, he became aggressive. She enticed him, allowing him to approach but never touch her. She waved an arm near his nose; he breathed deeply of the perfume of her skin; the dance became more animated as he tried again to partake of her fragrance, as exciting to a Balinese as a kiss is to us. But she repulsed him and chose another from the audience, an older man obviously fond of eating.

There was a laughing shout from the crowd as at first he appeared awkward. But it was only a ruse to amuse the audience—the man was a skilled dancer. The girl responded to him, danced more sensuously with him than with the other. Suitor after suitor danced, each adding his interpretive and more than suggestive movements to the accompanying roars of delight from the crowd.

From my place in the front row I could see Helen on the far side of the courtyard with the women. She was standing high on a pile of bricks. The dancer, with a sly smile, advanced toward me, the only non-Balinese there. The gamelan increased its tempo and the girl gestured in my direction. She reached toward me and there was a rumble of masonry as Helen's pile of bricks collapsed. I breathed with relief—or was it disappointment?—as the girl selected a young Balinese behind me as her next partner.

Dancing, music and theater are a part of life for every Balinese. He who does not have the talent to participate supports the gamelan and dancers that almost every village has. To reach the degree of perfection to which the critical Balinese aspire, training is begun very young. When we moved from the beach hotel at Sanur to the mountain village of Ubud, we spent hours watching the training of the young legong dancers. The Tjokorde Agung, a jolly, progressive rajah who uses his independence-depleted power to preserve and promote the Balinese traditional culture, was accepting guests, and almost any evening from behind the carved sandstone walls of his modest palace we could hear the gamelan. A famous dancer, now old but as supple as ever, led five-year-old girls through the complicated postures of the dance, thrusting their heads and hands and bodies savagely, relentlessly, into position until the movements were perfect.

Living with the Tjokorde Agung was to experience the Bali of Vicki Baum and Colin McPhee, of Walter Spies, Le Mayeur and Miguel Covarrubias—writers, musicians and painters of American, Dutch, Belgian and Mexican nationalities who lived and wrote on this island in the thirties. Each guest room is separated from the other parts of the palace by flowered and tree-shaded walkways or by walls where the carved figures of mythical lions and birds have grown green whiskers of moss. We ate the spicy Balinese food by lamplight with the Tjokorde on a raised pavilion that was once used for the vital ritual of tooth filing, without which no Balinese can enter heaven; only animals and demons have irregular or pointed teeth.

And a few minutes' walk from Ubud—across rice fields laced with string to control the intricate systems of scarecrows—were villages where the thump of rice pounding and the whisk of handlooms still persisted—unaffected by the rice mills of town that rob this staple of its nutriment or the cheap cloth in the stores that alienate the people of their desire to create. Here the women go about their tasks, their arms rhythmically raising and dropping the heavy rice pestles in the hollowed logs. They hummed softly at their work, sarongs draped to the ankles, their round full breasts delicately contoured in gold by the slanting sun filtering through palm fronds. In the old days, they complained, only prostitutes covered their breasts, while now the government in Djakarta, mistakenly believing that foreigners consider such natural dress a sign of poverty or primitiveness, are forcing them to wear blouses when they go to town.

For a while we were guests in Jim Pandy's home, and here was still another Bali. Jim, a gentle, sophisticated painter, lives on the beach at Sanur surrounded by his books, his records, and his treasures of Balinese art collected from all over the island. From the pavilion near the water where we watched the eastern sky reflect the setting sun, to the lanai where we sipped *berum*, the sweet rice-and-honey liqueur, to the guest house where we slept, to the open-sided pavilion where we dined, his home is a spacious garden. White pebbled walkways meander past statues graced with hibiscus blossoms and wrapped in black and white magic cloths; the sea washes over brown coral, and in the moonlight the shadows of men gathering shellfish are wraiths against the dark water. Perhaps nowhere is the artist more appreciated by his own people than on Bali, and in Jim's gallery the best of the silverwork, the stone and wood carving, the weaving and painting are displayed with a taste that is as traditional and as modern as is Jim himself.

Shortly before we left Bali there was another early-morning knock on our door. "Just a minute, Njoman," I called, wrapping a sarong around me and hoping that Njoman had another surprise for us. But it wasn't Njoman. Two somber-faced Indonesians in Western clothes stood on the porch. One of them flipped open his wallet in good FBI fashion.

"I understand you have a dog," he said.

Just then Dinah poked her long nose through the door.

"The animal will have to be shot," the other man said bluntly.

Stunned, I shoved Dinah back in the room, almost stuttering as I asked what they meant.

"No dogs are allowed to be brought to Bali from outside," the first man explained.

"But we have all our papers. Even the dog has a permit," I protested, showing them Dinah's certificate from the Ministry of Agriculture in Djakarta.

The men looked at the papers. "This says nothing about Bali; we have our own laws here. The dog will have to be shot."

"I'm sure there is some mistake. I want to see your chief." And I locked Helen and Dinah in the room.

At the headquarters I showed Dinah's permit and all our clearances. I told them how in Djakarta I had asked specifically if Dinah needed any other papers to travel in Indonesia, how in all of our applications I had listed Dinah as accompanying us, how I had been assured that everything was in order, that we would need nothing more.

"That was in Djakarta," the police chief said. "They don't know our laws." And he opened a tattered book to an old Dutch law dated 1926 stating that because certain islands of Indonesia were free of rabies, no dogs could be brought from Java—heavily infested with the disease—to these areas. *And the law prohibited the importation of dogs into every island in Indonesia except Java and Celebes.* . . . I was positive that it was all a misunderstanding. Dinah had had a particularly heavy immunization against rabies. I pleaded for time to contact Djakarta before Dinah was disposed of. They agreed on condition that we muzzle her and keep her in our room or on a leash at all times.

With Njoman Oka I tried to telephone Sumarjo at the Ministry of Foreign Affairs. He was in Jogja. I called Jogja, but he had left again for Djakarta. I telephoned Djakarta but he had not arrived yet. Some friends were leaving for Djakarta that morning and they offered to hand-carry a letter for us. And then Njoman had a suggestion.

"There is only one man on Bali who can save Dinah," he said. "Let's go see the Military Commander."

At Military Headquarters there was no tea, no small talk, no hesitation. I showed our permits and letters and went through the long explanation again. The Commanding Officer of Bali was in charge of all of Nusa Tenggara, the name for the Lesser Sunda Islands, and his word was law all the way to Timor. A young, muscular and handsome officer of few words, Colonel Supardi listened while his Chief of Staff, Colonel Suparmin, took notes. When we were finished he told us to wait. Only then was tea brought and before we had finished it we had another permit. Dinah was free to travel with us to Timor.

Our last days on Bali we spent driving up and down the island's eastern coast. From Karangasem in the north where Lombok Strait is the narrowest and the cliffs drop straight into the sea, to Sanur in the south where only a few inches of water cover the reefs, we scouted for a place to launch Tortuga on her journey to Timor.

Near the fishing village of Kusamba the road passed within yards of the Strait. There were no cliffs and no reefs, and the night before our departure we camped near the Cave of the Bats, that demon-filled passage leading no one knew how far into the bowels of the earth.

The priest in charge of the altars in front of the cave warned us not to go in too far, and a passing peasant offered —for a price—to bring out one of the bat-gorged pythons that lay comatose inside, but the layer of thick slimy droppings on the floor of the cave, the pale dogs that scavenged the dead bats, and the foul miasma that blasted from the entrance were enough to discourage more than a quick glance. It took no imagination to visualize the most evil of all demons writhing in the depths of that Pandora's Box.

As we passed Kusamba a few fishermen were pulling their prahus up on the beach and we asked them about the Strait. They glanced skeptically at Tortuga and examined the sky.

"The stars are wrong, *tuan*," they said. Their knowledge of the Indonesian language was as sketchy as ours and we assumed they were speaking of astrology, which governs every action of the Balinese. But to them our journey was ill-fated from the start; the dark of the moon was no time to be about, and especially no time to be near the Cave of the Bats.

Chapter Four

WE left Bali shortly after dawn when the sun was garish in the east and the shacks of the saltmakers were golden against the black sand beach. It was an easy approach down the steep slope. Close to the edge of the Strait where the sand was wet, Tortuga's tread marks were crisp at first; then as water seeped in they crumbled, becoming streaks of silver on black. In a few minutes they would disappear. It would be as if we had never passed, and somehow the thought was not reassuring.

As before, I steered Tortuga in circles, listening, testing. When the compass card indicated due east I increased our speed and Tortuga slipped over the long ground swells into the sun.

Ahead of us the outrigger canoes of the Balinese fishermen we had met the night before skated across the water like giant water spiders. Now, as we passed, they waved us toward shore.

"Better go back, *tuan*," they called, "go back."

But aware of the Balinese dread of the sea—to them the abode of the very lowest spirits—we waved in return and charted our course for Lombok, the first island in an almost untouched chain that stretched more than a thousand miles to the east. Our goal: Timor, near the end of that chain.

As Tortuga bobbed beneath us, her wake a feathery white trail fanning off into the blue of the sea, I felt a little like the sailors of Columbus's day who believed that the earth was flat and that if they sailed too far they would slip off the edge into a bottomless void. We were leaving the warmth and laughter, the music and dancing of Bali and slipping off into a world of which we knew very little.

We were aware, of course, that centuries earlier, Arab, Indian, Portuguese and Dutch traders had pioneered our route. And Sir William Dampier, the English buccaneer, and Captain William Bligh of *Bounty* fame had sailed these waters. But it was to the great English naturalist, Alfred Russel Wallace, that we looked for information about Nusa Tenggara, formerly the Lesser Sunda Islands.

Some one hundred years before, Wallace had crossed this same channel in search of data to confirm his theory that Lombok Strait, at 20,000 feet the deepest in the Indies, was the division between the Asian and Australian worlds of animal and plant life. From Bali westward abound the luxuriant tropical vegetation, the elephants, tigers, wild cattle and monkeys of Asia. But east of Bali, Wallace thought, he would find only the thorny arid growth, the cockatoos and giant lizards so typical of Australia. His findings verified his theory and for many years the so-called Wallace Line stood undisputed. Though today some naturalists disagree with this theory, believing Nusa Tenggara to be a transitional area, Wallace is still considered a pioneer in this field.

Beyond this we knew little of what we would find in Nusa Tenggara. In our long stay on Java we had met only three Indonesians who had ever been east of Bali. This was almost *terra incognita*—even the Dutch in their 350-year rule had waited until the early 1900's to pacify the wild tribesmen in the interior of some of the islands. And today, except for a few Javanese officials and soldiers who consider themselves exiled, the islands east of Bali are only frugally serviced by the new Indonesian government in Djakarta. Only in the few towns could we expect to find evidence of the twentieth century. With little of commercial or historical importance beyond the sandalwood of Timor and the Dragon Lizards of Komodo, these are the islands that were bypassed by time.

Perhaps another reason the islands of Nusa Tenggara had remained isolated so long was the strength of the currents in the straits that separate them. As Wallace wrote: "These are so uncertain that vessels preparing to anchor in the bay [of Ampenan, Lombok's chief port] are sometimes suddenly swept away into the straits, and are not able to return for a fortnight. What seamen call the 'ripples' are also very violent in the straits, the sea appearing to boil and foam and dance like the rapids below a cataract; vessels are swept about helpless, and small ones are occasionally swamped in the finest weather and under the brightest skies."

The Sailing Directions of the United States Hydrographic Office were no more encouraging, but Tortuga had proven herself seaworthy and we were confident, though ahead lay the longest nonstop crossing we had ever made. Barely visible some fifty miles to the east lay the mist-shrouded mountains of Lombok. Somewhere at their foot was the small port of Ampenan, our destination for the day.

With Tortuga steady on course I climbed from the hot cramped cabin and sat atop the open hatch. By tilting my head down slightly I could see the rugged war surplus tank compass mounted on the center post of the windshield, and with a small movement of my foot on the steering wheel I could correct our heading should a large swell send us astray. Or, if even this was too much effort, I could lean to one side or the other. Tortuga's steering is sensitive; even the restless stirring of Dinah as she moved from hers to my more comfortable seat altered our course. But veteran amphibious Jeeper that she is, she soon settled down to sleep.

Helen stayed below to plot our position. I watched her take a bearing with a small pocket compass on a high rocky islet northeast of us and on one of the peaks of the little island of Nusa Penida to the south. With a parallel rule she transferred these bearings to the compass rose on the chart, moving the rule so that the lines crossed our course line. Where they intersected she drew a small circle on the chart, marking our position. She measured the distance from the circle to land, made a few calculations and entered in our log: *0700, on course 090 degrees, speed four knots*. Satisfied, she patted the small image of Ganesh, the elephant-headed Hindu god of good fortune which Jim Pandy had given us before leaving Bali, and then joined me topside.

Churning smoothly ahead, Tortuga was alone on the sea now. The Balinese fishermen had long since returned to their village. Their boats with the slender snouts and painted eyes to frighten the demons of the deep were pulled high on the beach, and there was no sound except the dull throaty voice of Tortuga's engine, the bubbling of her wake and the flapping of her flag in the light breeze of the southeast monsoon.

Beating down from a brilliant sky, amber spears of sunlight pierced the Prussian blue of Lombok Strait only to glance from some iridescent fish or diffuse through a patch of algae. The gentle rocking of the Jeep had an almost hypnotic effect. Even Dinah seemed to feel it. She snored quietly on the seat below.

With the sun warm on our backs, it became an effort even to take our hourly bearings and plot our position on the chart. Except for those tiny penciled circles we had little sense of movement; all else in the broad expanse of Lombok Strait seemed static.

By noon our course line extended smoothly toward the center of the channel, but our one-o'clock plot showed a radical deviation. Hastily Helen took another bearing. Without our being aware of it the current had changed direction with the tide; we were being carried with the ebb toward the Indian Ocean.

Increasing our speed to six knots, close to Tortuga's maximum, I compensated our course for the current while Helen took still another bearing. Far to the north, Ampenan was already out of reach. Hoping for some help instead of hindrance from the current, we changed course for a sheltered cove that appeared on the chart several miles to the south of our original destination.

Toward midafternoon the current grew stronger, and when the wind swung around toward the north the heavy chop built up to the tide rip that Wallace had described. Short, erratic waves slapped against Tortuga's bow, jarring us off course first one way then the other. Spray shot high from the bow, was whipped aft by the wind until we were drenched. Even Dinah yawned uneasily at the motion as Tortuga plunged her bow in the troughs and reared crazily on the crests. But Tortuga's predecessor had weathered much rougher weather than this, and we crawled confidently below to the shelter of the cabin.

For another hour I concentrated on keeping Tortuga on course. Our progress was all dead reckoning now; we were close to the middle of the channel and the land was lost in mist on both sides. We tried to keep on a course plotted from our last position, compensating for the southerly force of the current and hoping we could touch land before we were carried out to sea.

Helen was the first to notice that something was wrong. Over the echoing whine of gears and the rumble of the propeller we heard a discordant grating. I opened an inspection plate in the floorboards between the seats. The propeller shaft thrust bearing was hot to my hand. An injection of fresh lubricant pushed out a grit-filled blob of black grease, but the damage was already done. I had a spare bearing, but it would take hours to change it—even if it were possible to work with Tortuga plunging like an angry bronco—and at the rate the current was carrying us south, by that time we would be miles into the Indian Ocean.

I had no idea how long the bearing would last. The propeller shaft was already vibrating and the watertight packing gland around the shaft was beginning to leak. I started the bilge pump and, reducing our speed to a point of minimum vibration, pointed Tortuga's bow toward the closest land, a narrow peninsula jutting into the strait near the south coast of Lombok. If the bearing would hold out another two hours, we might touch land a few miles from the mouth of the strait. If it didn't, we'd be adrift in the Indian Ocean by nightfall.

About four o'clock—by this time we had forgotten about keeping a log—we could see the peninsula clearly; we were almost abreast of it but still being carried south by the current. I had the feeling we were grabbing for the brass ring—

but if we missed the first time there would be no second time around. I increased our speed again. The propeller shaft wobbled so much the water was streaming into the hull around the packing gland. The bilge pump was working full time.

Slowly we closed on the peninsula. Shortly before dusk, as unnerved as we had ever been in Tortuga, we pulled up on a coral beach near a small village at the tip of the peninsula. The current had carried us eighteen miles south of Ampenan —within two miles of being swept into the Indian Ocean. We demoted Ganesh from good-luck talisman to rank of souvenir.

After having spent several months on Java, Bali and Madura we had become fairly confident in our Bahasa Indonesia, and it was with some assurance that we greeted the few villagers that came running to the shore. In response we received blank stares. With less assurance I repeated my words, adding in apology that we didn't speak the language very well. At the words "Bahasa Indonesia," a boy in his teens spoke up with a laugh:

"*Saia djuga, tuan* [We don't either, sir]."

The people of Lombok had their own language, Bahasa Sasak.

As predicted by Wallace, the area where we came ashore was sun-scorched and brambly. It seemed sparsely settled, but as we had experienced all over the other islands we had visited, people seemed to sprout from the ground like Jason's dragon teeth, and within an hour we had collected an amiable throng of visitors. They crowded around the Jeep as Helen fixed supper, exclaiming at the wonders of our stove and the water that flowed from a pipe. One old lady, gray and wrinkled, but slender and straight as a girl, cried "*Minta lihat, minta lihat* [I want to see]," but by that time it was too dark, and we promised her a good look in the morning. Before dawn she was back—with a handful of precious eggs as a present.

The same people, reinforced by others who had walked for miles to watch, were there all day as I worked black-handed on the Jeep, removing the floorboards, cleaning the fragments of steel from the bearing retainer, fitting a new bearing, replacing the assembly and lubricating it. I checked the alignment of the propeller shaft; it was slightly off which could account for the bearing having given out. It was hot slow work in the confines of the cabin—the bottom of an amphibious Jeep being completely sealed underneath, nearly all work must be done from the inside—but by evening the shaft was realigned, a new packing gland was fitted, and Tortuga was ready.

Later, an old fisherman pointed out a route up the coast where the current was not so strong. He warned us to stay close to shore, and traced on our chart a course over reefs, between rocks and through channels that seemed impassable. But he assured us we could get through with Tortuga's three-foot draft. The next morning we sailed the fifteen miles to Labuhan Tring, the closest place where we could get a road into Ampenan.

Expecting nothing but dirt trails on Lombok, we were pleasantly surprised to find a broad, paved and tree-flanked road leading to Ampenan. The town, largest on the island, had an almost prosperous air with its red tile roofs and neat houses, its schools and tiny, Chinese-run shops.

At the police station—one of the conditions accompanying our privilege of traveling through the Lesser Sundas was that we report immediately upon arrival on each island to the police, customs, immigration and military officials—we presented our credentials over the usual cup of tea. The officials inspected Tortuga and inquired incredulously about our crossing from Bali. I was just asking where we could find the customs officer when a Jeep stopped in the driveway outside. The customs officer had found *us*. Such enterprise, I feared, could only mean trouble. I was wrong.

A smooth-faced young man in crisply starched suntan uniform introduced himself.

"I'm Tjipto Soemirat, Chief of Customs here," he said in good English. "Where are you staying?"

I confessed that we had just arrived, that as yet we hadn't looked for a place. Chip, as he insisted we call him, broke into a quick smile.

"Then you must stay with my wife and me." He introduced the attractive Javanese girl accompanying him. "There are no hotels on Lombok, and the losmens are all full. Besides, we like to entertain foreign guests." With a grin he added, "We don't have many."

Shortly we were settled in the spare room of Chip's simple but comfortable stucco home on the outskirts of Ampenan. Tortuga was parked in the yard in front and soon crowds were forming at the gate. The calls to see Dinah, too, grew louder and louder until she nonchalantly condescended to allow Chip's children to parade her about.

We were fully as captivated by the children as they were by Dinah—five sprites with gleaming black Buster Brown haircuts and wonder-filled but mischievous eyes. The four girls and the boy stood politely to be formally introduced as Chip went down the line:

"This is Siska, this is Pariah—"

"Pariah?" Helen interrupted.

"Her name is really Aria." Chip laughed. "It means highest class, from the old Indian word *aryan*. But she was born in poverty—I was still a student; so I nicknamed her Pariah."

"Oh, he names them all for a reason," Iesje, Chip's wife,

losmens "a reason logement" its a little hotel and gouvernement possessions only for gouvernement people added. "Siska means Autumn Child." She held out her slender hand to the third girl. "This is Bea, meaning Right Duty. I'm not sure the name fits," she said affectionately.

"And this"—Chip beamed—"is my son Indra, the God of Thunder." Then he hoisted the last one above his head and bounced her there. "This little one is Lisa. I don't know what it means, but I named her after Lisa Larsen—you know, the *Life* photographer? I saw her once in Djakarta at a press conference. The photographers were barred from getting close to President Sukarno, but she wanted a closeup. She crawled on her knees right through the legs of the bodyguards and got her picture. What spunk that girl had! So—we named our youngest Lisa."

Within hours after our arrival we received a message from the chief of a neighboring village of Sasaks, the indigenous people who make up the majority of Lombok's population. The message was relayed by a friend of Chip's, Laludjaja, a thin scholarly man, a teacher, a Sasak himself and a student of Lombok's history.

"There is going to be a circumcision ceremony," he told us, "and the chief has invited you to come along. He asked that you bring your Tortuga."

It seemed that the boys who were to undergo the ordeal were not too enthusiastic and the chief thought that a little diversion might make things easier for them.

The village was several miles from Ampenan and on the way Laludjaja pointed out the few remains of historical significance. At Mataram, once the capital of the powerful Hindu dynasty that ruled all of Bali and Lombok after the Madjapahit Kingdom fell, the grounds of the Prince's Palace are now a public park. At Narmada, another princely residence, naked boys swam in the huge pool and dove from the grotesque statues around the edge, while in the shade of stone walls richly carved in the decorative Balinese style, a group of teen-agers strummed guitars and sang rock 'n' roll songs. But most of the fine old monuments and buildings that once graced the area had been destroyed during the Lombok War of 1894 when the Dutch conquered the Balinese princes and established their own authority.

"Now only a few temples in the Balinese tradition remain," Laludjaja told us, "and many of those have reverted to animism." He pointed to an open shed beside the road where a heap of stones wrapped in white cloth sat on a wooden bench. "Rocks, especially, are revered here on Lombok. They are called the source of the soul. Those stones are believed to have come from the top of Mount Rindjani here on Lombok. Rindjani, you know, is Indonesia's tallest mountain, over twelve thousand feet high. The name comes from an old Chinese word meaning 'place where the child is born.' "

As we jounced over a dust-filled back trail Laludjaja went on to tell us how animism was once the religion of all the Sasaks who migrated many centuries ago from the west. As in most of Indonesia, Islam had made a strong impression on Lombok, converting large numbers of the people but never doing more than obscuring the underlying animism that is still so strong. Two groups of Moslems developed on Lombok. One group tries to follow the five rules of the Koran: eat no pork; take no strong drink; pray five times each day; make the pilgrimage to Mecca; give alms to the poor. The other group prays only twice each day and has no compunctions about eating pork and drinking. Apparently the village where the circumcision was to take place was a member of the former group for we saw no pigs and there was nothing strong about the sweet orange soda we were served.

The thatched village, hidden in a grove of coconut trees, was decked with palm leaves and festive streamers of colored paper. Circumcisions, along with births and marriages, are the greatest occasions in the lives of Moslems. Friends and relatives from the whole area had come to pay their respects and help with the preparation of the food.

Under a palm frond and bamboo shelter, women in loose-cut black blouses and black sarongs—black seemed to be the modish color—tended long lines of blackened pots where rice was steaming over glowing wood coals. Men sat grating the cream-white meat of coconuts, and in one corner hung the wide-horned heads of sacrificed buffalo, for even among this more conservative group of Moslems the animistic practice of buffalo sacrifice on important occasions is still observed.

Later, when the work was done, the shelter crowded with young girls sitting and chatting on the ground. Their hair was rolled in tight flat buns and the Balinese influence was strongly evident in their earplugs of spiraled palm leaf and their self-assured, almost arrogant manner. Few even bothered to acknowledge the baskets of fruit brought to them by the young men attending the party.

"I should think she would at least say thank you," Helen commented to Laludjaja after watching one particularly attractive girl ignore five gifts of fruit from five different admirers.

"But she can't marry all five of them," Laludjaja laughed. She can accept a gift only from the boy of her choice. For the young people these gatherings are mostly a time for courting."

In contrast to the rigid prohibitions in other Moslem countries against the mingling of unmarried young men and women, Indonesian custom permits much greater freedom. The young people have some influence in the selection of a partner though the parents must still approve of the choice and make all the formal overtures of settling a bride price, and arranging the details of the marriage.

The circumcision ceremony that day was a time for eating as well as courting, however, and there were mountains of food—mounds of rice, eggs fried in coconut oil, tiny silver fish consumed heads and all, and a vast variety of sugared rice and coconut cakes, molded into cones and diamonds and colored pink or green or shiny black. Lombok is named for the Javanese word for chili pepper, and they must have used the season's crop in the main course, a scorching buffalo-meat curry that made us reach for a cooling banana after the first bite.

If the rest of the people felt as lethargic as we did after the feast, we wondered how they could carry the boys in the procession preceding the circumcision. As it turned out they didn't have to—at least not that day. The reluctant children decided they wanted to see first a *prisean,* a primitive duel where two men with buffalo-hide shields and long rattan sticks belabor each other until one draws blood. The indulgent elders put off the circumcision until the next day.

The following morning we were back at the village, and the children, apparently satisfied with the prisean they had witnessed the night before, had agreed to go on with the circumcision. Three boys and two girls, each about twelve years old and all elaborately costumed as princes and princesses of the ancient court, were carried through the village atop carved, painted and gilded wooden lions and mythical birds. We asked about the presence of the girls.

"Now they merely accompany the boys," Laludjaja replied. "It's a carry-over from the time when female circumcision was practiced."

"But why are the boys so old?" I wanted to know. "The operation must be terribly painful at that age."

"It is, and they receive no anesthetic. Actually, to many of the people the significance of the ritual is lost. Ask them, and they answer 'adat' it's the custom, the way their forefathers have done things for hundreds of years. Few but students of the Koran know that Moslem circumcision is a symbol of Abraham's willingness to sacrifice Ishmael. The boy must be willing to suffer pain for Allah."

Evidently the boys weren't quite willing yet for at the last minute they won another reprieve, this time to watch a shadow play. The circumcision, we were told, would take place "tomorrow."

It was that afternoon that Chip, with a long face, brought us two radiograms. One, in a hundred-word message, stated that the Ministry of Agriculture had reversed itself and would not give Dinah permission to continue the journey; that for her safety she must be sent back to Java. The other radiogram was from Consul Jack Lydman in Surabaja inviting Dinah to stay with him while we continued without her.

But there were no ships scheduled soon to stop at Ampenan, and the Indonesian Airways plane that landed infrequently on Lombok would not accept her. There was no way to get her back to Java except to take her in Tortuga back across the Lombok and Bali straits. That night Chip did not come home.

In the morning, his eyes swollen from lack of sleep, he told us he had spent the night trying to find in the book of regulations some provision in the law that would circumvent the prohibition against dogs entering Nusa Tenggara.

"But the law makes only one exception," he said sadly, "and I can't see how it applies to us. Only circus animals are permitted, temporarily, to be imported into the restricted areas of Indonesia."

Almost in one voice Helen and I exclaimed, "But that's how she came in—as a circus dog!" And then we told Chip of the

day months earlier when we arrived in Indonesia. His relief
was almost as great as ours.

The central plain of Lombok, irrigated by ample water
from the high mountains bordering it, was green and fertile
as we drove the 45 miles east across the island. Terraced rice
paddies alternated with fields of ripening corn and neat rows
of tobacco. Here are raised the golden-brown, deerlike cattle
that are the island's principal export to other parts of Indonesia, and here live most of the million or so inhabitants of
Lombok. In many places dozens of teams of buffalo or oxen
were plowing a single small field. The deep, sonorous tolling
of the immense wooden bells slung from their necks and dangling against their forelegs played accompaniment to this gotong rojong, the community effort that is an Indonesian
motto.

Chip was there to see us off when we left Lombok's dusty,
windblown eastern shore. He was there waving as we bounced
down the rocky beach and into the sea under a marbled sky.
Though we had known Chip only a week, we felt we were
leaving a friend. Chip, with his sympathetic understanding, his
quick wit and abundant hospitality, has restored our faith in
customs officers the world over.

It should have been an easy run across the sixteen-mile Alas
Strait to Sumbawa, but though bad weather was not due for
at least another month, an unseasonable squall brought sharp
winds and blinding rains that obscured the sea and darkened
the water so that the reefs were suddenly invisible. We put
in at a small, uninhabited and unnamed island, waterless except
for the pockets of worn rock that quickly filled with rain.
Dinah, always the first out of the Jeep, flushed our only company, a legion of hermit crabs in a dozen speckled colors that

scuttered away across the coral-scarred sand. We parked in the shelter of the few low bushes that projected from the brown grass and set up camp.

By the time the rain stopped and a rainbow wreathed the coast of Sumbawa it was too late to go on. We stretched a tarpaulin from Tortuga to the bamboo pole we carried for testing the depth of the sea, and read in its shade. Dinah was swimming by herself and we were sipping coffee when an excited bark brought us running around the side of the Jeep. A sailing prahu, perhaps 40 feet long, dropped the large rock it used for an anchor just outside the reef, and three disheveled men paddled a canoe ashore. What were we doing there? they wanted to know. They warned us of *orang djelek*, bad men, from the north. They volunteered that they were good men— but they asked strange questions.

"Do you have any guns?"

I hedged.

"Is the dog dangerous?"

I didn't have to answer that one; Dinah was pressing close to my side, baring her teeth, waiting for my signal. They bummed cigarettes and asked for money. They would not tell us their names and they were evasive about where they were from. Despite their assurances, they didn't look like paragons of virtue, and we began to wonder whether they were some of the hijackers we had heard still prey upon the small craft along the coast. They asked if anyone knew we were there; we told them we kept in touch with Java by radio. We had nothing but a receiver, but the dials seemed to impress them and they left. But when we saw the tip of a mast enter a bay to the west of us, the boat itself hidden by a hill on the island, we spent the rest of the afternoon at the Jeep, ready to take off.

After a wakeful night we were up at dawn. The mast tip

was gone. We never learned the identity of the ship nor that of its crew.

At Mapin, a village so small it shows only on detailed charts, a few men in a dugout paddled toward us.

"Is there a road here?" I called in Indonesian. They seemed to understand my words, but not the meaning of my question. I pointed to the spare tires on the Jeep.

"It goes on land too," I told them. "Is there a road here?" At their stupefied nods, I shifted the power to wheels, disengaged the propeller and rolled up the beach and across a salt flat.

It was then that the few scores of bamboo-and-thatch houses on stilts erupted. In seconds we were the center of a mob of shrilling, gesturing, pushing humanity. The Moslem influence seemed stronger here than on Lombok; the men were bolder, while the women stayed in the background, their stark, white-powdered faces staring from slits in the flame and green sarongs that were drawn over their heads so that they looked like Arabs. The area around the Jeep was a bobbing mass of black pitji caps, and through a forest of legs peeped the wide-eyed faces of children. It was a noisy, but friendly welcome for the first Westerners to touch here since before World War II.

There was no immigration or customs or any other kind of official at Mapin. They told us we should report at Alas up the road. Hospitality on Sumbawa, however, was not restricted to officialdom, and we climbed the four-foot-high ladder to the village chief's hut where, for an hour, we sat drinking sweet coconut milk—for a change—while the villagers alternated at the windows and door, blocking what little air could filter into the small stifling room.

The "road" was a twisting, jolting, gravel trail along Sumbawa's indented north coast. We had gone only a few miles when two men on a motorcycle flagged us down. Obviously in authority—one man carried a Sten gun, a rifle and a pistol —they instructed us to follow them.

The one street of Alas was jammed as we made the rounds of the homes of the officials, having tea with the mayor, the police chief, the customs officer, the immigration officer, the Army Commander and the mayor again, who invited us for lunch. By this time the thought of anything to eat or drink was more than we could bear, but the mayor said so genially, "It is the custom here that no one can leave hungry. But wouldn't you like to bathe first?"

We would, and we were led to the back of the house to the mandi. After a few minutes of sudsing, splashing and rinsing, with a few more just to cool off, we joined the mayor and his family. We didn't have far to go. They, along with the rest of the town, at least all that could squeeze into the house, were waiting outside the door to the bath.

The mayor's wife beckoned to Helen.

"You're very dark from the sun," she whispered. "Come, here is some powder."

She offered Helen some ghostly-white rice powder in a cup and led her off to make her more presentable, Helen protesting all the while that Americans work hard to acquire that beautiful golden-brown color that Indonesians come by naturally.

The dining room was bulging—with spectators, not diners —as we sat down to lunch. The windows were solid with faces; fathers held their children over their heads so they could see, and the air vibrated with comments on how we looked and how we ate. The food—nasi goreng, and fried fish with the eyes staring from blue plates, krupuk and sweet rice cakes

—overflowed the table. Gently at first, but later of necessity with more vigor, we maneuvered our arms into eating position, apologizing when someone's midsection made forcible contact with our elbows. During the meal the mayor kept up a running conversation on the medicinal value of the curl of dried seaweed he wore around his wrist. Excellent for curing rheumatism, he said. He had another piece of the prized charm which he gave us before we left. The second relay of spectators was taking its place at the windows, and the disappointment of those who had not yet inspected us was audible as we thanked our hosts and headed for Sumbawa Besar, the island's capital.

It was late afternoon before we left Alas, too late to drive the 40 chuckholed miles to Sumbawa Besar. We spied a side trail and eased Tortuga under the low-hanging branches to a clearing a hundred yards or so from the road. Except for a few black monkeys we were alone for the first time in months. Or so we thought. Our bunks were in place and we were already dozing when the *kulkuls* started. In the months that followed, these hollow log drums were a nightly punctuation to our sleep, and usually the message they carried was about us. A few minutes later a well-meaning delegation from a nearby village came whistling loudly up the trail. They had seen us leave the road, they said, but had not known who we were until the kulkul message reached them.

"You must not sleep here," they insisted. "You are welcome in our village."

It took much persuasion to convince them that Tortuga was very comfortable. But not wishing to offend them, we promised to stop by their village in the morning.

We did not add that after the day's press of people we needed the solitude, an aspect of our Western culture not generally understood by Asians. With their large families and communal living, privacy is an unknown concept; to leave a guest alone, even for a moment, is considered rude.

Sumbawa Besar, though smaller than Ampenan, had a sultan. A small man with tortoise-shell glasses and a quiet, friendly dignity, he lived in a large, two-story, Normandy-style house that seemed completely out of place among the

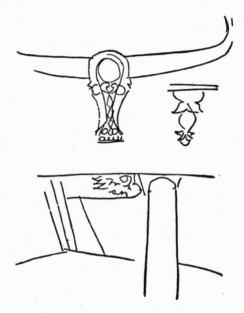

squat, Dutch-type stucco houses and the bamboo-and-thatch kampongs that crowded in on the town. His old palace, now deserted except for a few distant relatives, was a long barn-like structure of unpainted wood that seemed on the point of collapsing. Beneath the ramshackle entrance, a rusted cannon from the days of the Dutch East India Company lay half-buried in the ground. Slope-roofed, woven-mat and thatch huts, with a few banana palms sprouting from dry earth between them, encroached on the foundations of the old building. Mothers and fathers and naked little children made the palace shake as they followed us up the ramp into a great empty room that was once the audience chamber. One of the village women wore an American five-dollar gold piece on a chain around her neck. In the gold-capped front teeth of some of the others were little heart-shaped openings enameled in red and green. Their heavy bracelets and earrings displayed far more opulence than did the shell of the old palace. Only when the few remaining court costumes, the faded silver brocade kains, the gold-handled krisses and the long gold fingernails that were a sign of royalty's exemption from labor were modeled for us did we have any idea of the extravagance of this past era. By government decree, the sultans are no longer in power. Instead they serve as appointees of the central government to administer the lands of their kingdoms until officials are elected to take their places.

The one European of Sumbawa was a German doctor who for six years had been under contract to the Indonesian Ministry of Health. With only a few hundred doctors in all of Indonesia, the Ministry of Health, assisted by a group of Americans from the University of California Medical School, has started an accelerated doctor-training program in Djakarta. But the shortage of doctors outside of Java is still critical. And even on Java, doctors are reluctant to leave the more lucrative opportunities of the big cities. Now the government will not permit new graduates to open practices in any but small communities, and then only after they have served a certain number of years as government doctors in remote areas. But even with this, with the exception of one Chinese, there were no Indonesian doctors east of Lombok, and the government had engaged several Europeans to fill the medical gap.

Dr. Pöch invited us to spend the night with him, and that

evening he spoke enthusiastically of his travels on Sumbawa.

"You should try to visit the Donggo people in the mountains," he recommended. "They are probably descended from the earliest inhabitants of the island. And you must see the dances of Dompu. The sultan there is trying to preserve the traditions of his people, and he is well worth meeting."

As this balding, slender, mustached man spoke, we marveled at his energy. He appeared at least a decade younger than his sixty-odd years. The director of the town's one hospital, on call 24 hours a day—he was summoned to the hospital three times that one night—he was the only doctor for all of Sumbawa's 400,000 people. We were sadly surprised to learn that while on one of his midnight calls his home was robbed.

A few miles east of Sumbawa Besar, at a small village, several men in white Western shirts and trousers flagged us down. Others, in their brightest sarongs, lined both sides of the road. We did not know that the Sultan of Sumbawa Besar had sent a message ahead to his cousin, and the village had turned out to welcome us. We were the first foreigners to stop at Lape Lopok since the war, the people told us; the children had never seen a white woman before.

A special dinner had been prepared: ground chicken fried into croquettes and served on pointed sticks, vegetable curry and sweet rice baked in tubes of bamboo. But I had difficulty paying attention to the conversation. The walls of the room were papered with pages from the Los Angeles *Times, Herald Examiner* and the Chicago *News* that dated back to 1938. The advertisements of the then-stylish clothes seemed as archaic as something out of *Godey's Lady's Book*. The newspapers, our host said, came years ago as bundles of ballast in the holds of ships, but now that the island was no longer on a regular shipping schedule they rarely saw them anymore. Incongru-

ously, plastered over the newsprint walls were political posters
—the Moslem crescent moon and star, and the slogan FRONT
AGAINST COMMUNISM.

The village, early the next morning, had that golden quality
of bamboo in the sun. The daily activities had resumed, and
though we could hardly see through the clouds of dust
raised by the hundreds of scampering children who followed
us, we wandered freely between the long rows of houses.
Each was alike, a small dwelling with the roof and floors of
split bamboo and raised on stilts about four feet from the
ground. Only in the walls was any individuality shown; of split
cane, they were woven in intricate geometric patterns that
varied from house to house.

As we passed each house we were invited in with a friendly
smile. We climbed the ladder and removed our shoes, washing
our feet in the bamboo bucket that hung by each door, buckets
that also served as a precaution against fire, the greatest danger
to a village during the dry season.

The houses were divided into two rooms: a cooking area
with a rude hearth of stones and a few clay pots, and a sleeping area with woven mats for beds and extra clothes hung in
bundles from the rafters. At the back of each house a platform of widely separated slats served as garbage disposal and
latrine, and packs of skeletal dogs fought over the refuse on
the ground.

Under some of the houses women sat spinning homegrown
cotton into thread on small wheels operated with their feet.
Others sat by handlooms stretched from stakes driven into the
ground, making the flying shuttle and polished hardwood slat
that compacted the threads audible even over the murmurs
of our following herd. Still other women sat in pairs, each
combing the other's waist-long hair with a bamboo comb,
rubbing in coconut oil to make it glossy and picking lice that

they crunched between thumb and forefinger or between their teeth.

It was eighty miles to Dompu, eighty miles of boulder-filled, pockmarked, dust-smothered punishment that we were forced to spread over three days of travel. Near the end of the dry season, the earth was parched and brown, the air heavy with heat, made worse by the still-smoking areas of burned forest where the people had cleared the trees for cul-

tivation. The most common method of clearing land in Nusa Tenggara, its cost is relatively low in labor, unspeakably high in depleted soil and erosion, and the fields, which with conservation and fertilization could produce a crop a year of much needed food, instead must lie fallow for several years between plantings.

Along the road, scattered groups of people, their pots, sleeping mats and bags of rice on their heads, were migrating from their permanent villages to the rough, makeshift huts in their mountain fields. The rains were due soon, they said, and then rice planting could begin. Their *shaman*, their Islamic astrologer, would tell them exactly which day after the rains began was the most auspicious for plowing and planting, and then for several months they would stay in the fields, guarding the crop against wild boar, monkeys, deer, wild cattle, birds and rats until the harvest was in. They carried spears, and a few days later an immense boar with tusks that curved in six-inch circles lurched across the road in front of us. A pack of dogs cornered it in a gully and its scream rose to supersonic pitch as the men stabbed their lances deep into its brain through the ear cavities. Helen, angered and tearful, pleaded with them to stop their insensitive torture, but they only laughed uncomprehendingly.

In sparsely populated Sumbawa we often drove for fifteen or twenty miles between villages. As in all of Indonesia at that time, the small shops in these villages of Nusa Tenggara, with their meager stocks of cloth, cooking oil, utensils and tobacco, and their ready fund of money for loans at usurious interest rates, were run by Chinese. In the months that followed we saw those shops tightly closed and shuttered, the Chinese expelled to larger towns or returning to China, and their businesses given over to Indonesians. Though most of these Chinese had been born of generations in their villages and, except for their names and religion, were indistinguishable from the Indonesians, their diligence, acumen and success were resented. In colonial days, the Chinese had been favored by the Dutch over Indonesians, and now, in the drive to rid Indonesia of all foreign influence, the Chinese—who, often Indonesian citizens, still look upon China as their homeland—are being economically and politically pressured to leave. But Indonesians are generally inexperienced in business, are not able to withstand the demands of their relatives for credit and merchandise, and within a few months many of the shops taken over by them were bankrupt, leaving the villages with no source of supplies.

Dompu is the center of one of three ex-sultanates on Sumbawa, each with its distinct language. Fortunately the Sultan spoke Bahasa Indonesia as well and his assistant some English. We called at his "palace," a little larger but otherwise no different than the other tile-roofed and blocklike houses of the town.

The Sultan of Dompu, in his khaki shirt and trousers, and black pitji, was not a prepossessing man, but there was an air of quiet authority about him. As in the case of the Sultan of Sumbawa Besar, the Sultan of Dompu was the appointed *kepala daerah*, the head of civil government of the district. The children of the town clung affectionately to his legs, and ran shouting around him. The older people treated him with deference, and his two servants still crouched low when they entered the room for to them he was still the Sultan.

Dr. Pöch had shown us some of the fine, hand-woven, silver-brocade cloth for which Sumbawa was once renowned, and after the introductions we asked the Sultan about it. He smiled sadly.

"The government has prohibited the import of silver thread. Machine-made cloth from Java is cheaper. Now the families who still have these cloths pass them on as heirlooms or use them as part of the bride price when their children marry."

He was equally sad when we asked him about the dances.

"Only a few old men still know them. We try to teach the young people, but they are more interested in your music. But you shall see those dances that are left."

In a Moslem society such as Sumbawa's, dogs are considered unclean—a strict Moslem must wash his hands and his clothes seven times if a dog's tongue touches them—but though we offered to leave Dinah in the Jeep, she was invited to share our room.

The following afternoon, to the accompaniment of drums, gongs, and funnel-shaped flutes that sounded like Persian bagpipes, we watched the dances performed in an open area in front of the Sultan's home. Each dancer was in costume, a strangely Arabian dress with a rolled, doughnut-shaped turban reminiscent of a Saracen soldier. A slow pivoting on one foot with arms outstretched like a bird arrested in flight displayed the admired coordination of the warrior. A two-man mock duel with clacking sticks in place of swords simulated war. A hopping charge with sword held high, a piercing battle cry and a long speech in low monotone proclaimed the dancer's loyalty to the Sultan, his willingness to sacrifice his life. The dancer was an old retainer of the Sultan's father, and we had the feeling that even though this was only a dance, the straggly-mustached old man meant what he said.

Later we were shown the ancestral weapons, the decayed spears, rusted swords, helmets, chain mail armor, and two pairs of silver epaulets awarded by the Dutch generations ago promoting the then Sultan to general and his wife to admiral.

That evening the young people showed us their dances. In white Western shirts and low-slung trousers, the boys—the girls did not dance—shuffled in a slow, sterile step to the rhythm of drums and tambourines. Neither modern nor classic, it was a weak heir to the virile traditions of Dompu.

As a parting gift the Sultan offered us his favorite pet, a well-trained and winsome little monkey with black eyes that peered quizzically from his wrinkled blue-gray face. To our regret, he hid in the folds of the Sultan's sarong and loudly indicated his distrust of Dinah. But the Sultan insisted we take something to remember Dompu, a large brass-plated metal platter from Holland impressed with a medieval taproom scene showing several stout Dutchmen drinking ale. The monkey was still screaming through bared teeth as we left Dompu's generous, sad ruler whose world had crumbled before the forces of progress.

All through Sumbawa we had been hearing reports about the people of the Donggo country, a tribe variously described by Sumbawans as cavemen, aborigines, Veddoids, Negroids, and even by some as missing links. Some people even doubted that the Donggos knew the use of fire, but all were unanimous in their skepticism that we could drive to the end of a long-neglected road from where we would have to hike into the mountains. When we saw a board nailed to a tree with the word DONGGO and an arrow scratched on it, we turned off the main road, little more than a dirt track itself, and followed a narrow trail that meandered toward the north of a wide peninsula jutting into the Flores Sea.

Tortuga's bow projected so far that visibility was limited, and as we bounced over ruts and around boulders, through thatched villages and banana groves, Helen sat atop the hatch to warn me of obstacles I might not be able to see. We had covered about five miles when I heard her shout in alarm for me to stop.

Ahead a weathered wooden bridge spanned a ravine. There was no sign, no barricade to indicate danger, but I stamped hard on the brake pedal. The Jeep slowed, then continued as the pedal went to the floor and the sharp, eye-watering fumes of brake fluid filled the cab. I snatched at the parking brake, but even at our slow speed Tortuga's 5,000 pounds had too much momentum. Almost as in slow motion I saw the remnants of the bridge creep toward us, the missing logs yawning black chasms into the ravine fifty feet below. We felt the front wheels drop through the first gap; they bounced on to a decayed log beyond, then the back wheels dropped through the rotten wood. We gripped anything we could reach as Tortuga rocked on the edge of the next gap, then steadied, stopped and hung there. Trembling, fearful we would dislodge our teetering Jeep, we climbed from the cab, stared at the rocks below, then at the trailer hook on Tortuga's stern. It had caught on an up-ended log within inches of falling all the way through.

It took four hours in the blazing afternoon sun and a score of men from a nearby village to shore up Tortuga's dangling wheels. Using our small hydraulic jack and timbers pried from the decrepit bridge, we levered the Jeep inch by inch until she was back on solid ground again. By the time we had replaced the ruptured brake hose from our stock of spare parts it was dark. With no other way to reach Donggo, we returned to the main road and camped just outside of Bima.

At Bima, Sumbawa's second town, a slightly smaller edition of Sumbawa Besar, we stopped just long enough to take on water and fuel.

"Your gasoline has been here a month," the Chinese shopkeeper said as the fifteen five-gallon tins were brought out. Silently we thanked the Stanvac efficiency in Surabaja that had soldered and crated each tin so that none were damaged or leaking after their long journey to Bima by sailing prahu.

With the four extra tins of fuel stacked inside Tortuga we called on Bima's mayor to obtain clearance for the journey to Komodo, the island of the Dragon Lizards. Resplendent in the gold braid epaulets and suntan uniform of a Dutch colonial officer, the Indonesian official received us kindly.

"Of course," he said, reading out letters of introduction, "I'll be happy to make all the arrangements."

He gave us a letter to the village chief on Komodo, and

while we waited, he telephoned to Sape, the village from near which we would leave Sumbawa, and asked them to send a man ahead by sailing prahu with bait to attract the lizards. The question of bait had bothered us for some time, for no one could tell us whether any meat would be available on Komodo, and without bait there was little chance of seeing the Dragons.

At Sape, near the strait separating Sumbawa from Komodo, the government rest house had also been advised of our coming. While we were eating our supper of eggs and nasi goreng, we heard a scuffling in the rafters.

"Big cats," Helen remarked.

"Not cats—rats," the caretaker replied.

After supper we made the usual courtesy calls on the village officials. At the home of the village chief we sat on the porch drinking tea, while half the children in town hung from the railing and crowded the steps. We asked if the man had left yet for Komodo with the bait.

"Oh yes," the chief told us. "By coincidence a deer had just been killed when the message arrived. One of the fishermen left with it this afternoon."

"What time did he leave?" we asked, wondering whether the bait would reach Komodo before we did.

The chief checked his watch. "He should be leaving now."

"But I thought you said he left this afternoon," I questioned.

"It is very fine bait," the chief replied. He called his servant, who carried in the staring head of a large deer.

"But if the fisherman is leaving now, why is the bait still here?"

"He will come for it before he leaves. He wants to meet you first and discuss the price."

"But that was arranged in Bima, and we will not leave until morning. We can make better time than he can."

"The fisherman will be by tonight, I think," assured the chief, somewhat less than emphatically.

But by the time we said good night the fisherman had not yet arrived. "Perhaps we had better carry the bait with us," we suggested, though the thought of two days' travel in the hot sun with a putrefying deer head was not at all appealing.

"Oh no," the chief said, "when our kepala daerah in Bima tells us to do something, it will be done. Do not worry. Your bait is on its way to Komodo now."

Pondering this bit of double-talk which exemplified so well the Asian propensity for telling someone what the speaker thought the other wished to hear, whether it was true or not, we returned to the rest house and turned in. That night we left the lamp burning and were grateful for the heavy mosquito netting as a ring of long, whiskered noses and orange eyes gleamed fearlessly from a hole in the ceiling over our beds.

It was a pink-tinted dawn when we arrived at the fishing village a few miles from Sape. A long breakwater constructed of lumps of coral projected into the shallow bay; two rows of thatch houses on stilts ran the length of the breakwater, and a small dugout canoe was tied near each one. A few shadows squatted on platforms extending over the water from the backs of the houses, but other than that it was quiet, for the hour was early even for Indonesians.

The end of the breakwater was too steep to serve as a ramp for Tortuga. People were stirring now, and I asked a man what the floor of the bay was like. No rocks, he told us, just sand. I waded out several hundred yards before the water was waist-deep, but the sand seemed firm enough to support Tortuga until she was afloat. There were reefs farther from shore and the tide was on its way out. If we delayed we might not find enough depth to get over them. I headed Tortuga into the bay, four-wheel-drive engaged and propeller spinning. We had covered perhaps a hundred yards when the floor of the bay turned to sticky silt. The water was too shallow to float Tortuga and too deep for the wheels to have any traction. I tried reverse but we only sank deeper in the mud. The water was already lower. Soon it would leave us hub-deep in silt and we would be stuck there until the tide came in again. We gathered as many of the villagers as were willing to help, and after agreeing on a price, a long string of men, hindered by children whose heads barely cleared the water but who were eager to share the reward, spaced themselves along the two hundred feet of nylon rope we carried. Slowly Tortuga moved across the bay like a kite being led by its tail, until the water was deep enough for the propeller to have effect. There was a wild rude scramble as I passed out cigarettes and rupiahs. The faces attached to outstretched hands began to look familiar and I selected one man to finish the distribution when I realized that most had lined up two or three times. The fisherman who was to carry the bait was from this village. As I was coiling the rope I asked if he had left for Komodo yet.

"What fisherman?" was the reply.

Chapter Five

IT was some sixty miles by sea to Komodo, too long for one day's run, and once clear of the mud and reefs that guarded the mouth of the bay at Sape, we charted course for Gili Banta, a small islet halfway to the island of the Dragon Lizards.

Sape Strait has one of the worst reputations in the Indonesian Archipelago—all through Sumbawa we had been warned of its whirlpools, riptides and currents—but that day the strait was calm. Clouds rose like genies from the still surface of the sea, and Helen washed clothes on the bow of Tortuga, using the sea and saltwater soap to conserve our fresh water. I read leisurely topside, only occasionally touching the steering wheel with my toe. But the reality of the warnings was brought home to us as we crossed a patch of agitated sea; a gust of wind blew one of my drying shirts into the water, and before I could turn the Jeep it was gone, a spot of spiraling red receding into the blue depths of a whirlpool.

Just before dusk we glided into the secluded cove of Gili Banta, a silver-pink crescent of fine sand and high stone cliffs. Giant turtles, a fourth the size of Tortuga, darted from our path.

The island's only occupants, we spent the following day in peaceful solitude. We set up a more elaborate camp, stretching a tarpaulin for shade and to catch rain should the heavy sky fulfill itself. We swam in the tepid, clear water. The cove seemed a perfect buccaneer's hideout, protected on three sides. At the base of the cliffs stood great time-sculptured rocks, bored through with holes as though Henry Moore had been there. We sprawled on the beach and dug our toes down to the wet sand. We closed our eyes and listened to music from Australia and news from Radio Moscow. According to the broadcast the auto strike in Detroit had reached violent proportions, and people were dying of starvation in the streets of the city. We dined on crab omelette, canned chicken, cheese, fruitcake and a bottle of wine, all gifts of friends when we left Djakarta. "Save them for a special occasion," they told us, and that day was indeed special. It was Thanksgiving.

Toward evening, when the air cooled a little, we climbed the rise to the cliffs above us. We could faintly see Komodo, a hazy outline devoid of identifying characteristics. We scanned the bay beneath us for a path through the reef. We would be leaving before dawn. The only village on Komodo lies on the eastern side; we would have to circle around the north coast and then head south through a narrow strait where almost thirty islands that are named and scores of others that are mere rocks form a maze that would make that of Minos seem clearly marked. On Thanksgiving night we checked the hour of the tide and plotted our course for Komodo, no longer wondering why ships never called at this tiny island.

We left our Thanksgiving isle at 5 A.M., steering a course for the north cape of Komodo. We had charted our course, estimating our speed at three knots, so that five and a half hours would bring us to the island's northeastern tip. From there a heading of almost due south for four hours more should take us through a corridor of reef almost to the shore of another islet that lies opposite the entrance to Komodo Bay. We had only this islet to guide us, for the chart showed the entrance to be concealed from the north by three tall rocks.

But as we soon learned, plotting a course on a chart is far different from actually following that course when at sea. On the chart the islands are spread in a neat bird's-eye view, and with a pair of dividers we could measure distances and calculate speed and time. But at sea, with the water glaring like a signal mirror, the islands overlap in a panorama that seems like one mass of land, and we could only estimate our speed and guess at the strength of the current.

We followed our easterly course for the calculated time, but when we headed south, the eddies, whirlpools and currents made a compass course impossible to steer. We navigated by eye, watching the color of the water and trying to stay close to the center of the channel through the reef. We knew only that the entrance to Komodo Bay was on our right, that it was hidden from the north and that we must watch for the three high rocks beyond which we should see the clump of palms around the village. But which three rocks? The entire east coast of Komodo was an eroded cliff that dropped sheer into the sea; brown rock was sliced with black ravines that from a distance made the area between look like individual islands. We stayed as close to shore as possible, zigzagging over reefs and around rocks that showed as pinpoints on the chart but which towered above us like skyscrapers. We felt very small in Tortuga, even smaller when the eddies around the rocks twisted us off course and whirlpools sucked at Tortuga's bow.

We had been underway from Gili Banta for seven hours when we finally distinguished a separate island from the expanse of mottled land to the south of us. From its configuration it could only be the island opposite the entrance to Komodo Bay. But we shouldn't have reached it for another two hours or more. As in Lombok Strait we realized that the current was carrying us south. Soon we would be past the bay, and the current was too strong to buck. I changed course toward the west, still not sure we were at the entrance. Then we saw the three rocks, the channels between them mere cracks with the sea rushing through. It was a choice between Scylla or Charybdis. Hoping the chart was right, I steered for the nearest one. The current carried us close to the steep sides; I floored the throttle and for once I was glad Tortuga was so small. We could almost touch the rocks as we passed between them and entered a wide bay. A couple of miles away a single patch of green, a grove of coconut palms, stood out from the brown grass on the range of hills beyond.

At the village of Komodo, nothing more than a few score of bamboo huts on stilts, the village chief knew what we had come for. This tiny sun-burned island's one attraction is its Dragon Lizards, prehistoric carry-overs from the age of dinosaurs. Carnivorous, dangerous—so we were warned—they grow to eleven feet and more in length, are the world's largest lizards, existing only on Komodo and a few nearby islands. No one knows how they got there, for the Lesser Sunda

Islands are of fairly recent geological formation while the lizards are related to the same species that walked the earth some sixty million years ago during the early Eocene period. Named by the Dutchman, P. A. Ouwens, who first drew attention to them, the Varanus Komodoensis have been attracting expeditions ever since their discovery in 1912.

Experienced in such things, the village chief—a descendant, as are all of the residents of Komodo, of some convicts who were exiled to the island by the Sultan of Sumbawa—had it all figured out. We climbed the ladder to his stilt-elevated house, and while the women peered at us through slats from the back room, the men, only one of whom could read, carefully examined our letters. We nibbled fried bananas and coconut cakes and sipped sweet black coffee. Then the chief outlined his plans.

"You will need some bait. We will sell you a goat. You will need eight men to guide you and to carry your equipment. The lizards are far from here, and you must go by water. You can rent two boats from us."

This was beginning to sound like a safari.

"I think *one* boat and *four* men will be enough," I replied. "And as for the bait"—neither Helen nor I liked the idea of killing an animal—"can't we buy some meat that is already slaughtered? I understand that the lizards prefer rotten meat anyway."

The chief thought a moment, probably about the profit he saw slipping away.

"There is no market here, and we eat meat only on holidays. But we will sell you an old goat, one that is almost dead already."

One of the chief's henchmen dragged the animal to show us. We stared appalled that it had been allowed to live. One leg was hanging limply, broken in several places. Its hindquarters were slashed inches deep, and the side of its head was ripped open, exposing a blinded eye.

"What happened to it?" we asked.

"*Buaja dharat* [dragon lizard]" was the matter-of-fact reply, and our respect for the ferocity of these creatures mounted accordingly.

After another hour of chatting, everything had been arranged to the chief's satisfaction, but he had one request. He drew me aside and whispered, "If you would take me for a ride in your kapal dharat I would gain much face with my people."

"And I," I replied with true Asian courtesy, "would gain much face if you would honor me by riding in my kapal dharat."

The "main street" of Komodo, in fact the only street, was a sandy path between two rows of thatched huts that extended for perhaps a hundred yards. But the shortness of the road only increased the chief's pleasure as he directed me back and forth, telling me where to turn, cautioning me in alarm when I exceeded ten miles an hour and leaning out the door, waving at his people who crouched well out of the way beneath their huts. But when I headed for the water for a short turn around the calm bay, he protested excitedly, "Oh no, my people have seen boats. Just stay on land."

The chief's two wives had already inspected Tortuga's bunks, stove and running water. Now, when they saw their man emerge unharmed from the Jeep, they wanted to ride too, and Helen gained much face when she took the wheel. The number one wife climbed in first, clutching her tight sarong to keep it from sliding up around her knees—to an Indonesian, an unpardonable exposure. But Tortuga's door is three feet from the ground. Despite Helen's coaching, she missed the step and the sarong separated at a crucial moment.

But they were still game for the ride; they gripped the seat in terror as Helen drove slowly between the long rows of huts, and when they climbed from the Jeep they managed to look very superior.

We made camp that night at the only place in the vicinity of the village where we could be reasonably sure of having any privacy after dark—behind the graveyard.

We wanted to conserve the water in our tank and the chief obligingly sent two men to the well for us. The water they brought back looked like black bean soup, so while Helen gathered wood from the beach and the brambly hills, I punched holes in the bottom of one of our empty gas tins and filled it with layers of coarse and medium gravel and a layer of sand. The villagers sat around perplexed by my makeshift filter, exclaiming as the water dripped through a milky white instead of black. We boiled it for hours while two of the more ambitious young men kept us supplied with wood in exchange for cigarettes and English lessons. When we were finished the water tasted like smoky barbecue sauce, but at least it was safe to drink.

By this time we had started to ration our food, too. But even more than for food we were hungry for something to read. At first the battered Armed Forces Manual that we had carried for years, *Survival on Land and Sea*, had alleviated our shortage of both food *and* reading matter. It's surprising how reading about edible worms, white juicy grubs and snake fillets can depress the appetite when one is only a little hungry. The book of Sailing Directions helped some too, but it didn't make the most encouraging reading, and even the most statistical-minded would find the Tide Charts somewhat less than engrossing. But that night on Komodo we were not thinking much about books or food. We were too excited at the prospect of seeing the Dragons.

The outrigger dugout with tattered sails that the chief euphemistically called a boat was ready the next morning long before we were, and I realized why he had wanted to send so many men. It took two men just to keep the leaking hull bailed with the half coconut shells they used as scoops.

From the sea the island of Komodo seemed a far more fitting place for an antediluvian lizard than for the few hundred people who lived there. Protruding from the shore, knobby growths of coral embedded with shells gave the impression of sea-scoured fossils, while in the distance the low, sawtooth mountains appeared like the scaly back of some larger monster, half hidden behind the scrubby growth of green and drab brown.

The sun was merciless when we arrived at a bleak beach and a faint trail leading to the interior of the island. There were scratchy tracks along the shore; the tide had softened their outlines, but the men were sure they had been made by a lizard. They pointed to a dark oval hole, perhaps two feet wide, in the side of a dry wash. Similar tracks scarred the entrance, the lair of one of the creatures.

Near the coast the earth was pushed up irregularly with giant ant mounds. The trail crossed parched areas that were patterned with mazes of sun cracks and we felt even more that we were in the haunt of some reptile from the past. But farther inland the terrain closed in. We pressed single file through patches of head-high, rasping *alang-alang* grass and we kept Dinah heeled closely beside us. In the clearings wild boar broke snorting through the dense undergrowth to the sides and occasionally a white cockatoo would fan its yellow crest and caw hoarsely from some stunted tree. Once, a brown flash with a white flag of a tail signaled the retreat of one of the many deer on the island.

It was midmorning and oven-hot before we stopped. Suleiman, the only literate man on the island and the leader of the four men accompanying us, pointed below to a dry wash overhung with low branches.

"The lizards crawl along here in search of food," he said.

Where the sun streamed on bright gravel through an opening in the branches, he ordered a piece of meat hung a few feet from the ground.

"The rest is up to the lizards." He yawned, and stretching out on the ground, promptly went to sleep. Somewhat disillusioned by this lack of concern for such reputedly dangerous animals, Helen and I waited tensely. After an hour in the heat we were half dozing ourselves and beginning to wonder if perhaps the biggest danger was not from the smell of the bait. Already black with droning, shiny flies, it exuded a fragrance that should have attracted lizards from all over the island's two hundred square miles.

By noon we were ready to believe that the Dragon Lizard of Komodo was about as legendary as the Holy Dragon of the Chinese from which the superstitious believe it is descended.

"Suleiman," I said, shaking him awake, "are you sure this is the best place?"

"*Ja, tuan,*" he muttered sleepily, "be patient. Some people wait for weeks without seeing a lizard."

He seemed prepared to sleep that long.

About midafternoon we heard a rustling, scratching sound coming from a heap of dry leaves at one end of the ravine. In the shadows we could see only vague shapes, but as our eyes adjusted we made out a python-sized head swinging slowly back and forth, its yellow tongue flicking as it sniffed the air and listened. It crawled cautiously from the shadows into the light, moving on squat, powerful legs that held it half a foot from the ground. At last, apparently confident that it was safe, it moved forward, swiftly, deliberately, leaving an S-shaped track with its tail.

Snuffling at the drippings from the bait, it looked up at the meat; it stretched its snakelike head once, and then, wriggling like a serpent with legs, it slithered off, confused. About five feet long, it was an awesome creature, but hardly the brave dinosaur we had expected.

We wanted to wait longer, but the men were getting hungry. They had eaten all the food they had brought for the day as soon as they arrived, and since then they had been eating ours which we had tried vainly to make last. It was the same with the water and the coconuts we had brought and when everything was gone, they insisted that it was too late for the lizards anyway.

For some reason, the next morning we acquired another boat and four more men—probably to bring our party up to what the chief considered a proper retinue for Dragon Lizard chasing. As soon as we reached the ravine they finished off all the food, in spite of our warning that we were not leaving until we had our photographs. With our own supply of food, water and coconuts in Dinah's protective custody, we went to our blind in the ravine.

Two lizards were already there. Larger and more determined—the meat had a far more attractive aroma now—they leaped at the bait, jostling and snapping at each other. I slipped from behind the blind and crept closer, but the two lizards paid no attention to me. I found that I could speak loudly, even shout without disturbing them. Perhaps they are deaf, I don't know, but certainly loud noises made absolutely no impression on them.

I signaled to one of the men to lower the bait a little. In an instant it was gone—a coconut-sized chunk of meat swallowed whole by a cavernous mouth. At that moment it was easy to believe that the larger lizards are able to pull down a full-grown deer, a goat or wild pig.

For the rest of the afternoon, while the men grumbled at having no food and water, even though we had relented and shared all of ours, we waited in the blind. Once we saw a monster amble down the ravine. He stopped near a fallen tree trunk, dwarfing it, and when I measured the tree later, by comparing sizes I estimated that he was at least ten feet long and a foot and a half through the heavy part of his body. He stood there, his head three feet off the ground, but he would come no closer. It was too dark to photograph him and when I approached he fled, frightening away our two smaller lizards as well.

With more time to spend, the chief told us when we returned to the village, we might see bigger lizards, perhaps even see them swimming in the sea or fighting other beasts. But we could sense the wind shifting day by day; we could smell the threat of rain in the air and the storms accompanying the change in the monsoon. In the afternoons the sky was dark, the sea turbulent, and we had half a thousand miles to go before we reached Timor. We prepared to leave for Flores, the next island to the east.

"But there is no road at Labuhan Badjo," the chief said when we discussed our route with him. He ran a calloused thumb over our map of Flores to the town just across the strait where we had planned to come ashore and continue by road. The map clearly showed a road from Labuhan Badjo. We had counted on that road to reach our next fuel supply at Ende, the capital of Flores, near the south-central part of the island.

"There is no road," the chief insisted. "It starts here, at Reo," and he pointed to a town considerably farther east along the north coast of Flores.

In dismay we studied the chart. It was almost a hundred miles by sea to Reo and another 200 miles overland from there to Ende. Tortuga's fuel consumption at sea, in calm water, with no current and at half throttle, was over five times what it was on land. We had not encountered still water since we had been in Indonesia, but even with no current to buck, those extra miles at sea would drain our tanks long before we reached Reo, let alone Ende. And there was no chance of sending for more fuel. Komodo is as cut off from the rest of the world as though it were on another planet. No ship called, and the twice-yearly visit of the prahu that supplied the village with the few necessities of life that it did not produce itself was not due for several months. There had to be a road at Labuhan Badjo.

"There is no road," the chief repeated.

Back at our camp behind the graveyard Helen and I methodically studied the charts, scaling again and again the distance to Reo. By steering a direct course between the many small islands and over reefs and shallows where the indicated depths were barely enough to float Tortuga, we estimated that we could cut the hundred miles to Reo to 85 miles. Using a calibrated stick, more accurate than the gas gauge, I carefully measured the fuel remaining in the tanks. What with getting stuck in the mud of the bay at Sape and the currents in the straits, we had used over half of our supply. There was not nearly enough to go even 85 miles.

For a long time we sifted our memories and checked our log, trying to correlate our experience in crossing other straits and navigating along the coasts of other islands. We studied the tide charts and the book of Sailing Directions of the U. S. Hydrographic Office. Slowly an idea took shape.

We had always thought of the currents as hazards or hindrances. But what if we could use them to help us instead? The currents are determined by the tides, and twice each day, when the water is rising, the flow would be in the direction we wanted to go. The Sailing Directions listed an unbalanced current in the strait between Komodo and Flores; for eight hours, while the tide is on the ebb, the current flows south at speeds of up to nine knots; for four hours, while the tide is on the flood, the current flows north at some four knots. Our own experience had shown that the flow of current is not limited to the straits alone; along the north and south coasts of the islands, where the waters fan out from the straits, there are also strong currents. Judging by the shape of Flores, a long narrow mass of land, there should be a current along the north coast at least as far as Reo. From an hour after low tide until an hour before high tide that current should be flowing in our direction. It could take a week; we could travel only when the tide was rising and the current with us. It would be folly to navigate those reef-infested waters at night, but at that time of the month the daylight tide came early in the morning when the sea was at its calmest. There was a chance, a very slim chance, that if we used that current we might still reach Reo before our tanks went dry.

Chapter Six

EARLY the next morning Tortuga bumped over the reef and into the deeper water of Komodo Bay. It was an hour after low tide, the current was at its slack point but already strengthening, and by the time we reached the main channel it was flowing north at almost its full force. With a three- to four-knot current pushing Tortuga along and her engine turning over at a gas-saving quarter throttle we could make good time. Rocks and islands sped by at what seemed full-throttle speed with but a whisper from Tortuga's exhaust —and the sea life, heretofore shy of an engine's foreign sound, was bolder.

Marlin threw up cascades of water with their mighty leaps. Occasionally a whale shark that could have swamped us with one swipe of his massive flukes would surface, knife across the water and submerge, leaving a trail of bubbles that disappeared almost as fast as the huge gray form they followed. There were sea snakes, ugly creatures of dirty brown and banded yellow, with flesh that seemed oily in the clear water. More deadly than cobras, they eased their wrist-thick, six-foot-long bodies alongside Tortuga, their blunt heads just above the surface of the sea, but at any movement from us their flat tails would plummet them into the black depths.

There were porpoises too, but these we considered old friends. They had escorted us along the coast of Panama and across the Strait of Magellan, and now as they looped in long chains across the surface, as they snorted and spouted their sprays of water high in the air, twisting and somersaulting, splashing and speeding across our bow, playing like a numberless litter of puppies, we almost forgot that with each turn of the propeller the fuel level in the tanks was falling and that only careful timing of the tides and the most economical use of the engine would get us to Reo.

The route we chose was the shortest but far from the safest. The Flores Sea and the straits that connect it with the Indian Ocean to the south are infamous for unmarked shoals and fallacious soundings. Our charts were the most up-to-date available in Djakarta, but no extensive survey of the area had been made since before World War II. Reefs suddenly appeared before us where none showed on the charts, and Tortuga's wheels bumped over shoals where soundings indicated more than enough depth for her three-foot draft. Ever since one day off the coast of Panama when we were running from a storm and were trapped in a pocket of reef, the light green of shoals has brought a trauma to Helen. But every mile saved was that much extra gasoline, and despite her protests I steered a direct course over the many shallows, between bands of reef and along shelves where the line between safety and danger was as sharply defined in the color of the water as the horizon between earth and sky.

But once a confluence of swirling currents swept us off course and a blue-green shoal of coral rushed under us. Reflexively I swung Tortuga toward the channel of deep water to the side, but the current carried us broadside over the shoal. There was a slope to the reef. I knew that if a wheel caught on a high projection, the force of the current against our beam could capsize us. And yet, like birds enchanted by a snake, we watched the reef loom higher and higher, the blues and purples, the greens, yellows and occasional pink, the fantastic shapes, the branches and convoluted brains and crustacean-specked knobs of coral kaleidoscoping brighter and brighter as the depth of the water decreased. And then a wheel rocked over a high point; Tortuga tipped and her beam went under as the wheel caught, then slipped over. Jarred into action, I floored the throttle until we were in the deep opaque blue of safe water. Thereafter we gave a wide birth to any lightening in the color of the sea, often wasting precious gasoline to avoid what turned out to be merely a school of flashing silver fish or a drift of seaweed.

Though we had noted the hour of high and low tide the day before and had allowed for the daily variations in time—the tide cycle occurs about forty-five minutes later each day—we could not be sure, closer than a quarter of an hour, when the current would actually change direction. We had planned to come ashore after four hours at an island that showed on the chart some eighteen miles from Komodo. But charts are intended for ships that anchor, not for amphibious Jeeps that must crawl from the water and up a beach, and the island we had selected proved to be a steep, cliff-sided rock. We continued, scanning with binoculars the dozens of small islands in the strait, checking their high-water marks for the tide level and watching for the swirls and eddies around their tips that indicated the current was changing.

It was nearing high tide and Tortuga's progress was slowing before we located an island that looked approachable, a small cone-shaped island rising sheer from the sea about 500 yards away.

As the current grew stronger I gave Tortuga more and more gas until she was throbbing. But though the propeller was churning a white froth behind her, she seemed to stand still. The current was close to Tortuga's maximum speed of seven knots and getting stronger. I shifted down to second gear and floored the throttle. Almost imperceptibly we moved toward the island. It took thirty minutes with the engine racing to cover that last quarter mile against the current. In those thirty minutes Tortuga burned more fuel than we had saved all morning, more than we had used in the whole twenty miles we traveled that day.

The next morning we charted our course northeast along the coast of Flores, an area known to be rich in pearls—and a hideout for small-time pirates from the island of Sulawesi (Celebes) several hundred miles to the north. We saw no signs of pearl fishing, but the mast tips of sunken prahus sporadically dotted the surface of the sea over the shallows.

It was a lonely coast; the dark mountains in the interior of the island were masked in heavy clouds and the few villages hidden among groves of coconut palms seemed deserted. The dugout canoes that should have been out fishing were drawn high on the beach and the nets stretched to dry between palm trees were untended. Only an occasional wisp of smoke filtering through the roof of a thatched hut betrayed any sign of life, and we had the feeling—perhaps everyone in a wild, strange and lonely place has this feeling—that our presence was the reason for the quiet.

As we continued along the coast the charts became more inaccurate, the reefs more numerous, the landmarks on which we depended to plot our position fewer.

Often we used the bamboo pole to check the depth before crossing some reef that appeared too clear in the green water. So featureless was the shoreline that for hours at a time we had no idea as to our progress, and it was only by the arrangement of the islands that fringed the coast that we could determine our position.

Using the engine only to maintain minimum steerageway, we traveled eleven miles with the current before poling our way over the reef to a desolate, waterless, treeless mound of an island. Our first thought was of the fuel. I measured the depth in the tanks and computed our mileage. We had almost made up for the fuel wasted the previous day.

As always after even a few hours at sea, there was a brief tense period when the ground still rocked beneath our feet and we still felt the vibration of Tortuga's engine. We passed the afternoon with the mundane tasks of lubricating and inspecting the Jeep, washing clothes in the sea and heating canned food that we had little inclination to eat. But with these finished an ennui set in. In an hour we explored the island from the coral reef that lined its shore to the rocky point that crowned its center. Apparently the overnight stop of some itinerant fisherman, a driftwood fire still smoldered near a crude, lean-to shelter and a hollowed driftwood log lay half-filled with putrefying fish. An uninviting place. There was no romantic beach, no graceful palms, nothing but scrubby bushes, drab brown grass and foot-scarring coral. We looked forward to evening when we could stretch full-length atop

Tortuga, relishing each rare breath of cool air and passing the hours in sleep until morning.

At low tide the next day, our exit was blocked by reef. When we landed at high tide the afternoon before, there had been ample depth to float us over the reef. Now the lovely branches of coral that had glowed a brilliant violet under four feet of water were a dull gray on the dry shore. Starfish as blue as a dawn sky lay limp and faded, orange sea slugs were shriveled and lifeless, and the purplish-black spines of sea urchins were drooping as the water receded and left them stranded in some shallow pool in the coral. Over everything hung the saline stench of exposed reef.

An hour after low tide, when the current had started flowing in our direction and we should have been underway, the water was still too low to float Tortuga over the reef. We tried to drive her over the shelf into deep water but a wheel dropped into a hole and we were stuck, unable to move in either direction, fearful that perhaps a sharp projection of coral had punctured a rubber seal in the bottom, frustrated that we were helpless to do anything but wait and watch the current that would have carried us swiftly along, gradually diminish in force. Impatiently, every few minutes we measured the depth as the water rose around Tortuga; it is strange how in a land where time in years is irrelevant, time in hours could mean so much. When at last we felt Tortuga rock free of the reef we had only an hour left to travel with the current before it reversed direction again.

And so the days passed, each one bringing us a few hours, a few miles, closer to Reo, each day with its cautious selection of a place to come ashore where we could be certain of getting over the reef in the morning, and each day the anxious measuring of our diminishing fuel supply.

With each day our knowledge of the currents increased.

We learned that by staying close to shore and just outside the rim of reef where the strength of the current was less we could leave before low tide, that those bands of agitation on the surface of the sea meant fast current that would carry us along at a fast rate, and that by moving close to shore again just as the tide was turning we could squeeze another hour of travel from the day.

By the fifth day out of Komodo our spare fuel tanks were dry, our main tank was considerably less than full, and our drinking water was almost gone. We were still thirty-five miles from Reo, too far for one day's run during the short time the current would be with us. But the charts indicated no more islands, not the smallest patch of reef-free beach where we could land for the night. We had no choice but to risk a final run, those last thirty-five miles to Reo, knowing that if we miscalculated the distance or the amount of fuel remaining or the strength of the current this could well be the final run.

That morning we were ready long before the tide turned. We had been lucky in our choice of a camp; a deep cleft in the reef, barely wide enough to clear Tortuga, dropped steeply into deep water, and for once it was our choice, not the tide's, to determine when we should leave. We watched bits of floating seaweed and driftwood, measured the time they took to pass between two points on the island, and when their motion toward the west slowed and little eddies swirled them in circles we eased Tortuga through the channel into blue water. By this time low tide was almost four hours later than it was when we left Komodo; the morning was well along before we could leave and a slight but increasing wind was already bristling the sea. We found the band of current, but this far from Komodo Strait its strength was diminished. We would have to average almost six knots to reach Reo before dusk.

Reluctantly I increased our speed to a gas-consuming half throttle.

There was no reading or washing clothes that day, nor much conversation. Dinah lay quietly below, sensing the tension. Even our friends the porpoises could not distract us from watching the quivering needle of the gas gauge. It had an erratic flutter; one moment it would read half full, the next it would fall to the empty mark as Tortuga rolled with the quick, choppy waves. I knew the gauge was not precise, and it was all I could do to resist crawling out on the stern and measuring with the stick through the filler pipe how much fuel was left. But waves were breaking over the stern as well as the bow. I told myself that just knowing would not change anything, that there was nothing I could do, that I must relax and keep my mind on my steering and avoid gas-wasting variations in course. But still, each time Tortuga wallowed upright between waves my eyes jumped to that shaky little needle, and each time I looked it was a little closer to that E at the bottom of the scale.

Late in the afternoon, when the current started to hinder us and the needle of the gas gauge no longer fluttered but instead hung at the empty mark, we moved closer to shore. As near as we could determine we were still fifteen miles from Reo. We looked for a place to land, but dark scrub jungle and mangrove roots reached like fingers into the sea. There was no place to beach Tortuga.

For another hour we crept along close to shore, just outside the reef but clear of the current that was now flowing back toward Komodo. We waited for the cough and sputter of the engine.

A knobby peninsula jutted north into the Flores Sea. To go around it meant bucking the current, chancing that the gas would hold out long enough to get us back into slack water on the other side, risking the possibility of being adrift without power in the mainstream of the current. But it was that or abandon Tortuga and take to the life raft, and we were both determined to stay with her until she stopped.

There was turbulence where the water swirled around the point of the peninsula. The waves rocked Tortuga at crazy angles, sloshing from side to side the few quarts of fuel remaining in the tank. The engine sputtered and stopped as the fuel pump sucked air. I switched on the auxiliary electric fuel pump, pressed the starter. The engine caught, putted a few times, and then as I swung the rudder with each wave to minimize the rocking the engine smoothed out and the purr of its exhaust was like a song to me.

We rounded the point, and it was as if the curtain of jungle had been drawn aside—and with it the curtain of despair from our spirits. We maneuvered across a broad expanse of bay, past rust-crumpled, half-buried landing craft and up the smooth gentle beach that skirted the town of Reo. We had been closer by nine miles than the chart showed, a fortunate error for when I measured the fuel we had enough left for only four more miles.

Chapter Seven

THERE was something different about the crowd that gathered on the beach that day. Many of the children and some of the older people wore silver crucifixes on chains around their necks, and unlike the Sumbawans at Mapin and Alas they did not crowd in around us. They greeted us with surprised but warm smiles and then stood back and watched quietly as I crawled beneath Tortuga to grease the salt-encrusted bearings and steering linkage. One of the men brought a coconut for Helen. His skin, darker than the golden complexion of the people on the islands to the west, was a light chocolate color, his features were more prominent, and his hair, instead of being straight, hung in loose, long ringlets around his face.

Within minutes of our arrival we heard a truck racing down the road from the main part of Reo. A strange hush fell over the crowd as the truck careened over a small bridge and skidded to a stop near an old concrete pillbox. Led by an Indonesian Army lieutenant and bristling with submachine guns, automatic rifles and fixed bayonets, a platoon of helmeted soldiers engulfed us. Each wore the mottled jungle-combat camouflage uniform of olive-drab and green and they all looked like they meant business. Helen and I stood quietly, restraining growling Dinah and hoping they wouldn't be as quick to shoot as they had been in Djakarta. A thought flashed through my mind: how ironical it would be to sweat out the long voyage from Komodo only to become the major characters in an "incident" on Flores. Apparently they were expecting something far more menacing, for after one look at Tortuga and her bedraggled crew they sheepishly stacked their weapons. The sergeant, a wide grin creasing his face, dug into a wooden case in the back of the truck, and with a "Welcome to Flores" handed me a bottle of beer. Warm though it was, nothing ever tasted so good.

"Sorry," the lieutenant said after he had looked at our papers, "but we can't take chances. Reo has been a beachhead for invasions of Flores too often." He pointed to the sunken landing craft in the bay. "Those are Japanese from World War II. And that prahu aground on the beach carried a rebel force from Sulawesi. We've had two rebel attacks already this year. When our lookout reported a strange craft in the bay, well, after all, you *could* have been heading a new invasion."

There was no gasoline for sale at Reo. No ships had called there in three months and even the Army had only what was left in the truck. But somehow, the next morning, the quiet-spoken, friendly lieutenant had found five gallons for us.

"This will get you to Ruteng," he told us. "There's a Catholic mission there. Perhaps they can help you."

From Reo to 4,000-foot-high Ruteng it is some forty miles along a low-gear trail that snakes into the mountains of Manggarai, the western part of Flores. After months in the hot lowlands where any exertion more strenuous than breathing raised shirt-drenching perspiration, the cool, crisp air of the highlands was an invigorating change. We felt the lethargy drift away and new energy seep into us.

But as much as the fresh cool air the mere fact that we were on land again was a boost to our spirits. Another phase of water travel was behind us, and the dark, clouded mountains that from the sea had seemed so forbidding took on an appealing wild beauty. It was lush green country, so different from sultry Sumbawa. Giant ferns and trailing creepers and elephant ears were jeweled with mist; gray-green, tangled whiskers of Spanish moss floated from trees so high we felt like ants beneath them; and in the ravines that parted the black earth, bamboo a hundred feet high and a foot in diameter thrust like feathered spears from a dozen hues of green, from growth so thick it seemed even a bird could not penetrate it. A stream tumbled from a moss-velveted cliff, and we shivered when we bathed among its rocks and clear pools, but they were shivers of pleasure. We sluiced the salt from Tortuga and washed our salt-stiffened clothes and combed the sand from Dinah, and she gamboled like a puppy.

But as far as washing Tortuga was concerned it was wasted effort. The skies opened and the rains that had threatened for weeks came with a rush of wind and a timpani of thunder. We tried to drive on, but the deluge was a tangible, opaque barrier that obscured even Tortuga's bow. We had won our race with the fuel, but the west monsoon had beaten us to Timor.

The morning after the storm was clear, and though the rain had reduced the road to a slippery, muddy path, we arrived early in Ruteng. An orderly little town with neat, tree-shaded streets and wooden houses roofed with red-painted corrugated iron, Ruteng is the administrative center of a *daerah* which could be compared to a county seat. There are offices and simple homes for the Indonesian Civil Service, and the few Chinese-run shops were allowed to remain in business though those in smaller villages were already closed or turned over to Indonesians.

We had just finished our courtesy calls on the government officials and were making our way through the throng of townspeople around Tortuga when we were startled to hear a bright, cheery hello.

"Hey, you haven't been away that long, have you? I hear there are fifty now."

With a laugh, a curly-haired priest in a white, ankle-length cassock pointed to the thirteen-starred yacht ensign that flew from Tortuga's flagstaff. And that was our introduction to Father Robert Stiller of Pennsylvania, a young man who would have seemed more at home on some college campus than in the remote thatched village that was his parish.

We had heard even before we arrived at Reo that there were missionaries on Flores, but we were not prepared for the elaborate and extensive facilities that have been established by the Society of the Divine Word, a worldwide Catholic mission group of German origin.

At the mission station we were introduced to the Mother Superior and the Rector, both of Dutch nationality but with Indonesian citizenship. The Mother Superior, her stiff capuchin framing a round, jolly, unlined face, took Helen gently by the hand and led her away to a room in the white convent. Dinah and I were established in a room in the parish house, a simple room with a washstand and wardrobe, a desk and shelves of well-thumbed books, and a hard bed with a pallet of kapok and coarse homespun sheets. Its occupant, a priest, was on leave; his saddle and rubber boots, as much a part of the habit of a Florinese priest as his cassock and rosary, were lying in a corner.

Later, Helen described her room in the convent as a healing haven of silence after the boisterous receptions we had received everywhere we traveled in Nusa Tenggara. It was a Spartan room of white simplicity—a scene from a Mary Cassatt aquatint. Later, when instead of kulkuls we heard from our respective solitudes the soft voices of vespers floating through the still air from the nearby church, we relaxed for the first time in weeks. And when we feasted on thick lentil soup, homemade cheese and butter, ham and mango sauce, all from the mission's farms and prepared by the nuns, Helen and I both agreed that heaven could wait.

That evening Father Stiller called for us. "I'd like you to meet the other Fathers," he said. "We spend most of our time in our parishes—mine is two days by horse from here. But this is Saint Nick's Day and we'll all be in the mountains on Christmas so we've planned a get-together for tonight."

Christmas. The word came as a shock. Somehow, on this island a few degrees south of the equator and halfway between Singapore and Australia, Christmas seemed as remote as our home and family in California.

In the recreation room of the sprawling wooden parish house perhaps a dozen priests were playing chess or reading. Some wore the brown frocks of the Order of Franciscans, others wore black or white homespun cassocks. A phonograph was playing Christmas and folk songs from Europe, and suddenly Christmas did not seem so far away after all.

One of the priests, a sturdy, amiable Dutchman named

Father Smits, filled liqueur glasses with orange curaçao. For the rest of the evening, until the mission electric plant shut down at ten, we sat happily bundled in sweaters we had not even thought of since leaving Java two months earlier and visited with Spanish, German and Dutch priests, part of the community of over two hundred priests and nuns scattered throughout the island. Many of them had spent upwards of thirty years on Flores, surviving fever, Japanese internment camps, and the excesses of nationalism during the period when Indonesia was achieving her independence—and any white face was an enemy.

The history of Catholicism on Flores, we learned, goes back four hundred years to when the Portuguese, then in control of the area, sent Dominican priests to the eastern part of the island. Later, when the Dutch assumed sovereignty of the Lesser Sundas, the Jesuits took over, and in 1913 the Society of the Divine Word began its work. Over the centuries the number of converts has grown to over half of the island's million-plus inhabitants.

But as much as religious training, the mission is concentrating on education, and with Father Stiller we wandered through the many well-kept buildings of the station; through the schools where over a hundred Florinese girls were studying home economics, hygiene and child care as well as history, mathematics and English; through vocational schools where young blacksmiths, masons, sheet metal workers and carpenters are being trained. All over Flores there are similar schools as well as elementary and secondary schools, seminaries and convents with thousands of students enrolled.

The classrooms and shops were well equipped, and since Tortuga was due for a tune-up and some general maintenance work, I requested permission to use the mission garage. Soon I had an audience, young men from Ruteng and from the mission school, most of them wearing white shirts with pockets full of ball-point pens. As they watched me clean the carburetor and fuel pump and repack the wheel bearings, getting greasier by the minute, they shook their heads and clucked their tongues in chorus. By the time I was finished crawling under and into Tortuga I could have passed for a coal miner. The crowd was overflowing the garage and the tongue-clucking had reached locust plague proportions. Later I asked one of the priests what it was all about. He sighed.

"The sight of a foreigner working with his hands comes as a shock to them. They think that for anyone who can read and write, manual labor is degrading. And when they learned that you are a university graduate, well, this is more than they can understand.

"Indonesia needs skilled craftsmen desperately, but even the graduates of our vocational schools prefer to work as clerks though they could earn much more if they practiced their trades." Half in jest he added, "You might have done us a real service if you had repaired your Tortuga in the main square in town where everyone could watch."

The next afternoon we heard that a *tjatji*, a whip duel, was to take place in one of the many compound-like villages on the outskirts of Ruteng, and Father Stiller offered to take us. We walked along a narrow, slippery path and across a stream where dark-skinned, sarong-clad girls were filling giant bamboo tubes with water to carry home. Father Stiller pointed to the thriving gardens of corn, cassava, rice, tomatoes and carrots on either side of the trail.

"A few years ago our people were tilling the soil with sharpened sticks. They still do in many parts of Flores. We try to help them with more efficient agricultural methods, tools and better seed. But it's slow work.

"Here on Flores each year there's a period when the people

are close to famine when their crop from the last year is almost gone and the new crop isn't ready for harvest. You'd think the people would jump at a chance to increase their production, but one of our priests raised a fine garden and the people just marveled over his tomatoes. 'Give us some seed, so we can grow fine tomatoes too,' they said. The Father answered, 'Of course, but first you must clear your fields of rocks and dig deep in the soil to bring fresh earth to the surface. And after you plant the seed you must keep out all the weeds. Then you will have fine tomatoes like these.' The people thought a bit. They told the Father that perhaps it would be better if he just kept the seed after all."

We came to the village, an oval of wooden huts perched on stilts, each palm-thatched roof crested with carved wooden horns, symbol of the buffalo cult prevalent throughout Indonesia. In front of one of the larger houses straw mats were spread on the ground, and the village chief, a stout man in Western shirt and trousers and a black pitji cap set squarely on his head, invited us to sit while his wife prepared the welcoming sirih. She was wearing her ceremonial headdress, a circlet of silver springy branches from which tiny silver fish dangled. Squatting gravely before us, she smeared the dark green leaves and red betel nut with creamy lime, folded the leaves into mouth-filling bundles, and presented them to us to chew. The offer was made somewhat less attractive by her own stained lips and blackened stubby teeth, the result of years of chewing the stuff.

Our "enjoyment" of the sharply bitter sirih—which is supposed to have a mildly stimulating effect but which for us stimulated only the flow of saliva—was fortunately interrupted as two men danced into the open area in the center of the village. Each wore a wooden mask, like an up-tilted welder's helmet, painted red with triangles and stripes of indigo and white and tufted with stiff plumes of white horsehair. One carried a rawhide oval shield and a length of rattan with a yard-long rawhide snapper, the other only a short springy stick and a thick cloth wrapped around his forearm. Sarongs were draped over long trousers and as they moved, small bells jingled from their ankles and rumps.

Cracking his whip the man with the shield circled his opponent. They both moved with shuffling steps like boxers, singing in loud voices of their bravery while the watching village girls beat an accompaniment on gongs and wooden drums. With a whistling snap and a sharp crack, whip struck stick. *Whish*, a softer thud and whip struck flesh, raising a welt that turned purple, then red as blood seeped through the broken skin of the victim's back. Showing no sign of pain, he laughed and did a hopping jig in derision of the other, and the two traded weapons for another round. Though it is said that the combatants never act out of hatred or anger, the object seems to be to flick out an eye or slice off a bit of nose. Similar to the prisean on Lombok, the tjatji is a fearsome test of courage and physical prowess.

On the morning we left Ruteng, Father Stiller had a request to make of Helen. His eyes crinkled at the corners, as his face, still boyish after three years on Flores and with another seven to go before his first leave, brightened in a grin.

"You know, Helen," he said, "ever since I've been here I've been telling these gals studying home economics what an American kitchen is like. I never thought one would roll right up to the school. How about giving them a demonstration?"

We were happy to oblige and the girls, most in their teens and all clad in the cotton print dresses that are the uniform of the day for schoolchildren throughout Indonesia, crowded in, watching intently as Helen worked the small pump handle mounted on the dash in front of her seat, filling a kettle with water and then boiling it on the one-burner alcohol stove. She took cups from one of the cabinets and made tea, and the faces of the girls flashed with smiles as something they recognized resulted from what must have seemed to them a mumbo-jumbo operation. Handsome girls they were, their teeth unstained by sirih—though many of them would chew the leaf when they returned to their villages. With their education and training they would bring high bride prices to their parents. Tortuga's galley, though it lacked garbage disposal and refrigerator, was a great success, and when we left, the girls gave us cookies and fresh brown bread they had baked.

The Rector had a request too. He gave us mail to deliver to mission stations along the way.

"During the rainy season," he said, "we're lucky if the mail truck gets through once a month."

After a few days on Florinese roads we understood why. Some four hundred road miles from end to end, Flores is one rugged ridge of volcanic mountains that drop steeply to the sea on both sides. The rains began again soon after we left Ruteng and the roads became an abominable mire. We realized then what one of the priests meant when he said we were a month too late to cross Flores and we cursed those five weeks of delay in Djakarta.

Indonesia is clear of the typhoon belt that periodically devastates the Philippines, but the eastern islands are on the fringe of it, and the storms accompanying the west monsoon often approach typhoon force. In the Caribbean we had learned to respect the native weather prophets and were convinced that there is more than superstition behind their belief that the moon somehow influences the frequency and violence of storms. We could expect intervals of relative calm between the phases of the moon, but from now on, in the afternoons at least, the rains would always be with us.

Each day the deluge came a little earlier and lasted a little longer. Always it came with that same violence that had stopped us the day we left Reo, that blinding wall that made driving impossible and forced us to the side of the winding, cliff-bordered road at the first rap of thunder.

The sun was never out long enough to dry us; life became a battle against the creeping, green-white mold that coated shoes, clothes, photographic equipment, everything. With the rain came the leeches, cunning little creatures that transferred themselves from dripping grass, found every gap in our clothing, burrowed through Dinah's thick fur, swelled with our blood from threads of wriggling black to finger-sized gray blobs whose decoagulating suckers left wounds that oozed red for hours after a lighted cigarette singed them into dropping off.

If the trails on Sumbawa were an endurance test, those of Flores were an obstacle course. Barely a day passed without our clearing slides or boulders or winching across some swollen stream where the bridge had washed out years before. In one stretch of eighty miles we counted almost forty bridges gone, and before crossing even those few bridges that looked safe, remembering Sumbawa, we stopped to inspect each one, jumping up and down on it and looking for rotten timbers. More often than not it would rock and creak beneath our weight and we would find some unmarked detour around it, a path through bamboo groves and vine-strangled jungle, a precipitous descent to a stream and a scrambling, four-wheel-drive climb to the road again on the other side.

But perhaps the greatest hazard was from falling trees. During the dry season the fields are burned to clear them for the next planting, but the fire spreads unchecked into the forests. Great hunts are declared by the villagers and more forest is burned to drive out the deer, wild boar and the fierce wild carabao which are run down with dogs and then speared. The rains come and the denuded soil erodes, exposing the shallow roots of trees which come crashing down at the first strong wind—always, it seemed, across the road.

Usually we could clear these trees by ourselves, cutting them with our machete into pieces small enough to winch away with the motor-operated capstan on Tortuga's bow. But once we were stopped by a downed giant. My machete rang and flew from my hand when I tried to cut into the iron-hard wood, and when I had to pull the whole tree clear, the heavy nylon rope for the winch merely stretched and dragged Tortuga's brake-locked wheels through the mud.

We had left mail at a mission outpost that morning, and the lone priest, a Belgian, had invited us to spend the night with him; anxious to make the most of a rare clear day we declined. Now as we returned for help Father Daem came running from his simple parish house, crying, "You are welcome, you are welcome!"

He arranged to have the tree cleared the next morning, and that night, with an oil lamp shining on a print of Roualt's Christ and a "before and after" picture of Father Damian, the Leper Priest, Father Daem shared from his Christmas package from home a can of kippers, some soup and a bar of Belgian chocolate. Unlike most of the priests of the Society of the Divine Word who become missionaries soon after being ordained, Father Daem was a volunteer. In his middle years, he left his prosperous parish in Brussels to build with his own hands in the mountains of Flores a clinic for expectant mothers.

As we traveled east across Flores we became more and more dependent on the priests for their understanding of the language and their entree to the people. We had found very little written in English about the Lesser Sundas, but many of the priests had made a life study of the islands' culture. They were generous with their knowledge.

The specialty of Father Verhoeven, a Dutch priest with Indonesian citizenship, is prehistory and archeology. In his office, surrounded by fossils of elephantlike stegodonts, giant bats and reptiles, implements from the Stone and Bronze ages and plaster casts of early man, we questioned him about the past of Flores.

Like an informal seminar the story unfolded. It was a story based mainly on anthropological studies—there are no written records of the early peoples—a story of numerous small and great migrations, of Veddoid people who might have come from India thousands of years ago, of Negrito elements, of Papuan types such as are found on West Irian, the Indonesian name for New Guinea.

The eminent Austrian prehistorian, Dr. Robert von Heine-Geldern, speaks of migrations in about 800 B.C. from the area of what is now the Balkans, the Pontian Migration across eastern Europe into Asia where it spread into the area of Tonkin in south-central China, giving rise to what he calls the Dongson Culture. These Asian Bronze Age people, it is thought by some, later moved on to the Indonesian Archipelago, bringing with them irrigated rice culture, ritual buffalo sacrifice, the working of metal, animism, and the custom of erecting stone monoliths.

According to the Dutch scientist, Dr. Jaap Kunst, strength is lent to this theory by the art motifs still present throughout the Islands: spiral breast ornaments found in Croatia are almost identical to the huge ear pendants we later saw in use by the Karo Bataks of Sumatra; some old Croatian weaving and the Dyak plaited mats of central Borneo are "so much alike as to be interchangeable"; the symbol of the Tree of Life and the representation of the soul riding on a horse to the Country of the Dead, both from west Russia, are very similar to those representations of the same as found in south Sumatra; a carving on an ancient tomb in Bosnia depicts the soul as a bird riding on a deer and even the art form and style are almost identical to those on a burial shroud from the Indonesian island of Sumba to the south of Flores. Similar motifs have been found at excavations at Harappa in Pakistan and at Sumerian ruins, both of which predate the Pontian Migration. Dr. Kunst lists dozens of such similarities; other scientists intimate a relationship between Indonesia and Easter Island in the Pacific. But all stress that it is dangerous to draw conclusions from similarities, ignoring the differences. As Father Verhoeven concluded:

"There is much theory but little proven fact. One thing, however, is fairly certain with regard to Flores. Hundreds of years ago the island had trade contact with the West. The Portuguese stopped here on their way to the Spice Islands. They traded for sandalwood and established several bases."

Father Verhoeven held up a string of opaque white beads. "These are Venetian, possibly from the time of Marco Polo who is thought to have stopped at Sumatra on his way back from China. And these five-sided, amber-and-glass beads are of the Roman period, while this serrated red-and-blue one is like those found in the tombs of Egypt. They were all found right here on Flores, possibly brought by Arab and Indian traders, but that was so long ago the people have forgotten their origin. In their legends the beads are gifts from the spirits or were found on mountaintops. The people place great value on them. With this string of orange Indian beads, for example, you could buy several buffaloes and perhaps a wife."

Other priests are doing research on the many languages of Flores and on the crafts. A Slovakian priest is encouraging the highly developed art of weaving in the *ikat* style, the same technique used in the burial shroud from Sumba. At Sikka, a southern seacoast village where the Indian Ocean crashes over reefs to a lovely palm-lined beach, we watched the ikats being made. Women sat beneath their houses or under trees using foot-operated wheels to spin into thread the homegrown cotton (a poor, coarse grade; cotton has not been raised anywhere in Indonesia in commercially successful quantities). Others tied the warp threads tightly with grass fiber. When the threads are dyed, the colors, usually locally grown indigo and red, will not penetrate the tied areas, and when the fiber is removed the motif is white on a dark background and forms symbols of animals or plants or lizards, the last an ancient fertility sign.

Each house had its loom, a crude affair with the threads stretched between stakes driven into the ground. Girls sat with their legs thrust forward, their hands whipping the shuttle back and forth so fast it blurred, changing colors and weaving stripes in traditional patterns that go back beyond memory, patterns that were perhaps originated by those mysterious people of Dongson.

But to us one of the most interesting studies was that of Father Rozing, a Dutch priest who is doing research on the music of Flores. The Florinese for centuries have blended their rich voices in multi-part harmony; all over the island we had heard them chorus in both village and church. Father Rozing was adapting their music to church themes.

Like Dr. Kunst, Father Rozing is convinced that there is a connection between the Balkans and Flores.

"Look," he exclaimed excitedly, showing us a double flute of bamboo from his large collection of Florinese instruments, "this is just like the double flutes used in Yugoslavia." He picked up another tube of bamboo about a foot long and two inches in diameter. Fibers had been split lengthwise around the outside leaving both ends attached, and these were raised with bridges made of small pieces of wood. It was something like a cylindrical guitar with the tones varied by the length of the fibers and the placement of the bridges. Father Rozing plucked the taut fibers, and soft notes like those of a muted banjo but with a wooden rather than a metallic quality filled his small parish house.

"This idiochord, a drum zither it's sometimes called, is like those made of cornstalk in Serbia."

He took the flute again and blew a trill on it. "Even the tonal scale is the same."

We heard an answering call from outside.

"That's an unbound flute, an interesting instrument. They have them in China and the Ukraine too."

We thought it was close, but the notes of a flute carry a long way, and we walked for several minutes before we found the source. High up on the hill behind the parish house a boy sat like Pan on a large rock. He was blowing into two lengths of bamboo that were spread at a narrow angle, fingering the holes of each one independently. The melody, sad and time-less, drifted toward us like the soft mist that was rising from the floor of the valley, crawling up the sides of the mountain to blend with the tinted cotton puffs at the crest of a long-dead volcano, rising to become part of the purpling evening sky.

For the people as well as for us the many mission stations were oases. Once, as we were chopping a path through another fallen tree, four men approached, mounted on the sturdy little horses that are raised in the Lesser Sundas. They were from a village along the coast where Bahasa Indonesia is known and we could talk with them. They were taking their father to a mission in the mountains, they said, but it was still a day's ride by horse and could we do anything to help the old man until they got there. He sat drooping on his horse, bundled to his eyes in heavy, coarse blankets, and though the day was hot he was shivering violently. His lips were blue and his fingernails pale. I was sure he had malaria.

To people in remote areas, it seems, every foreigner is a doctor or at least has medicine, and we had pulled thorns, swabbed iodine, plastered Band-Aids and dispensed aspirin all the way from Djakarta. We gave the old man some quinine tablets, instructing him to take two now. We handed him a cup of water, but he chewed the bitter pills and swallowed them dry. Helen and I puckered our faces at just the thought but he seemed to relish the taste, for the same reason apparently that the people prefer iodine to antibiotic ointment and uncoated aspirin to sugared pills. If the treatment doesn't hurt or taste bad it isn't doing any good.

At almost every mission station on Flores there is a clinic of some kind, but with only one doctor for the island's more than a million inhabitants the priests double as medics. At Soa, an isolated village in central Flores accessible only by a boulder-strewn road that is little more than a horse trail, we arrived while Father Mommersteeg was treating some of his ailing parishioners for yaws, a horrible skin disease that produces running, ever-deepening ulcers and is a major scourge in Indonesia. With almost masochistic pleasure they received the injections of penicillin, a drug which with one dose will cure the disease—but can do nothing to prevent reinfection when the patient returns to his village.

The bamboo-and-thatch huts of Soa are built around what looks like a huge amphitheater. Tiers of great stones that might once have served as altars for pagan sacrifices form walls at different levels, and in the center is a *peo,* a kind of totem fetish. Nearby is another pole topped with an image of the Virgin Mary.

"It's quiet now," said Father Mommersteeg, a veteran of twenty-three years in Soa. "Most of the people are in the fields. It's planting time, and by adat or tribal law there can be no feasts until the harvest is in. But in a few months the Feast of the Carabao will be celebrated."

Adat, we knew, controls every aspect of an Indonesian's life. Be he Christian or Moslem, adat decrees when he must plant and harvest, what rites must accompany births and deaths, even what activities a menstruating woman may participate in. We pressed the Father for details about the Feast of the Carabao, and somewhat reluctantly he continued:

"The people fear that their breaches of adat will bring sickness or plagues of rats to the village. They want a scapegoat, something to suffer for them. So they tie a buffalo on a long rope in the center of this open area. They throw spears and knives at it until it's wild with fear and pain, until it bleeds to death.

"It's a dreadful custom, discouraged by both the government and the Church. But it's been going on for centuries and I'm afraid it will be a long time dying out. You see, there's still another factor involved."

Father Mommersteeg led us to a hut where dozens of buffalo skulls hung on the walls. "The man who donates a buffalo to the feast gains great prestige in the village, and to a Florinese prestige is all-important. This family used to be one of the wealthiest in the village—until it gave away all its buffaloes for the Feast of the Carabao. Now it has great prestige, but that's all."

As we were leaving, the village chief invited us to share a drink with him. A wrinkled old man with quizzical eyes peering from beneath a faded red turban, he led us up the ladder to his stilt-elevated hut. We sat on the bamboo-slat floor as he poured *tuak*—a palm wine—from a thick tube of bamboo into shallow cups of coconut shell and ceremoniously handed them to us. Beneath the floor, gray, bristly pigs scratched themselves against the stilts, making the whole structure shake. From the rafters hung spears with red and yellow feathers and baskets with fine geometric designs. The chief signaled us to drink; like watered milk in appearance, the tuak had a pungent, not unpleasant taste that quickly quenched our thirst. A fine old mellow vintage, it had been tapped from the tree that morning.

The palm from which the wine comes—it is really more of a beer than a wine and only slightly intoxicating—grows all over Indonesia, but on the predominantly Moslem islands the liquid is rarely tapped. On Flores nearly every village has its palms, and rigid taboos govern the taking of the sap. Forgiveness must be asked of the tree spirit when the bark is cut and the bamboo tube to catch the liquid is affixed to the trunk. A menstruating woman must never approach the tree; by adat she is unclean and the fermentation will stop. And when the tube is drained, prayers of thanks must be offered and a little must be left for the spirit. But if the taboos are observed, each morning the tube will be full, and a large tree will keep a family in tuak for many years.

Father Mommersteeg rode with us to Mataloko, the central Flores headquarters of the mission, an enclave of schools and shops with a parish house, a convent and a huge church. Surrounding the station are the rich, rolling hills of the mission's farms that supplied the dairy products and meat we were enjoying so much after months of canned food.

On the way to Mataloko we stopped at another village of Father Mommersteeg's parish. On the far side of a hill, it was hidden from the road, a cluster of crude shacks overlooking a great flat valley of mottled green. In the center of the village, man-high slivers of rough stone were thrust into the ground like a jagged inverted comb. At their base were horizontal slabs of stone that straddled other rocks to form small cavities beneath. The people had no memory of who constructed them nor their purpose except that they were in honor of the ancestors. Similar forms have been found on Sumba to the south of Flores, in Sumatra, Laos and Malaya, giving rise to many theories. Among the most interesting if not the most plausible is that of British archaeologist William J. Perry, who proposes they were erected by a hypothetical migratory people which he calls the Children of the Sun. To these same people he attributes the dolmens and menhirs of the druids in England and France and some of the mysterious stone monuments of South America and Easter Island.

All through Flores we detected a patient but resigned optimism when the priests spoke of their work. From several we heard that Islam was spreading into the mountains from the coast where for centuries it has had roots. Understandably, it is the men who take most eagerly to Islam, which permits four wives, while the women prefer the monogamous dictum of Christianity. But how did the old religion of animism affect the mission's work? Father Mommersteeg put it this way:

"Animists believe in one supreme power, the creator, a belief that makes it easier for us. But they also believe that everything has a spirit or soul, some good, some evil. And that's where we have trouble. We want them to associate the good spirits with God, but they say that since the good spirits would never harm them anyway, why bother with them? Only the bad spirits have to be appeased."

In some parts of eastern Flores the appeasement of the bad spirits takes a gruesome form. Adat decrees that to protect a newly constructed house the head of a young girl must be buried under the cornerpost.

At another village we learned of a custom which if investigated further could have far-reaching effects. It was a poor village, high on a hill, and the huts, scattered without pattern, squatted on low stilts, and the thatch hung almost to the ground.

Several women came running to meet us, but one oldster turned her back. The priest tried to joke with her, but she just sulked.

"She's a little angry with me right now," the priest said. "Says I'm depriving her of her rightful income. It's not true, of course. I'm only trying to raise the status of the village."

"What has the status of the village got to do with her income?" we asked.

"Because of an old, old custom that has either died out elsewhere or never existed any place but here, this village is not thought of too highly by the other villages in the area. It's the custom of this village that when a boy calls on a girl the two of them go behind the cloth screen. The boy is allowed to spend the night—provided he is gone by sunrise and leaves a suitable present for the mother. The trouble is that the girls have a hard time finding husbands. The boys come from miles to call, but they don't marry them. I've persuaded some of the girls to send the boys home early, but the mother of one, the one that's angry with me, says that she spent her life raising her daughter and now that the girl can bring in a few presents I have no right to interfere."

"But what if the girls become pregnant?"

"They never do—unless they forget to drink their tea every morning. It's brewed from a plant that grows in the mountains. When they marry they stop drinking the tea and the normal functions continue."

Forgetting I was speaking to a Catholic, I exclaimed, "Why, this is what science is seeking. What a boon this would be for India, for China, for Java, for all the countries that are faced

with populations that are growing faster than their food supply and resources."

The priest made no comment, and frustrated by my lack of
knowledge of the language I could never learn from the people the name of the plant.

At Ende, capital of Flores, we picked up our next supply
of fuel and made arrangements to send back by the next truck
the gas we had borrowed at Ruteng and Reo. For three days
we waited in Ende for the swollen rivers that had washed out
the road to eastern Flores to subside, and for three days it
rained with a brainwashing insistency. It had taken us two
weeks to reach Ende from Reo, and we were little more than
halfway across the island. We had to be underway; it was still
several hundred miles to Timor. But the rain was our prison.

We began to hear and see rain in our sleep, the rattle of rain
on metal roofs, the slash of wind-whipped rain against windows, the gentle insidious droplets gathering on leaves, running in trickles to the sharp points of palm fronds, falling in
thin strands of crystal and breaking with silent thumps into
our consciousness.

On the fourth day the weather cleared somewhat and we
received word that the road was passable. The hundred-ton
mission ship was in port, and before leaving we spoke with
Brother Marianus, her bright-eyed, good-humored chief engineer, about our route for the rest of the journey to Timor. To
each of our questions about the likelihood of trouble with
weather, currents or reefs he replied with a noncommittal
"*Ja*, maybe." Later, when he saw Tortuga, he was more ex-
plicit. "*Jaaaa*, maaaaaybe," he said.

It was a gray day when we left Ende for Kelimutu, the
Mountain of the Three-Colored Lakes, reached by a short
branch from the main road to eastern Flores. In an old Dutch

guidebook it says the round trip from Ende to Kelimutu can be made in a few hours, but that was many years ago. Now the "passable" road was a river-sliced, furrowed trail. At one ford where the river boiled in brown froth over boulders almost as large as Tortuga we lost several hours winching and pushing up the steep bank. Darkness caught us before we reached the cutoff to Kelimutu.

We spent the night at the convent of Djopu where some eighty Florinese sisters are in training. It was two days before Christmas and their dark faces, framed in starch-white capuchins, were alive and gay as they decked the altars with flowers. The contrast was striking; the grandparents, perhaps even the parents, of some of these girls practiced the Feast of the Carabao or buried heads at the cornerpost of a new house or drank the tea of sterility and practiced what amounts to premarital prostitution. There was a look of satisfaction on the face of the old German nun who supervised the young sisters, and a look of nostalgia on Helen's as we sat quietly together and listened to records of Handel's *Messiah*.

That night was the last quarter of the moon and the storm struck on schedule. Djopu is secluded in a valley with protective mountains on all sides but we could hear the storm coming. The wind and rain screamed down the hills, raging through the trees and pressing against the metal roof of the parish house until it snapped like some giant's cricket toy. A window flashed open and the candle was snuffed as if the wick had been cut. The lightning came, bleaching the countryside with the white of magnesium flares. Thunder sent Dinah cowering under the cot, the kind of thunder that makes a sonic boom seem like a firecracker. It reverberated across the valley and jarred the walls and when we thought it had reached its peak it went on to the pulsating crescendo of a naval broadside.

But the storm that night was an assault on more than the senses. It leveled seven houses and de-roofed several more, and we wondered what it would be like on the sea.

The next morning the sky was clear of the long-threatening clouds, but there was still a dark overcast. The peak of 6,000-foot-high Kelimutu was shrouded in haze and there was little hope of seeing the true colors of the lakes. But after the storm we wanted to give the rivers to the east at least a day to subside. Despite the overcast we headed for Kelimutu.

The long-unused side road was scratched through an area of great ferns and bamboo. It wound through gullies and along the sides of steep hills where even in four-wheel-drive the tires cut divots from the soft earth. We lost the road once when the country opened into rolling hills choked with elephant grass higher than Tortuga. With Helen sitting on top to guide me we pushed ahead, tanklike, flushing wild boar, orange orioles and some long-tailed black and white birds, and a deer. It was like moving through a cage of green, and I closed the windows to keep the grass-clinging leeches from whipping inside. Our altimeter registered a little over three thousand feet when an eroded bridge stopped us. There, in a silence overlaid with the stiff rustling of grass and the shrill click of cicadas from a grove of towering trees farther up the mountain, we spent Christmas Eve.

The tall grass crowded in; no breeze reached us, and we stretched our bedding atop Tortuga. The sky had cleared and the stars were very bright and very close. The stars are bright and close like that over our home in the mountains of California, but below the equator, in the mountains of Flores, we saw the Southern Cross instead of the Big Dipper. We lay there quietly on our backs, our arms behind our heads, not speaking. Dinah, out on the bow, made the Jeep rock as she squirmed to get comfortable. Then, in a soft, faraway voice, Helen said, "I wonder how the folks are. And Don and Darlene and the children."

It had been three months since we had been in a place we could receive a letter from our parents and our brother and sister.

Helen's voice brightened. "I'll bet they'll all be with Mother and Dad tonight. I'll bet it's chilly and they'll have a fire in the fireplace and they'll toast marshmallows and make popcorn and open presents."

Helen was quiet again; I was thinking of the family too. And of the other Christmases we had been away from home. The year before we had been with an Englishman in India, and on Christmas morning his Indian friends, Hindu and Moslem, came to wish him a happy holiday. They piled all three of us with garland after garland of orange marigold and some sweet white blossoms until we were overwhelmed with the fragrance and had to spread the strands in order to see through them.

Two Christmases we had been in Alaska, truly white Christmases they were, with the sun at midnight coating the ice floes of Cook Inlet with the rosy glow of old wine.

And then there was a Christmas on a Patagonian sheep ranch. The wind was howling through the wall of poplars around the ranch house like a pack of wolves at a full moon. There was an Englishman with a French name from the Channel Islands, and an Australian, an Irishman, a Welshman and the two of us and Dinah. We sat around a fire, passing the *maté*, warming our hands on the hot gourd and sipping the *yerba* tea through a silver straw. The table was sagging with two immense turkeys, meat *empanadas*, plum pudding and a dozen side dishes. When we could eat no more we tied white handkerchiefs around our necks and in the traditional Patagonian way we filed to the kitchen to toast the cook with apple champagne.

On Flores that Christmas Eve we toasted *in absentia* the old German nun at Djopu. She had packed a basket for us with ham and black bread sandwiches, sweet rolls, white cheese and cubes of fresh pineapple and a bottle of her special white wine made from grapes she had grown herself.

Christmas Day dawned like pink crystal as we climbed on foot to Kelimutu. It was volcanic country and above the fringe of trees the reddish-gray earth was scooped in long black furrows radiating from the craters of the lakes. From the razorback ridge we could see the incredibly blue Indian Ocean stretching in shimmering bands of sunlight to the south. All around us the valleys of Flores were shedding their early-morning veil, revealing a mottling of more shades of green than a painter could conceive—from the darkness of the flat-topped forests to the velvet of grassland to the almost yellow of new bamboo.

We climbed higher to a rounded peak. Below was a diadem: a moonstone, a turquoise and a garnet—the lakes of Kelimutu, their colors as saturated and sparkling as the gems they resemble.

A chemist would explain the colors of the three crater lakes in terms of their mineral content, but to the people, Kelimutu is a stage of heaven: to the warmth of the green lake go the souls of young men and virgins; to the cold of the milky-blue one go the souls of old people; while the Burgundy-red lake is the soul-haunt of thieves and murderers.

By this time our supply of canned food—which we had thought more than enough to reach Timor—was reduced to a few cans of hard biscuits and a jar of jam. It would have been gone long ago except for the hospitality of the missions. We had tried in Ende with little success to replenish our supply, but import restrictions had made foreign canned goods almost impossible to obtain outside of the larger stores on Java, and transportation deficiencies had severely limited the distribution of the few canned products of Indonesian manufacture. With little optimism, at Maumere on the north coast of Flores, we made the rounds of the five or six Chinese shops handling food. We wandered from shop to shop, followed by a growing throng of small fry all eager to direct us to the place of business of some fourth or fifth cousin, but we found nothing more exciting than a can of bitter pickled cucumbers from Hong Kong and a string of red chilis. And then we discovered a veritable treasure trove. Behind a stack of copra bags that exuded anything but an appetizing aroma we found some rusty American cans that must have been left over from pre-independence days. We couldn't tell what was inside— their labels were water-stained to illegibility—but we were certain it was food. And in the last shop we located some Balinese corned beef and some Javanese meat and red beans, both fortunate finds. We had tried them earlier and found them excellent. What's more, Dinah liked them too, and her canned horsemeat was about gone.

That left only one hunger, something to read. At the mission near Maumere even that lack was alleviated, and not with hymnals and prayer books—though we could have used one of the latter before we reached Timor. With a generous wave of his hand and a "Help yourself" sophisticated, cultured Father Baack offered us our pick of his extensive library of paperbacks. Happily clutching a stack of Hemingway, Wouk, Steinbeck, Faulkner, Farrell, Waugh, Greene, Maugham and Tennessee Williams, we headed for Larantuka at the eastern tip of Flores.

We made only one stop between Maumere and Larantuka. At Hokeng, about halfway, we met Brother Sebastian who managed the mission coffee grove, a jolly man whose appearance and lively personality could well have been the inspiration for Chon Day's character of the same name. Slovakian by birth, English-speaking by preference, and the bearer of a United Nations passport by necessity, Brother Sebastian was planning to spend his year's leave in Milwaukee—"To learn to make cheese and beer." If his success with beer and cheese approaches his skill at making Advocat (a Dutch drink composed of brandy and eggs) his popularity among the other brothers and priests will soar even higher.

Handing us two bottles, he said: "I used to make it with the yokes of eggs and Cognac. But now there is no more Cognac so I use whole eggs and arak."

Arak is a brandy distilled from rice or palm wine.

Brother Sebastian touched his ample stomach. "I cannot drink it myself, but the Fathers, they say it is very good."

The road through eastern Flores plunges abruptly from the low mountains down to the coast at Larantuka. At one place where the panorama spread from rocks and tall, broad-leafed trees to expansive dark jungle broken by patches of lighter grassland, we paused, thinking of the next phase of the journey. Far below us was a sprawling village of grass huts with conical roofs. It had a wild, unsettled look, like some of the African villages. Beyond was the limitless sea, a glaring gray sheet spotted with the hazy islands of the Solar group across the strait: Adonara, Solar and Lomblen. And beyond these, too far to be seen, were Pantar and Alor, the last islands before Timor, islands where the people were reputed to be as wild as the village below us looked.

It was about noon of the day before New Year's when we

arrived in Larantuka. Immediately we grew an ever-lengthening tail of shouting children and grownups who had no trouble keeping up with us as we bounced over the potted, tree-shaded road toward the beach. Though it was too late to cross that day we wanted to examine the approach. From now on we would have to limit our travel to the morning hours. The afternoon winds and squalls of the west monsoon were too unpredictable. Already the water was riffled with whitecaps and in the center of the strait where the current is strongest—eleven knots we were told—the waves heaved up to meet the wind.

A long, low pier projected into the strait. A ship had been sighted, and the pier was piled with bags of copra and coffee.

Leaving Dinah in Tortuga, Helen and I walked along the pier, examining the mottled bottom of the shore through the clear water. It was coarse sand bleeding to lumpy coral and billowy, entangling seaweed, but the water deepened rapidly and we would be afloat before we left the sandy part.

The Jeep by this time was inundated with people. All we could see was the flag and the two sharp points of Dinah's ears projecting through the hatch where she was apparently standing to catch a little air. We had left her to watch Tortuga, but with Dinah children can do anything, and they were crawling all over. One of them poked Dinah in the ribs—if an adult had done that he would have lost a hand—but she just yawned, exposing her strong white teeth, and then grinned, her tongue flapping loosely in the hot air. I heard the boy who poked her say to a companion: *"Ada gemuk, baik makan."*

Dinah wasn't as fat as she had been when we left Java—nor were we—but I couldn't let this reference to her as a fat, juicy morsel pass uncontested. That the Florinese eat dogs came as no surprise. It is said of some tribes of Sumatra that "there is no form of animal, as long as it carries meat on its bones, which is not eaten by the Bataks. They even have no horror of putrid meat, and dogs which suffer from skin disease and no longer can walk are killed and eaten." We never heard that the Florinese were quite so omnivorous as all that, but just in case, I employed a tactic that had worked well in central Flores where sleek, healthy and huge Dinah had been similarly eyed with the pot in mind. I assumed a very grim expression.

"Oh no," I told the boy, "you can't eat *her. She* eats *people.* I think you would do fine for supper." And to his companion, "And tomorrow, you for breakfast."

Their eyes opened saucer-wide and they moved back with slow cautious steps. As an added convincer I gave Dinah the command to "Watch." She bared her teeth in a halfhearted snarl and gave an obedient woof—which would not have fooled anyone who knew dogs, for her hackles were down. But after that the children walked wide circles around Dinah and the adults suppressed knowing grins.

Larantuka was long a Portuguese trading center, and the influence is still evident in the larger stature of the people and in names like da Costa, da Silva, and d'Alves. Many of the old Portuguese church relics, some dating from the 1600's, are still in Larantuka, and a Philippine priest took us to the house of a member of the Confrerias, an old church fraternity, to see them. It was the Confrerias who had safeguarded the yellowed ivory crucifixes, the silver chalices, the faded altar vestments, during the long years when the Protestant faction in Holland forbade Catholicism in the Indies and during the Japanese occupation of Flores. Still active, the red-robed, banner-carrying Confrerias escorted Monsignor Manek to New Year's Day mass the next morning, our last day on Flores.

Monsignor Manek was the first local priest to be ordained on Flores. At the time of our visit he was Bishop of Larantuka, one of three bishops on the island, but later, when the rank of the diocese was raised, Monsignor Manek, in preference to many European priests of greater experience and seniority, was elected Archbishop of Flores, proof of the avowed policy of the mission eventually to turn all responsibility over to the Florinese. I remember well the rainy afternoon with Monsignor Antonio Thijssen, the dynamic Bishop of Ende, whose personality and thirty-year tenure on Flores made him the logical choice for Archbishop had a European been so honored. In his enthusiastic way he told us of the mission's efforts to become self-sufficient in food, to raise enough extra coffee for a cash crop, to put the mission printing shop on a paying basis, to train enough Florinese priests, nuns and lay brothers to replace all of the Europeans. In the meantime the mission was walking the flimsy tightrope of good relations with the government, knowing full well that any one of the mercurial changes of government policy could result in the eviction of those priests of Dutch extraction, even though almost without exception they had devoted their lives to Flores and had taken Indonesian citizenship. I remember Monsignor Thijssen's smile, sad but hopeful, as he said, "You might almost say that we are working toward our own destruction."

At Monsignor Manek's request we delayed our New Year's Day departure from Larantuka until after mass.

"Your Tortuga would be formidable competition," he explained with a grin, "and I'd like the people to stay in church."

When mass was over, the shore was white with all of Larantuka, it seemed, in their holiday best, watching as we eased Tortuga into Flores Strait. The ship that was expected had arrived; a freighter, it tooted a wheezing blast on its whistle and signaled us to come alongside, but for once the current was with us. We waved and tooted back and headed for Waiwerang, Adonara's southern village, sixteen miles to the east.

Chapter Eight

THE islands of the Solar group are a compact
mass of green mountains separated by swift narrow straits.
The wiener-shaped Solar to the south hugs the coast of Flores,
nearly blocking the view from Larantuka of the Indian
Ocean. To the east is Adonara, like a fireman's axe with the
pointed western tip curving down toward Solar and the cutting edge to the east honed by the sea to a long, sweeping con-
cavity. And beyond is Lomblen, the largest of the three, a
great shark sprawled between the Flores Sea and the Sawu
Sea where some of the major naval engagements of World
War II took place. All three islands are knobbed with volcanoes, some smoking, some rumbling, some silent, a hodge-

podge of sharp, truncated or rounded cones plunging abruptly to the sea.

From Larantuka we could see Adonara clearly, only two miles away across the Flores Strait. Farther north the water shallows to a 75-foot-deep millrace less than a mile wide. Twenty years ago we would have crossed directly to Adonara, but the road that once circled the island is no more—a victim, as are the roads in all of the Lesser Sundas, of lack of funds and lack of interest of the new government.

Once into the mainstream we headed southeast, cutting diagonally across toward the south tip of Adonara, letting the current do most of the work. We steered east into Solar Strait, keeping close to Adonara. Even from a distance the ruins of the old Portuguese fort on Solar were distinct through the binoculars, a rubble of brown stone fused with the dark green growth of four centuries.

Some four hours after leaving Larantuka we circled in to land at Waiwerang. From the strait we could see only a long shed and a stone pier where copra was stored and loaded. We had been sighted and a small group was already gathering, a line of white shirts or brown chests flanked above and below by checked sarongs and black pitjis. I shifted Tortuga to wheels and surged over the coral and up the beach amid the relative quiet of popeyed stares.

But the quiet did not last long. The news of our arrival spread through the village like wildfire. Men of all ages, abetted by women and children, descended upon us, shouting down our greetings, filling the narrow, shack-lined ways so we could barely crawl along, reaching into Tortuga, pinching and tweaking our flesh, screaming and waving their arms until we thought our ears would split and our bodies fall apart and poor Dinah go mad trying to defend us from all sides at once.

We had landed at Waiwerang because the trail from there to the eastern part of the island was supposed to be still passable. It would save us at least ten miles of sea travel and close to five gallons of gasoline. But this reception was too much. Without running the people down there was no chance of reaching the road. I decided to try for the beach again. But how?

The mob, there were hundreds, was all over us, climbing up the sides and on the bow, into the hatch. I didn't see a friendly face in the lot. I could not risk injuring someone with the Jeep. I remembered too well what a mob in India did to a car and its occupants for just grazing one of the sacred cows. They had overturned the vehicle, and with the trapped driver still screaming inside, had set fire to it. But I think I was as angry as I was frightened. I reached for one of the signal flares we carried for emergencies, a hand-sized tube that goes off with a ten-gauge bang and then another and sends two balls of red flame several hundred yards into the air—or into a crowd if one is so inclined, which I was. If we could distract them long enough to head back for the strait, Tortuga would break records for a reentry.

I was twisting the firing ring on the flare when the bedlam around us stopped as though sliced from its source with a knife. The people fell back, and we were encircled by a new group, sturdy, stern-faced youths, silently holding hands in a ring around us. Stunned, it was our turn to stare openmouthed as a burly European burst smiling through the throng.

"Welcome to the Island of Murderers," he said.

"Well, the name certainly fits," Helen quavered.

"Oh, these aren't the murderers," our rescuer replied, indicating the now thoroughly cowed villagers of Waiwerang. "These boys guarding your craft are the wild ones. I'm Father

Van der Hulst. Been here twenty-six years. Come along to my place in the hills and I'll tell you all about it."

With Father Van der Hulst leading the way in his pickup truck—which he used mainly to haul copra for his parishioners from the hills down to Waiwerang—we followed along an overgrown trail to his headquarters at Hinga. The back of the truck was packed with the boys who had rescued us, and all the way these "murderers" were singing hymns while we muttered in amazement at the way they had tamed those hundreds of wild men at Waiwerang. Later, when these same boys exchanged their Western shirts and trousers for war paint and spears and staged a mock attack, we understood.

Father Van der Hulst had some calls to make in a nearby village and we tagged along. It was similar to the villages on Flores, but there were two sounds we had not heard before. Competing with the incessant shrill of cicadas and the lilt of some unseen bird was a rhythmic dull clunk and an equally rhythmic but slower asthmatic whistle combined with a thump. Curious, we wandered in search of their sources.

We stopped to watch a woman initiate her daughter into puberty. With her little brother astraddle her hip, the girl stood stoically as her mother shaved the front part of her head bald, a warning to the men of the village that she was approaching marriageable age and must not be molested.

We located the first sound at the back of a large wooden house. A crone—she could have been one of Macbeth's witches—sat over an open fire. A large flat stone was hot from the flames and with another rock, like a neolithic hand-axe, she was pounding corn, one kernel at a time, the golden lumps flattening into black flakes with a muted, sizzling pop. We tasted it, thinking it might be similar to our popcorn, but it was tough and chewy.

We wandered on in search of the second sound. It seemed to come from everywhere and nowhere, a wheeze and a thump, a wheeze and a thump. We passed several houses with black chickens split down the breast and nailed flat to the walls, and in the cemetery there were a few fresh graves with more dead chickens on them. We surmised they were some sort of magical charm to keep whatever spirit caused the death of those in the new graves from striking elsewhere.

At one end of the village was a small bamboo shed, and as we came closer the wheeze and thump grew louder. Inside were three men and a deep bed of white-hot coals. Two of the men, their bodies streaming wet in the heat, were working a bellows made of tubes of bamboo six inches in diameter, moving the hardwood pistons in and out with long smooth strokes. The third man, older than the others, was watching a gray lump of iron change into an immense glowing ruby. Hanging on the wall was a finished product, a battle-axe with a beautifully worked, foot-long blade in the shape of a parallelogram and an edge that would have pleased even a barber.

Back at the parish house we got a hint as to what these battle-axes were used for—and why the people of Waiwerang had been so quickly cowed.

"You see," Father Van der Hulst explained, "there are two rival clans in the hills of Adonara. Like the Hatfields and the McCoys in your country, they've been having a running feud for hundreds of years, sort of a vendetta that goes back to the 1500's. Legend has it that it started between two brothers, but no one really knows. Each year, even now, many people in the mountains are killed and their houses burned. The people along the coast are terrified of becoming involved. They become very quiet when the mountainfolk come down.

"Oh, by the by," he added, "the people of Waiwerang have found an excuse for their actions when you came ashore." He laughed. "You can take it for what it's worth. It seems the local soothsayer predicted some visitors from outer space and they just wanted to see if you were real."

Apparently Waiwerang is still looking for spacemen, for much later we learned that several ships refused to call there anymore after their crew members had been treated similarly.

The road to the east side of Adonara branched from the road to Hinga and we were able to avoid passing through Waiwerang. We left early; it was a clear morning, but in the distance, clouds were building up again and we made a fast run across to Lomblen. By contrast, only a few people gathered on the shore. They stood quietly when we came ashore near the mouth of a small river—where what we had thought was a log we saw later was a fourteen-foot crocodile.

At the small mission station we went over our proposed route with Father Goerts—and learned that most of the roads shown on our map were either nonexistent or so neglected as to be impassable to anything but foot traffic. All but thirty of the remaining 165 miles to Timor would have to be by sea, and the storms preceding the change in the moon were predicted any day. We did not feel any better when the priest told us that Indonesia's only whaling village, Lamalerap on the south coast of Lomblen, had already given up hunting the huge mammals for the season because of rough seas.

We had always taken rather lightly the warnings of the Javanese and Balinese fishermen who dread the sea even when it is calm. But these people of Lamalerap are a different breed. For them whaling is not a business; they hunt the whale for meat and for oil for their lamps. They are hardy, fearless men who take their frail canoes far out, sneaking alongside to spear the animals, and they do not hesitate to jump to the back of a thrashing wounded whale to administer the *coup de grâce*.

If the sea-wise hunters of Lamalerap fear the west monsoon, who were we to challenge it? We began to wish we had accepted the invitation of Brother Marianus at Ende to sail back to Java aboard the mission ship.

That night, after the two priests and the lay brother had turned in, Helen and I spread the charts on the floor of our room. The air was sweltering with that tropic heaviness that forbodes bad weather. Dinah lay panting on the concrete floor, her nose raised. We moved on our hands and knees from chart to chart, scaling off the distance to Timor, sliding the oil lamp from Lomblen to Pantar to Alor. In the lambent yellow light the dark patches of reef against the parchment shade of the charts seemed alive like the sea.

Far into the night we talked, our voices scrambled by the mosquito netting on the bunks and Dinah's staccato panting and the echoes bouncing from the walls of the bare room. Helen ventured that perhaps we should return to Flores. But it was almost as far back to Ende as it was to Timor, and we had no idea as to whether the road was still passable. On the other hand the whalers of Lamalerap hunted in the unsheltered Indian Ocean while our route lay to the north where the Alor and Solar groups of islands might act as a shield against the force of the sea. But then we had seen at Djopu what a west monsoon storm could do, even with a ring of protective mountains.

We knew what lay behind us; we had no desire to face the roads of Flores again. But there was something else. What lay ahead was still a mystery, and I remember feeling the force of that nameless attraction that makes men do foolish things for no reason except to see what lies beyond the next mountain—or the next island. Reaching this goal, Timor, that we—or rather I—had set, seemed as important to me on

Lomblen as Ushuaia on the far side of Tierra del Fuego had seemed when we had stood on the shores of the Strait of Magellan and watched a sixty-knot wind streak the water with white-crested combers. Now, as then, Helen left the decision to me, a decision I knew I had no right to make and one I was to regret before the week was out.

The next morning the yellow smoke and trails of sulphur fumes from the cone of Gunung Api, Fire Mountain, one of Indonesia's most active volcanoes, streamed in a flat wind-compacted band as we left the large bay on Lomblen's north coast. The jade waters of the bay were shot with the brown of reef, and swells from the sea beyond gave Tortuga a pitching motion that grew as we approached the narrow channel at the entrance. We headed northeast by east to clear Lomblen's north point, and the force of the wind-driven waves against Tortuga's port quarter made her list at a weird angle, her starboard bow digging in and the stern raised like a mosquito about to sting. All morning we could feel the wind strengthening, see the whitecaps building up; a school of whales cavorted a few miles off shore, but even through the binoculars their spouts and the smashes from their flukes were hardly distinguishable against a sea agitated by a far greater force.

We steered a course by eye, staying close to shore and always watchful for a place to run to. The low bow angle limited our speed to three knots, and we pressed our luck, continuing past noon when we should have been ashore, trying to squeeze as many miles from the day as we could.

By midafternoon the sea was too rough to continue. We headed closer to land, cruising slowly in search of a place to come ashore. We passed a village, a shabby place with a coral-lump breakwater. A crowd that looked as wild as Waiwerang clustered quickly, signaling us to come ashore, but there were no smiles there either. They were angry when we went on; the words they shrilled at us were picked up by the wind and we could hear them long after we passed the village.

On shore the people kept pace, the crowd growing as the afternoon wore on. We increased our speed, taking on barrels of water over the bow, but each time we headed for the beach they were there, shrieking, and we put out again. The water was black and the reefs obscured when darkness forced us to put in at a small cove on the island's northeast point. The crowd had grown to over a hundred by that time, and rather than land and risk a repetition of Adonara we tied Tortuga to a rock a few yards from shore. Amid a din of jeering comments from the beach I left Helen in Tortuga and with my hand clenched around a flare I took Dinah ashore in the raft for a short walk. But Dinah was in no mood for another Waiwerang either and her lunges kept the people at a good distance.

Patiently I tried to explain who we were, where we were going and why—this last with no success at all. I told them we would not leave before morning and that they could all see then. Too tired from fighting the wheel all day to eat, too nervous from dodging reefs to sleep, we stretched out atop Tortuga and tried to ignore them, but the crowd merely increased in numbers and noise. In spite of the blackness we cast off the rope and were moving farther into the bay when someone started to whistle.

For a moment we were wordless. Where had he heard that song? These were not mission people; they would not have access to a radio. But during the war, Australian commandos had operated in this area. An American submarine had gone aground on a nearby island. But somehow the answer to that question did not matter. As he continued I whistled along with him. "*Terima kasih, bung* [Thank you, brother.]," I said when we finished. "*Kumbali, tuan* [You're welcome, sir]," he answered. Though the people stayed all night, the light from their small fires burning face-fringed holes in the blackness, there was no further sound and we rested well, the memory of that whistled "Of Thee I Sing" or "God Save the Queen" lingering it seemed long after sleep came.

There were many smiles and even a few pets for Dinah as we cast off at dawn.

It was fifty-five miles to Alor, even in calm weather too long for one day, but we had two choices for a stopover. There was Pantar, an island almost as large as Lomblen and with a population reputedly so savage that even the missionaries have given up. And there was a tiny speck of coral and sand marked "uninhabited."

The small island was less than halfway between Lomblen and Alor, the north tip of Pantar considerably more. To land on Pantar near the halfway point we would have to steer south several miles off our route. This was the practical reason for choosing the small island. The real reason was that the word "uninhabited" and the quiet it promised were irresistible.

We arrived at our island before noon. There was a reef some twenty yards from shore, but even at low tide there would be plenty of water over it. Beyond was a flour-white beach that slanted steeply upward to some forty acres of brown stubbly grass. The dead cone of a small volcano thrust several hundred feet into a sky swept clean by the wind of dark clouds.

There was one tree on the island, a flat-topped runt whose thin foliage offered just enough shade for Tortuga. We stretched our tarp for more shade, and with our foam mat-

tresses to sprawl on and Father Baack's books to read we settled down for an afternoon of bliss; after all, paradise is relative, and that's what we called our refuge, Paradise Island.

Dinah, as usual, had been the first out of the Jeep. She
stretched her age-stiffened hindquarters, cramped from hours
of bracing herself against the pitching of Tortuga, and headed
for the water, eager for a cooling swim. She scooped a piece
of half-buried driftwood from the sand and with her gray
snout powdered with white brought it to me. I was content
to read, but Dinah is not discouraged easily. She showered me
with a violent shake of her saturated fur and dropped the stick
in the middle of my *Sanctuary*. I threw it out into the water
for her, and with strong, deliberate strokes she retrieved it
and started back, her head high out of the water and little
whimpers of excitement or pleasure escaping her tense jaws.
It was good to see her paddling so smoothly, buoyed by the
water, for on land her movements were becoming uncertain
and slow and she waited for help to get in and out of the
Jeep. Sadly, Helen and I realized that this was probably her
last expedition.

For a while we joined Dinah in the lime water. Between the
shore and the reef the bottom was silver with sand, and we
floated, the soft currents swirling around our legs, gently mas-
saging away the tensions of the day.

Lazy thoughts crept through my mind. How nice to be a
fish, to spend forever moving silently through this warm
water, with no fear of storms on the surface.

"Shark!" Helen screamed. Something snatched at my arm
and I stiffened. But it was Helen, hysterical because Dinah had
seen the two black triangles slitting the water just beyond the
reef and was swimming toward them—anything moving
on the surface is an invitation. I grabbed at her, caught her tail
and jerked hard and her head went under. Coughing and sput-

tering she lost interest and headed for shore with Helen and me right after her.

We fell on the sand, palsied with reaction. Suddenly the thought of being a fish was no longer appealing. The fish could have their spheres of limited emotion, their fear only of death, their hunger only for food, their drive only to reproduce themselves. How much better to be a human being, with more than instinct, with a conscious knowledge of someone to love and protect, with the capacity to feel fear for someone or something else besides one's self, with a mind to transport one to other worlds and back again, to become alive at danger or challenge, thrill to uncertainty, reason the alternatives, reap the harvest of accomplishment or failure and if the latter to wonder why and try again. I knew then that to drift with the current or retreat before the wind could never satisfy me for more than the moment, and I was happy we had not returned to Ende.

Our island, we learned, was not uninhabited after all, nor did we spend the rest of the afternoon in unbroken peace. Six or seven wild goats grazed at the base of the volcano, somehow absorbing enough moisture from dew or grass to eke out an existence. Salivating, mentally at least, at the prospect of fresh milk, we plotted how we could catch one. That failing —the goats were as timid as deer and twice as nimble—we resorted to the guessing game we had been playing ever since we stocked up on the unidentifiable canned food at Maumere. The rules of the game were simple: we could heft or shake the can, but whatever came out we had to eat it. They were small cans and we generally opened two for a meal. The combinations were sometimes less than appealing: grapefruit juice and wieners; or margarine and baked beans; or grape jelly and tuna. That day we were lucky. In the first can was spaghetti, in the second were green beans. We had our protein after dinner—the eggs in Brother Sebastian's Advocat, creamy whipped eggs subtly blended with potent arak. We decided that this was the only way to eat eggs.

The interruption came in late afternoon. With a low, deep growl that from her means trouble for the recipient, Dinah charged the beach. A canoe with four men standing in it had spotted us. They seemed to be heading for Pantar but they swung their sun-bleached striped sail on another tack and changed course toward us. I studied them through the binoculars, short, black men with kinky hair that stuck out from their heads like coil springs, giving them a rather sinister bouffant look. They wore loin cloths and carried spears. Helen and I stayed out of sight behind the Jeep and for a few minutes they tacked along the beach with Dinah bristling and barking apace with them. Wary and confused, they moved slowly out to sea and left us. We opened an extra can—corned beef for Dinah.

Just before dusk, with our bare feet splaying in the sun-tinted sand, we strolled along the beach looking for seashells. We found a nautilus that was too big to cup in both hands, a flawless spiral, brown and white outside, with a pearly interior, the kind Cellini mounted in gold, the wine flagon of kings.

There were other blessings from the sea that night: a contentment that comes with the quiet of complete isolation and a cool breeze that brought sleep.

Toward dawn the breeze grew to a wind that tore at our tarp, waking us. We broke camp quickly and were underway before the sun was up. Stretching before us were the thirty-odd miles to Alor, rough seas, and increasingly darker skies.

It was mid-afternoon when we swung south into Pantar Strait and headed for Kalabahi Bay. The tide was on the ebb, and we felt the pull of the current as the blue water coiled into whirlpools, oily black nozzles pointing toward the bottom of the 1,500-foot-deep strait.

Three circular islands, each progressively larger, are strung like Christmas tree ornaments in the center of the strait between Pantar and Alor. The water was coursing to either side of them, and from the chart we could see little choice as to which side to pass. We decided on a direct route to the entrance of the bay, passing the two northerly islands on the west and then swinging to the east of Pura Island, the largest.

All day we had been pushing Tortuga, trying to make time, for it was a long run from Paradise Island to Kalabahi. But now as the current propelled us into the narrowing channel we wanted most to be able to slow down. The two small islands swept by in a blur; we cut back the throttle to the minimum at which we still had rudder control, but still we must have been doing close to fifteen knots. At the narrow part of the strait, Pura Island, sitting like a ball in a funnel, was bearing down on us much too fast.

I couldn't see the entrance to Kalabahi, but I knew we should reach it before we passed the middle of Pura. Kalabahi is the only town on Alor, and it lies at the end of a 10-mile-deep bay that is more like an estuary in the way that the current reverses with dangerous suddenness as the tide turns. Looking for the entrance to the bay, I swung Tortuga to port. We passed a sharp point of land and too late I saw it. We were swept on and I floored the throttle, but the current from the bay was against us too, and we were shoved south toward the floodgate that is the passage between Pura and Alor.

There was no time to decide what to do or what the consequences might be. A flat reef projected from the shore at the south of the entrance to the bay. It was almost awash, its mottled brown exposed by the ebbing tide. I headed for it; the front wheels, in gear now, grabbed at the sloping coral. We felt the bottom of the hull rasp over the low ledge, and then, with the propeller and rear wheels working too, Tortuga eased from the water. It was several moments before I realized that I had deliberately run her aground, something we had always feared would happen accidentally.

It was almost two hours before the tide turned and the water surged back into the bay. The sea rose, and with a sizable dent in Tortuga's bottom but a vastly boosted confidence in the strength of her hull, we floated clear of the reef and headed for Kalabahi.

Drab and rundown, Kalabahi was smaller than the other main towns in the Lesser Sundas, but there were just as many officials. By the time we had taken tea with the police chief, the military commander, the mayor, the customs man and the rajah—the tribal chieftain through whom in former times the Dutch ruled—we were so ballasted I doubt if Tortuga would have floated us.

There were five Europeans at Kalabahi: a Dutch priest and lay brother and a German doctor and his wife, a young couple who were on their second two-year contract to the Indonesian government. The fifth was Dr. and Mrs. Harald Klevenhausen's six-month-old baby girl, a platinum-blond cherub who was the envy of all the darker mothers in town.

With 130,000 potential patients, Dr. Klevenhausen had good reason to look tired, but when we remarked on it that night at dinner he just shrugged.

"Malaria," he said. "I've had twenty-seven attacks of it in three years. There's 100 percent incidence here, plus yaws, tuberculosis, dysentery and leprosy. I came here to study tropical medicine. I came to a good place."

Dr. and Mrs. Klevenhausen lived in a tin-roofed, masonry house near the soccer field—it seems that every town in Indonesia, no matter how small, has its soccer field. The home was immaculate, simply furnished with wicker chairs and wall hangings of handlooms.

The night was warm and we sat on the porch. Dinah was breathing hard in one corner and the Klevenhausens's dog in another, both studiously ignoring each other. Night-flying moths and beetles pinged against the chimney of the oil lamp, with a slight sizzle fluttering to a pile on the concrete floor.

There was that air of the adventurer about Dr. Klevenhausen, a dash and confidence. An ex-naval officer, an avid sailor and sportsman, he was tall, sandy-haired and slender but with a robust quality that was not dimmed by his frequent bouts with malaria. His clear blue eyes smiled easily and warmly, but once, when he spoke of some of the villages in the interior of Alor, I saw that in anger those eyes could turn to ice.

"They still take heads," he said. "The Dutch never did stamp it out. The mountains are so steep that horses are useless and during the rainy season some of the trails are impassable even on foot. The villages are fortresses isolated on hilltops and they have little contact with each other—except during raiding parties. Many of them have never seen a European."

"How about Pantar?" I asked. I told him about the boat that had approached us while we were on Paradise Island, and how Dinah had chased them away. From his answer we gathered we were lucky they did not come back with the whole village; they probably would have if they hadn't been confused by the sight of Dinah and the Jeep.

"Why, even in the villages where I'm known I have trouble sometimes," he said. "In one place south of here they held me for several hours. They can be most unpleasant. You'd better watch out when you pass Kolana on the east coast. Whatever you do, don't land there."

We questioned Dr. Klevenhausen about his work.

"Well," he said, "we have a small hospital here, but there's no electricity and when I perform surgery my wife has to hold a flashlight for me. Only now we can't even get batteries, so I took a headlight off my Jeep and use that."

Which was a most practical use for the vehicle since the one road still usable ran only around the bay and a few miles north to the coast. When the doctor visited his eight policlinics he traveled by prahu and by foot, taking two months to make the rounds of the 20-by-50-mile island. And when he came back there was often some epidemic to control. That night he got little sleep. An outbreak of bacillary dysentery was reported, but there were not enough drugs to fight it.

The next morning the doctor called the old sailor who captained his prahu, and together we studied the charts.

A wrinkled, grayed Moslem, he swayed on his bare feet as though still at sea. He looked automatically at the sky and scratched his wisp of a beard.

"This is bad time," he said. "Soon the moon will change, after tomorrow maybe three days more, then storms and rain for maybe two weeks."

Three days to reach Timor, sixty-five miles by sea in three days.

The nonexistence of roads marked on the map and the resulting extra miles by sea from Lomblen had again reduced our gas supply to the danger point. The doctor and the priest had none to spare though they offered us the few gallons they had to last them until the next ship called, whenever that might be. The police chief and the military commander were no better off. Without much hope we made the rounds of the shops. *Tidah ada* in Indonesian, *no hay* in Spanish, no soap in English, they all mean the same and that was the answer at each place. Until at one shop run by a Chinese who was affectionately nicknamed by the doctor, Last Hope, we heard an encouraging, "I'll see." We topped off our tanks and prepared to leave the following day.

"Before you leave," Dr. Klevenhausen remarked, "you must see the *mokos* of Alor. We have the rest of the afternoon."

With the doctor and Father Weiss, the young priest, and the police chief who refused to leave town without a number of well-armed soldiers, we joined a convoy of two Jeeps and drove around to the far side of the bay to one of the tamer villages. But when we got there we learned that the chief had just died. The mourners wore loincloths or shorts clinched to their waist with wide leather belts that bristled with arrows. They waved bows and wide-bladed short spears and danced a very convincing charge.

The police chief, a fine-looking Indonesian of Arab extraction, seemed worried. "They say their chief was poisoned by someone in the next village. *Aduh*, this could mean much trouble."

We drove on a few more miles to a scattered village of steep-roofed, open-sided grass huts. The doctor spoke a few words to the chief, and then a group of loinclothed, turbaned warriors brought out the mokos—cast bronze drums.

With great interest and excitement Helen and I examined the mokos. Of all the mysteries of the Lesser Sundas these are among the most fascinating. There were seven of them, each about a foot and a half high and a foot in diameter, tapered in the middle like an hourglass and with four ear-shaped handles quartered around the circumference. They were open at one end and closed at the other with a sheet of bronze that sounded like a bongo when thumped with the hand. Some had Hindu motifs; all were coated with a heavy dark patina.

One in particular caught our eyes. Around the base were

intricate floral patterns cast in the bronze, vine-hung bowers interspersed with symbols like the Javanese Tree of Life, inside which was what looked like a crown topped with a *fleur de lis*. Around the top were more of the same but between them were two grotesque human figures, limbs outstretched like frogs, their hair stuck out in the same frizzy bouffant as the men we saw at Paradise Island. Their torsos were skeletons with the rib cage and organs crudely portrayed, the genitals prominent.

There are literally thousands of mokos on Alor, only a few in other parts of Indonesia. The Alor people find them buried in the ground; they say they are gifts from the gods. But where did they come from? The people have no knowledge of working bronze, and no copper ore has been found on the island, though it is present on Timor. The few kettledrums discovered on Java, Bali, Sumatra and Borneo are generally conceded by prehistorians to have originated with the Dongson culture, though pieces of a mold of the type used in the lost-wax process have been found on Bali, which would indicate that at least some were cast there. But the drums from outside of Alor are usually larger and of much finer workmanship, and the motifs bear little resemblance to those of the mokos.

Some archaeologists claim the mokos were brought in trade. They have identified three periods: the oldest, those thought to have been made by the Dongson people and brought to Indonesia sometime during the millennium before the birth of Christ; those cast on Java and Bali before and perhaps even after the Hindu period; and those made strictly for trade in Makasser on Celebes only a few hundred years ago. The Alor people recognize three types of mokos too, but their determination of the age is somewhat less than scientific. They claim to be able to distinguish between the periods by smelling the inside of the mokos. Amazingly, they rate the age of the three types in the same order as do the archaeologists.

But if the mokos were brought in trade what were they traded for? Alor has nothing of value. It is known that Indian and Chinese traders sailed these waters two thousand years ago. Sandalwood was highly prized and Timor, to the south of Alor, was a principal source. But Timor has no good har-

bors on the north coast. Could it be that Alor with its two deep protected bays became the trading post of the Lesser Sundas? There is no evidence to point to this. And why would the mokos be found buried in the earth? Why are there no legends to hint at an explanation?

I asked the chief to test the moko with the phallic human figures. He sniffed long and carefully and proclaimed it to be from Makasser. But I wondered, is it reasonable that the Makassarese, among the earliest of the converts to Islam and as fanatical in their beliefs as any, would have created symbols that are in direct violation of the Moslem prohibition of portrayal of the human form and particularly a phallic portrayal?

Could it be that all of the mokos are Dongson? Could it be that on one of those early migrations, a group of Dongson people came to Alor with their mokos, their bronze daggers (one of which, the only one in all of Indonesia, was found on Flores), their animist rites and the other customs that have spread throughout the Archipelago? Could it be that instead of prospering as they did elsewhere, that this group was overwhelmed by a fierce indigenous population or wiped out by a virulent plague? In either case, the mokos, which are thought to have had a mystic significance, might have been buried, either to protect them from the attackers or as an offering to the spirits that they might be spared of the pestilence. Shorn of legends and mystic significance they would be found by later migrants, perhaps the dark-skinned, frizzy-haired Papuans from New Guinea or the Melanesians which the Alor people of today so closely resemble. There is no evidence to back this surmise either, but legends rarely die with time alone, and to the people of Alor the mystery of the mokos is as obscure as it is to the archaeologists.

"You know," Dr. Klevenhausen said, grounding my flight of fancy, "mokos are a symbol of wealth. Every man strives to obtain at least one. You can buy almost anything with a moko—land, a wife, even a human head. If one village takes a head from another, the victim's family is honor bound to retaliate, and that victim's family in turn, and so on. But sometimes they will accept a moko instead, and then the killing stops—until the next time. Other times, the moko itself is the spark. Whole tribes will go to war over especially prized mokos."

With a note of pride the police chief interjected, "Not long ago we confiscated a moko that has kept two villages at war for 150 years. It's under guard at headquarters; the villagers value it at 350,000 rupiahs."

I made a rough calculation. At the official rate of exchange that would be over $10,000, a sizable amount, more, probably, than all the men of Alor together could earn in a lifetime. So-called civilized nations have gone to war for much less.

One of the warriors brought us coconuts to drink. With one whack of his long sword, as easy as lopping off a head, he cut through husk and shell. He turned the sword point to cut into the exposed white meat and release the milk, but Dr. Klevenhausen took it from him and used his own knife, whispering, "Always open your own out here. In some of the villages there isn't enough water to bathe and the people use their knives to scrape their skins clean."

As we refreshed with the cooling coconut milk—it seemed that no matter how hot the day the milk was always cool—I watched the braves standing around the mokos. They were smiling, and, except for their weapons, they seemed no more fierce than any of the other people we had met. They were certainly friendlier than the folks at Waiwerang.

"Don't be misled," Dr. Klevenhausen retorted. He stepped to one of the warriors and drew an arrow from the fan of dozens in his wide belt. Its three-foot shaft was unfletched and the tip was a six-inch, double-edged sliver of steel.

"This is for wild boar or deer." He drew the crude four-foot bow and aimed at a man-thick tree some two hundred feet away. Without the swish of a feathered shaft, the arrow quivered into the trunk, sinking two inches into the hard wood. "I was lucky," the doctor said. "They can do it every time."

He showed me another arrow, a blunt one. "This is for birds. And this one—"

"Must be for fish," I finished as he handed me a wicked-looking arrow with a tip made of twisted wire and eight backward-slanting barbs.

Dr. Klevenhausen smiled, but there was no mirth in his eyes. "This is for men. It's a war arrow. Ugly, isn't it? But for them it's not enough. When they go to war they sharpen dried hollowed chicken bones and press them over the tips. When the arrow hits, the bone splinters deep inside the wound."

The original dumdum bullet.

The next morning early, though still suffering from his latest attack of malaria, Dr. Klevenhausen, with Father Weiss, accompanied us the eight miles to the bay on Alor's north coast.

"Remember," he called after us, "the change in the moon—and don't stop near Kolana." I felt like Caesar being warned to beware the Ides of March.

From the Jeep that morning Alor's mass of mountains looked like a crumpled wad of green crepe paper discarded by a mighty hand on the dark surface of the sea. For almost forty miles due east the chart indicated a coast broken by sharply rising cliffs. It offered no protection from the increasing west wind. The following sea humped Tortuga's stern, driving her bow down so she scooped like a shovel through the waves, the water rolling back and curling up the windshield. We passed several villages, Likiewatang, Kabe, Limbur, Adagai, Kenariman and Taramana, keeping well out to sea and hoping that Tortuga's low profile, combined with the high swells, would reduce the chances of our being spotted.

By late afternoon we had covered only twenty miles but the sea was too rough to continue. We came ashore at the first break in the reef we could find, crawling up a steep, boulder-studded beach to a flat spot near the slide-covered road that in former times had encircled the island. A few stumpy poles stood where a telephone line had once run, but the wire was gone—to make the tips for war arrows, the doctor had told us.

Though the chart indicated no villages within miles, we faced Tortuga toward the sea and cleared a path through the boulders, ready to take to the water if necessary. Somehow it seemed a little melodramatic.

About dusk, as we were eating, Dinah growled. I grabbed her and her paws clawed the gravel as a lone Alorese walked by. He wore a simple breechclout and a belt full of arrows and carried a bow. He passed within twenty paces of us, but the unnerving thing was that he paid no attention to us, never turning his head even when I waved. This had never happened before; always we had been overwhelmed with curious people until at times we had pleaded for privacy. But now we were wishing that this brave would show a little more friendliness instead of stalking on so grim and silent. He made one sound. When he passed out of sight beyond the slide covering the road he whistled a peculiar birdlike chirp. It was answered from the direction from which he had come.

We set up only one bunk and took turns standing watch that night. We did not feel a bit melodramatic. But though we heard other whistles—or imagined we did—we saw no one and as soon as it was light enough to see we were underway.

Usually we could count on the mornings being calm, but that day the wind was already strong when we left. We had pumped the fuel from the bow tank to one in the rear, and with Dinah crouching as far back as we could shove her, the weight was shifted aft enough to raise the bow. The wind and the following sea moved us briskly along as far as Alor's northeast point. There, after almost five months of traveling east, we changed course. We headed south for the Portuguese half of Timor, the closest land beyond Alor.

There were villages along the east coast too, and we stayed well out. But with the wind and waves hitting us squarely abeam, our progress slowed. I gave Tortuga more gas and moved closer to the protection of shore. The storms weren't due until the day after next but already the sky was purple and sudden gusts of wind were lashing the waves to foaming crests that glared stark against the dark shore.

We were nearly abreast of Kolana when a brief but powerful rain squall blew up. It was not the storm Dr. Klevenhausen's old captain had warned of. It was just an everyday afternoon squall. But in seconds it blotted the coast from view and whipped the sea to a fierce chop. We set a compass course and pushed Tortuga at full throttle toward the shelter of a reef-rimmed cove beyond.

The shingle beach looked steep. I shifted into four-wheel-drive and hit it fast. Tortuga's wheels bit into the gravel, clawed futilely, then shuddered and stopped. I started the engine for another try and a chilling knock echoed from behind the fire wall.

For me that was the most paralyzing moment since we left Bali. As long as the engine was right I had been confident that Tortuga could take us anywhere. But now—

I don't know how long I sat there behind the wheel trying to think what could be wrong. There had been other crises in our years of amphibious-jeeping and when they passed I always marveled at Helen. She became almost hysterical when we crossed a reef that was under less than ten feet of water; she blanched when we traversed terrain where the Jeep tipped a little too much, both situations which I almost enjoy. But when the real trouble came she was calm. In a blustering *chocosano* off the coast of Panama it was Helen who hummed the Navy Hymn while I could only grip the wheel. When Tortuga's engine died and we broached while surfing ashore through twenty-foot breakers off Costa Rica, it was Helen who quietly encouraged me as I tried frantically to get it started. And now, in a low voice she was encouraging me again when I knew that no matter what was causing the knock I could not make major repairs under those conditions. As gently as I could I asked her to let Dinah stretch her legs while I checked the engine. I wanted time to think.

The oil level was normal. Perhaps we could make it back to Kalabahi on foot. Across those mountains? Impossible. Along the coast then. Through all those villages? Ridiculous. I checked the ignition timing and the oil pressure; they were all right too. What about the rubber raft? Paddle forty miles against that wind? Who are you trying to fool? No, somehow we had to reach Timor.

I had a can of upper cylinder lubricant, and with the engine running slowly I fed that through the carburetor, hoping that if a valve was sticking this would free it. But when I pressed the accelerator the knock returned. I added heavy transmission lubricant to the engine oil and tried again. The thickened oil seemed to cushion the knock. It was still loud, but I began to feel we had a chance. If we left in the early-morning hours when the sea should be its calmest, if we kept our speed down, we might still make Timor.

Helen ran to warn me that a group of men was approaching from the direction of Kolana. Hurriedly we backed into the deep water of the bay. It was almost dark but I could make out nine of them. They were all dressed and armed like the man who had passed the day before except that these carried what looked like shields, brown ovals slung over their backs from head to buttocks. They could have been dried-palm-leaf rain capes—or they might have been war shields. They stayed well away from the beach, watching. One of them trotted toward Kolana and the others squatted near a fallen tree a few hundred yards from us.

Later, as Tortuga drifted about her anchor in the middle of the bay, the rising moon—it was almost full—made the gray coral seem to grow beneath us, matching our own increasingly gray mood. Ugly formations like giant brains seemed to rise through the clear water, and to my worry-muddled mind the sea spirits so real to the Balinese seemed real to me too. "At last," they seemed to say, "at last you've gone too far. You've tempted Loro Kidul once too often. The Goddess of the Southern Sea is angry." Beyond the cove I could hear her anger in the raging wind and the waves gnawing at the shore.

Through the long night Helen and I stared across the pale water, past the beach now silver in the moonlight, over the row of coconut palms to the sheer black mountains beyond. I could not suppress the thought that perhaps we had tempted fate once too often. I remembered the Cave of the Bats, and across the thousand miles from Bali the prophecy of the old fishermen boomed through my mind: "Go back, *tuan*, the stars are wrong."

At three A.M., in the black of morning when the moon had run its course, I warmed up the engine. All night I had resisted the impulse to start it. Perhaps I thought that like some bad dream I would wake up and the knock would be gone. Perhaps it was just that optimism of mine that in happy times Helen says borders on folly. Slowly at first, then faster, I ran the engine. I listened, tensely. It was quiet and smooth! I saw a smile creep over Helen's face. The engine came up to operating temperature; the high-pitched clunk returned, just as loud and just as ominous as before.

The men on the beach were still there too, and more had

come from Kolana. They heard the engine, and from the sound of their angry voices they had not expected us to leave so soon. Their cries faded as I steered Tortuga out of the cove and into the wind and current of Ombai Strait.

That was an eerie moment, the first time we had ever navigated at night; in the matchlike glimmer of the compass light Helen's face carried a worried frown as she plotted our course over the shadowy barrier reef and around Alor's southeast point. Once clear of the lee of the island the full force of the heaving Indian Ocean swept down on us and I knew why the whale hunters of Lamalerap feared the west monsoon.

Helen gave me the course, 110 degrees, almost southeast; allowing for a twenty-degree swing with the current, we steered 130 degrees for Dili, capital of Portuguese Timor, thirty miles away.

Mesmer used a bright object to focus the attention of his subjects. The illuminated face of the compass had that same effect, a spot of light in a world of blackness. The sky was black, the sea was black, there was no horizon and the mass of Alor at our stern was a nebulous shadow that hovered, following us, never retreating. I switched on the headlights. Invisible Timor lay somewhere beyond those probing cones—puny ineffectual rays, one moment pointing skyward to nothing, the next arcing down to be lost in the depths of 10,000-foot-deep Ombai Strait, two insectival antennae rising to feel the froth on the boarded combers bearing down on us from the west, twitching a frantic warning of their approach but only as Tortuga was already rocking with the blows. They told me nothing; they distracted me. I switched them off and the world was black again except for that bewitching little spot on the compass.

Crouching way back in the Jeep, Dinah was whimpering. Her feet scratched for a grip on the smooth plastic cover of her cushion, but the waves bounced her ball-like from the sides of the cabin, each dull thump followed by a little grunt of pain. Helen moved back to cradle her, but the shift threw the weight too much to port. We were heeling from the wind already. She returned to her seat, kissed me on the cheek and rubbed my arms; they were beginning to ache, tense from keeping that little bright spot centered on 130 degrees. I wondered if it was like this in space, the darkness, no sense of movement, no point of reference, no idea how far we had come from Alor.

Dawn broke with exquisite suddenness, the "red sky at morning sailors take warning" kind—streaks of rose fire, flowing gold and the purple threatening clouds over Timor's eastern mountains, disappointingly far away. Helen took a bearing on Alor's Mount Tamasa and Mount Kolana and plotted our position. In three hours we had covered less than three miles, an average speed of under one knot. Reluctantly I gave Tortuga more gas; the gap between us and Alor increased, but so did the knock from the engine.

After another hour—it was seven A.M.—Helen took another set of bearings. Our speed was two knots, but it was still almost 25 miles to Dili. If we changed course and steered instead for the nearest land, Maubara at bearing 160 degrees, we could cut six miles from that distance, three hours at our present rate. But that would head us into the wind too much. We would be bucking the waves. And there were two little spirals on the chart just off Maubara which the Sailing Directions translated as whirlpools that were known to swing large ships out of control.

The other alternative was to head for a point farther east, between Maubara and Dili, saving almost five miles. But there was no port there, and when we applied for our visa to Timor, at the Portuguese Embassy in Djakarta, the Ambassador had warned: "You can't just storm the beach anywhere, you know. You must enter through an official port." He was grinning when he said it, but he wasn't joking. At the time we had assured him we would comply; now such formalities seemed unimportant. I chose to remember only the grin. I swung the wheel and the compass card floated around to 145 degrees. We headed for an empty stretch of beach on Timor twenty miles away.

In our hurry to leave Alor we had taken no time to eat, and by nine o'clock we were beginning to feel hollow. Helen opened a can of red beans. Tortuga was pitching too much to use the stove and we ate them cold from the can. Dinah, unmindful of the lumpy bruise over her eye, crawled forward gingerly to get in on Helen's three-way feeding act: a bite for me, a bite for her and a bite for Dinah—different spoons of course. There were a lot of mouths missed and a lot of beans spilled and a lot of confusion as to which spoon was which.

During the short period at midmorning when the tide changed, the sea calmed enough for us to prepare coffee and sit topside. But when the wind swung contra-current the two forces met in great foam-topped breakers that spilled over Tortuga's deck and cabin, pouring into her hatches and driving us below again. Traveling cross-current and cross-wind Tortuga fishtailed along the troughs, her flag board-stiff in the near-gale, her nose ramming through the crests, the muffler across her bow growing thick with white salt as the brine, sudsing its hot surface, exploded into steam. The knock from the laboring engine was a shrill tattoo. From our low position in the seats we could see only the steep waves curling over our heads and the deep troughs before us. Except when some swell carried Tortuga to its crest, both Alor and Timor were beyond our ken and we had only the bouncing card of the compass to keep us on course.

The mounting wind and waves slowed our progress more, and by noon, nine hours after leaving Alor, we were still eleven miles from Timor. We were desperate to reach land; that ever-growing metallic cadence from the engine was maddening. If only we could stand up for a minute, stretch our legs, feel something solid beneath us. But Tortuga seemed some insane living thing, a buffalo at the Feast of the Carabao, bucking and plunging to escape the tormenting sea. Helen's knuckles were white from gripping her seat, my fingers were numb on the wheel and Dinah's whimpers had become a pathetic confused whine. Without any thought for the consequences I increased our speed again and the rumble of the propeller became counterpoint to the complaint of the engine.

For two more hours Tortuga waddled toward Timor. I tried to hit the swollen sea so the bow would ride over rather than through the waves, swinging the wheel as they approached and returning to course when they passed. Slowly details became distinct through the binoculars: a lighthouse; the red roof of a military post; the row of trees marking the road to Dili; then, a craggy coral beach. When the last swell pushed Tortuga ashore, her hull dented and scaled with rust, her paint blistered, her engine thumping, and her crew very subdued, very tired, and very grateful, I knew in a small way how Captain William Bligh must have felt when after being cast adrift by the mutineers of the *Bounty* he ended his own small-boat journey on this same island 173 years before.

Chapter Nine

N ATURE'S *cheval de frise*, a barrier of platter-shaped, rapier-spined cactus extended far inland from the shore, separating us from the road to Dili. There were low tunnels through it, meandering paths tracked with the spore of wild pig, but no opening big enough for Tortuga.

To the east our exit was blocked by a gully where some long-dead river once sluiced into the sea. We drove west, along a shelf of grass-bound sand between the cactus and the high-water line, easing Tortuga along in the lowest gear. After about a mile the cactus opened onto a clearing with a watchtower and a low shed, apparently some military emplacement. I stopped the Jeep and walked forward cautiously, whistling loudly; I did not want to be a target again. But the place was deserted. Beyond was the road, broad, graveled and bordered with eucalyptus trees. A telephone line paralleled it; the wires were strung tautly from proper poles, not looped from trees as on Flores and Sumbawa.

In contrast to the militaristic urgency of security-conscious Indonesia, where the officials came looking for us if we delayed in reporting, our arrival on Portuguese Timor went almost unnoticed. There were no police to "greet" us; with a polite *"bom dia"* the sturdy, chocolate-skinned Timorese stepped aside as we passed, and we drove the thirty slow miles to Dili with little more than a glance of surprise from the few officials we met bicycling en route. The police chief at Dili was equally unconcerned when, out of long habit, we reported to him immediately on arrival.

"There's no hurry. Come back tomorrow to register—or whenever you're rested," he said.

One thing, however, was the same. There were no hotels. The closest, the only one on Portuguese Timor, was at Baucau, some sixty miles farther east, a resort frequented by Australians who flew in from Darwin. But at least there was a restaurant, just one, an awninged, vine-covered, bricked patio fronting the sea, with one Timorese waiter, an air of intimacy, a *table d'hôte* menu and Portuguese wines. We dawdled over a lavish meal of grilled white fish, beef filets, and demitasses of rich, dark coffee, the finest coffee we had ever tasted.

Fortified, we looked for a place to stay. After some searching we located a rundown, plaster-peeling room for a dollar a day at the back of an import house near the waterfront. The manager's wife was a harridan, her cats noisily resented Dinah, and the place needed a good scrubbing. But it was a roof and when the storm the old Moslem predicted struck the next day we were happy to be under it. We would have been happy to be anywhere as long as it was not on the sea. The Timorese knew it was coming too; on the long gravel beach that skirts Dili, their outrigger dugout canoes were drawn high and lashed securely. We heard it, a rumble, some vibration that started as just a feeling inside us and grew to a night-terror at day, a darkness split by earth cracks of lightning, thunder that quaked the windows and walls of our room. A radio bulletin reported that two sailing prahus, manned by Makassarese, Indonesia's best seafarers, were blown a thousand miles and wrecked off the coast of Australia. Water charged over Dili's seawalls in a flood of foam and sand. The wind flattened the trees into lopsided caricatures. A driving rain, a hard tangible force, obscured the harbor though it was only yards from our window. With a numbed elation, almost a fascination, we watched, thinking that but for one day Tortuga would have been out there, a sparrow in a hurricane.

When the storm faded into a steady rain—broken rarely by a touch of sun, a pallid disk in a smoky parchment sky—we opened the shutters and sniffed the washed air and like groundhogs on the first day of spring ventured forth to explore the wonders of Dili. It was hardly what we might have expected for a capital, even of a territory as small as New Jersey-sized Portuguese Timor. But then just thirty miles away was Alor, and to our prejudiced eyes Dili, with its motley collection of jerry-built housing, and Chinese-run shops, its two paved streets crossed by dirt lanes and board sidewalks and shaded by tall, spreading trees, was a tropical London—complete with Harrods.

In the one-room store, more like a north-country trading post, Helen metamorphosed, with no incubation period, from expeditionary to *femme fatale*, coy glances and all, and would not be budged from the perfumes, soaps and lace from Portugal. I strolled to the other end—losing Dinah en route at a stack of very fragrant dried beef—past German hardware and Japanese porcelain to a tantalizing display of Australian canned food, German beer, and Portuguese wines. There were plastics, yardage, bags of coffee, flour, sugar, rice, everything, anything. Cradling a ten-liter flagon of red, some yellow cheese, two tins of pumpernickel plus assorted fruits, vegetables, and meats for the journey to Indonesian Timor, perfumes and soaps for I pretended I didn't know when, and a pair of handmade red slippers for no better reason than that Helen had to have them, we returned to our room at the Ritz.

In this tiny outpost of empire we felt a contact, meager though it was, with the outside world that we had not known for half a year. There was a flight a week to Darwin; each month a freighter from Dutch New Guinea picked up its cargo of coffee, hides, wild beeswax, copra, and rubber, and twice a year a ship from Portugal called. But even more, we could write letters without worrying than an Indonesian censor would imagine some vague, unintended offense in the most innocent of phrases. We could receive letters that had not been surreptitiously steamed open, the act detected not by the censor's stamp which never appeared—but by his excess of glue that on resealing stuck envelope to contents. And, if we had cared to, with a minimum of formality as compared to the tedious weeks of office calls in Djakarta, we could have flown to Darwin and back for a holiday. But we preferred to stay in Timor; there was an intriguing quality about this most distant of Portuguese territories. How, we wondered, had Portugal, one of the world's last colonial powers, managed to keep her far-flung possessions—the Azores, Madeira, Cape Verde Islands, São Tomé and Principe, Portuguese Guinea, Angola, Mozambique, Goa (which a short time later was lost to India), Maucau and Timor—in an age when colonies are out of fashion.

Using dividers and chart, Helen navigates a choppy sea.

Helen was the only barber within miles as we made our way through the Lesser Sundas, a chain of islands flung from Bali to Flores.

ABOVE—Tortuga II among the islands of Lesser Sunda. The 15-foot amphibious Jeep carries enough gasoline for 150 miles at sea or 750 miles on land. BELOW—An outrigger greets Tortuga as we approach Komodo, only village on the island of the same name.

RIGHT—World's largest lizards live on Komodo. Here Helen snaps a photograph of the awesome creature. BELOW—Falling trees were the greatest danger along the main road across Flores. Using Tortuga's power winch, Frank tugs logs from the road.

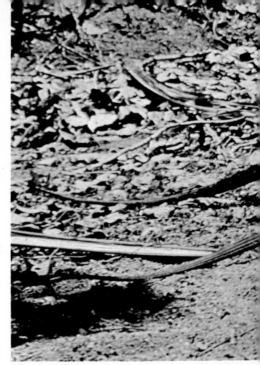

RIGHT—Komodo dragons. BE-LOW—Komodo had never be-fore seen a motor vehicle. Here Helen helps one of the wives of Komodo's chief alight from her first car ride. Larger than native dogs, Dinah caused a furor.

Courtesy National Geographic Magazine, © National Geographic Society

BELOW—Raising his leather shield, a whip dancer readies his rawhide snapper to lash out opponent's eye or slice off the tip of the nose.

LEFT—The men of Alor dance a convincing charge. CENTER—Timorese soldiers intrigued by Frank's camera. BOTTOM—Darkly handsome women perform exotic, serpentine dance on Portuguese Timor.

ABOVE—Gangs of men fore and aft tug Tortuga across raging, rain-swollen river.
BELOW—River-wise Timorese carry Helen over treacherous currents. Portuguese Timor.

ABOVE—Animist faith of Lesser Sundas endows every natural object with a spirit. Near Soa, Flores, needlelike stones have witnessed pagan rites for thousands of years.

UPPER RIGHT—Adonara warrior (sporting a wristwatch) launches a mock attack. Son of a headhunter, he is now a Catholic priest's aide. The palm fronds are battle camouflage.

LOWER RIGHT—Created during the Bronze Age, bronze kettledrums are used as currency on Alor, in values from 50 cents to $3,500. Warriors in background hold four-foot bows.

Loading operations for the return to Java: ABOVE—Tortuga approaches the *Karawatu* to be hoisted aboard. There was a moment of panic when a twisted cable spun Tortuga toplike 40 feet above the water.

ABOVE—Sumatra: The roofs of the houses dip in the middle and sweep gracefully to sharp points at the ends. Chairs, benches, and tables are carved of stone. CENTER—Ibrahim, our Sumatran guide. BELOW—A military convoy escorts us through Sumatra, where armies of rebels and bandits keep government troops constantly busy.

ABOVE—Indonesia holds the largest oil reserves in the Far East. This Sumatran refinery rises out of an inky swamp near Palembang.

LEFT—A solitary Moslem reads the Koran in Medan's mosque. Nine-tenths of Indonesia's people hold to Islam, but animism, Hinduism, and Buddhism survive.

ABOVE—In battle regalia, warriors demonstrate for Frank how their ancestors fought when headhunters and slave traders scourged the island of Nias. BELOW—Nias youth soars over the six-foot "jumping stone."

ABOVE—Indonesian army officer, in jungle camouflage, tells the women of Air Bangis, only recently retaken, to call their men back from the mountains. BELOW—Journey's end.

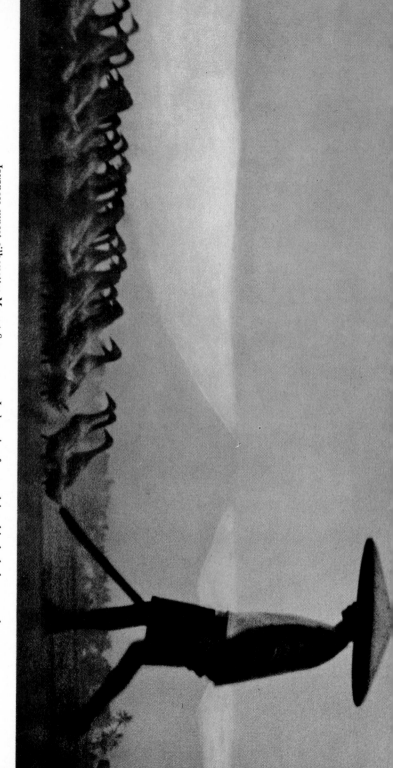

Javanese sunset silhouettes Mount Semeru as an Indonesian farmer drives his ducks homeward.

Courtesy National Geographic Magazine, © National Geographic Society

The answer was not apparent in Dili, just rousing itself to rebuild after the destruction of World War II. In spite of Portugal's neutrality, for more than three years Timor had been occupied, first by Australian and Dutch troops and then, in retaliation, by the Japanese. Strategically located, and in Japanese hands an ideal base for an invasion attempt on Australia only 300 miles away, the island had suffered heavy bombardment; Dili's harbor was still littered with wrecks; all but one building had been leveled. And almost every bridge in the territory had been destroyed by the tiny band of Australian commandos who, shielded and provisioned in part by native Timorese, for almost a year kept 15,000 Japanese soldiers confined to the area around Dili.

By the end of the war the sandalwood that was once a lodestone for ancient traders was gone, Timor's coffee plantations were overgrown, her cattle herds decimated, her economy shattered, most of her white Portuguese population dead of starvation, sickness or reprisals. When we saw Dili, only the newly built Administration Building, the clinic, church, and the residential area for Portuguese officials gave evidence of what Dili could become—if, as these officials pointed out to us, Sukarno is satisfied with the recovery of New Guinea. To them this seemed unlikely; at the time of our arrival a group of Indonesians, claiming to be political refugees and asking asylum, had been jailed for allegedly trying to incite the Timorese to rebel against the 400-year rule of the Portuguese.

We saw a clue to Portugal's success as a colonizer one night when Senhor and Senhora d'Almeida, a hospitable couple from Goa who spoke that lilting brand of English we found so charming in India, took us to the Club Dili, the town's one social center. An American film was playing, a Korean War story, and waiting for it to start was a cross section of Dili: Timorese men and women, their skins even darker against the white of their Western clothes; Chinese were there and Portuguese: businessmen, planters, shopkeepers, soldiers, civil administrators, skin colors ranging from the deepest black to pale white, all talking and laughing, drinking together. And in the auditorium, except that places were reserved for high officials, there was no segregation in the seating.

In India the complaint we heard most against the British was their color bar; in Indonesia the Dutch were criticized because only a favored few Indonesians were accepted socially. And in both places almost everyone knew about Little Rock. Americans were bitterly classified right along with the colonialists because of it. On the other hand, the French, like the Portuguese in their colonial policy, are integrationists, and yet they are losing their colonies too.

A few days later, Senhor Abilio Monteiro, Administrator of Dili, a suavely handsome Portuguese in the gold-braided, starched white uniform of an officer in the Overseas Service, brought us word that the Governor wished to see us. There was no question as to what to wear; this was not Indonesia where informality is the order of the day, where we were quite likely to find an official at home in pajamas or in the office in shirtsleeves. I had not worn my suit since we left Djakarta, but that morning as we climbed the stairs to the Governor's office in the cream masonry, two-story Administration Building we were formal too, a very soggy formal despite our freshly pressed clothes; Dili during the rainy season resembles most an overheated steam bath.

His Excellency, Governor Filipe Themudo Barata, a robust man in his early fifties, rose from his dark hand-carved Jacobean desk as we entered. A matching bookcase against the wall displayed handsome, leather-bound volumes, all Portuguese titles. The Governor greeted us with a warm handclasp and a reserved expression—he had that same quality that later we noticed in all but a few of the Portuguese we met on Timor, a melancholy that could easily be misinterpreted as aloofness. He motioned us to the tall-backed red plush chairs.

"Mr. and Mrs. Schreider," he smiled, dispelling any suspicion of aloofness we might have had, "we had given you up. You were expected months ago."

I mumbled something about a few difficulties en route.

"Ah yes, your vehicle, I understand, is not functioning. No matter, just leave it in our maintenance shops."

Governor Barata had taken office only a few months before, but it was soon apparent that he was very knowledgeable about the history of the territory from the time it was discovered by the Portuguese, only twenty years after Columbus first crossed the Atlantic, right up through the events of World War II. As he spoke of the war and its effect on Timor, he reached for a box on the table beside him. It was light yellow in color, smooth-grained, and from it emanated a delicate spicy fragrance—the sandalwood that lured traders from Arabia, India and China centuries before the Europeans knew the island existed, sandalwood prized above gold by the ancients, its oil used in soap, perfume, incense, and cosmetics.

"The tribal chieftains of Timor gave me this when I took office," he said. He unfolded the white flag that was inside the box. It was covered with dozens of dark brown spots, each with a name printed beside it. "Each chief put a mark here in his own blood as a symbol of his loyalty. We are proud of our Timorese. During the war only a few thousand collaborated with the Japanese. Most remained loyal even though their Portuguese administrators were interned.

"But what of your plans?" he asked. "Two visitors from Portugal have arrived. A tour has been arranged for them, and if you wish you are welcome to go along."

The first leg of the tour was to be by plane, the rest by

Jeep, and early the next morning we took off from Dili's muddy airport aboard a small, four-engine de Haviland Heron. We fastened our seat belts and held Dinah; the wheels splattered through brown puddles, bounced over the rutted grassy runway and then, airborne, the plane spiraled in tight circles over the town, no more impressive from the air than from the ground. The hospital, Governor's Palace, Bishop's Residence and a few homes of planters perched on the hills above Dili, and then—nothing but a sculptured green carpet of low jungle broken by a scattering of dark rain clouds, a vast emptiness with black rocky peaks projecting through flat blankets of mist, dead volcanoes thrusting up into a gray sky. Dinah, ever curious, peered through a window—and promptly dropped to the floor, to stay there until we touched down at Suaia on the south coast.

The two men from Portugal for whom the tour had been arranged, documentary cinematographers, were checking their equipment. I wandered toward the cockpit and the pilot waved me in. He was one of the rare outgoing Portuguese we met, burly, with a booming laugh, an ever-present smile and—I was happy to know as the plane shuddered in an air pocket—a fourteen-year accident-free flying record on Timor.

"There," he shouted over the engines, "that's Tata-Mai-Lau."

He pointed to a craggy black mass lost in the clouds, Timor's highest mountain, over 9,000 feet.

We had hardly reached flying altitude—it was only sixty-five airline miles to Suaia—when the plane started circling for a landing. The overcast opened and we saw the sun. The mountains, gashed by the brown veins of rivers, sloped off gently toward the Timor Sea. Light green pastures were pricked with thousands of brown cattle. There are more than half a million head on Portuguese Timor, more cattle than people. We nosed down toward one of the fields. Was that the landing strip? It was no different from the pastures except there were fewer cows on it.

"Landed here hundreds of times," the pilot assured me, and I ran back to crawl into my seat belt.

When we stepped from the plane it was like stepping back to Alor; the cattle herders, mounted on wiry little horses, carried long spears and looked just as wild as the Alorese.

A small tractorlike vehicle drove up and we all piled on. With the driver, the Administrator of Suaia, the pilot, co-pilot and the two film men there were eight of us with room for four, and we clung to the sides as the high wheels churned through mud and across streams toward Suaia.

After a mile or so we stopped at a village, a few conical huts of grass, round haystacks with roofs that went right down to the ground without the formality of walls. There were no windows, no chimney; smoke from the cooking fire inside seeped through the thatch, blackening it with a smaller cone at the top, like a rim of lava around a volcano. The door was a low cavelike opening closed by a fan of palm leaves. A woman sat near one, her full, bare breasts partially covered by her long blue-black hair. The driver spoke to a man who ran bowing, sweeping off his hat, from one of the huts. He grabbed a bucket and ran to a deep hole a few feet away.

"We need some fuel," the driver explained. In a moment the Timorese was back and pouring a clear amber-green liquid into the tank of the diesel truck, pure petroleum ladled directly from the earth as easily as dropping a bucket down a water well. It had undergone no more preparation than straining.

There are a few such wells on Timor, but though an Australian oil company has been exploring for some time, no commercially adequate deposits have been found. Other minerals are just as scarce. Manganese was once exported in small quantities, and it was once thought that there were rich reserves of copper, a belief based on the chunks of almost pure metal the natives occasionally turn up with, but no high-grade ore has been discovered. We began to wonder, not only how Portugal had managed to keep Timor, but economically speaking, why she wanted to.

At Suaia, an administrative post with only a few buildings, an exotic serpentine dance was performed by darkly handsome women in long black sarongs accented with bright pink, a line of swaying forms and gently waving white scarves. Small wooden drums beat in a rhythm that was more Latin than Asian.

By noon we were on our way back to Dili, a thirty-minute flight that dragged on to an hour as the pilot swung cautiously far east to avoid a rain squall and slanted steeply upward to clear wing-quaking downdrafts. He circled long over Dili before touching down on the soggy field. Ten days later all Timor mourned this man. On a flight between Darwin and Dili, the Heron with the pilot and ten others was lost without a trace over the shark-filled Timor Sea.

For the next two weeks we followed on the heels of the two film men. Rain and overcast skies constantly upset their shooting schedule, but during the few sunny hours the Timorese turned out in all their finery. We knew we were getting the red-carpet treatment, that we were seeing only the best of Timor. But even so it was difficult to believe that the Timorese were exploited. Never, outside of India, had we seen women with so much jewelry—silver bracelets to the elbows, brilliant handloomed sarongs, tortoiseshell combs studded with silver coins.

"We have trouble keeping coins in circulation," one Ad-

seemed disembodied in the dim light of the fire, like actors on a stage with black-light spotlights playing over them.

Several arms threw more wood on the fire; the arms grew bodies, then faces as the flames rose; eyes flashed yellow in dark faces, the cries became shrieks and we saw the men were kicking something along the ground as if in some macabre soccer game, slashing at it with their long swords. Dawn brightened, and the women, as agitated as the men, beat the drums and gongs faster and faster, screeching a high-pitched wailing song. Two of them, disregarding the mayhem of swords and spears, scrambled monkeylike across the ground and snatched at the remaining pieces of the object. They held them aloft with eyes in a fixed glazed stare as the men danced around them. It was a frightening display even after we could see that it was only a large melon they had been using as a head.

There are eight administrative divisions in Portuguese Timor, and we visited all but the enclave of Oe-Cussi, a bit of Portuguese territory on the north coast isolated from the rest of the province by almost fifty miles of Indonesian Timor, and as Goa was to the Indians, a thorn in the pride of the Indonesians. We traveled by Jeep supplied by the government with an expert Chinese driver who must have been a frustrated Grand Prix racer. He tore over the atrocious roads with an abandon that made even Dinah close her eyes. We climbed from the coast to the rolling grassy hills, through forests of eucalyptus, bamboo, moss-hung casuarina, and groves of coconut palm, flushing cockatoos, pigeons, doves, ducks, complaining monkeys and an occasional deer. We lurched by sparse villages and through coffee, tea, rubber and cacao plantations, most government-owned at least in part.

Our driver, like all the Chinese in Portuguese possessions—

which recognize Nationalist and not Communist China—
claimed Nationalist sympathies in contrast to Indonesia where
the reverse is true. Overseas Chinese seem to be pragmatic in
their politics, on the surface at least, being Nationalist or
Communist as the country of their residence leans. A rather
thin, sharp-faced young man, he spoke only Portuguese,
Chinese and Tetum, the last the most common of the twenty
languages on Timor. We anticipated no problem, however;
we had dusted off our Spanish, and after the first few days in
Dili—where our sentences usually came out weird mixtures
of Indonesian, English and Spanish—the Portuguese-born
officials had no trouble understanding us. But the first time we
spoke Spanish to our driver he replied, "Solly, no speak English." And thereafter, though we used more and more the Portuguese pronunciation, he was convinced he could not understand us. Whenever we pleaded with him to slow down he
gave us a big smile, a bigger shrug—and kept the accelerator
floored.

About the only time he slowed was when we came to a
river. Here he was a paragon of caution. He would stop, survey the puzzle of deeply rutted tracks on either side of the
ford, and then, with what must have been sheer intuition,
cross at exactly the right place.

But once, where the river had risen in a flash flood and
wiped out the tracks, he hesitated. A large truck, caked with
mud, stood on the far bank, and a Timorese was waving frantically, warning us not to cross there. Over the roar of the
water he shouted, pointed to his truck, and made that unmis-
takable sign, a forefinger drawn across the throat.

"What happened?" I asked the driver. He gave me that
smile and shrug.

The Timorese waded across, the water tugging at his waist,
to show us the best place to ford. I asked him in Spanish what

happened to his truck—we would be fording rivers like this on our way to Indonesian Timor—but he didn't understand either. I asked him if he spoke Indonesian. Guardedly he replied that he did, a little.

"But I am not Indonesian," he added emphatically. "I am Portuguese." He went on to explain that the truck had crossed at the regular ford but had hit a deep hole, newly eroded in midstream. The engine had stalled and the current had washed more earth from beneath the wheels; the vehicle had overturned, filling with water and mud and clogging the engine. It had been hauled out by another truck the next day; that was three days earlier and he was still waiting for a mechanic to arrive from Dili to clean out the motor.

The night before we left Dili for Indonesian Timor, we dined with Senhor and Senhora Monteiro in their new stucco and dark-paneled home. It was an elegant candlelight evening with the warm glow of sterling on a Portuguese lace tablecloth and a line of crystal wineglasses standing like soldiers at each place. There were anchovy hors d'oeuvres, chicken livers in aspic, shrimp bisque, a fresh green salad, choice bits of beef in wine sauce and cradled in whipped potatoes, café mousse, and of course the fine aromatic coffee for which Timor is justly famous.

The rain that had been falling steadily for days had let up; there was a rare freshness to the air, and we sat on the veranda overlooking the empty harbor that before had raged with a thousand devils and now was a serene dappled-gray surface. We sipped till late the clear anise-flavored Lagrimas do Christo, the tears of Christ, or the treasured one-hundred-year-old Malaga that was an heirloom in the Monteiro family. But there was a sadness to the evening; the radio announced that the Australia-based search for the Heron, its survivors or wreckage, had been abandoned with the discovery of a life raft—empty. Until other arrangements could be made Timor was as cut off as any place in the Lesser Sundas.

There had been other nights like this with other Administrators throughout the territory, men who with their wives and small children—the older ones were invariably studying in Portugal—lived a sophisticated lonely life, competent men who had spent a minimum of twelve years in training and service before reaching the level of Administrator. Most were experts in agriculture, irrigation and law with a knowledge of engineering and economics in addition. But even with able men such as these—the British, French and Dutch were able administrators too—one question came again and again to our minds: how had Portugal retained control over her overseas empire, which totals more than twenty-two times the area of the mother country, when the tide of nationalism is rising all over Asia and Africa, when empires are crumbling overnight?

It is a little over a hundred miles from Dili to Atapupu, just across the border in Indonesian Timor where we planned to board ship for the return trip to Java. We left Dili early; Tortuga, her stuck valve repaired, was purring like new, and we hoped to make Atapupu that same day. But the rains started again, and unable to see, we stopped at Ermera, high in the coffee country in the western part of the territory. We had visited there earlier on the tour, and the Administrator, Senhor Luiz Ricardo, was as hospitable as before. A slight man who radiated a sparkling ebullience, he welcomed us to his large tile-floored home and that night after supper we sat around a fire in the living room while thunder drowned the crackling logs and lightning streaked through the windows, overpowering the flare of the red flames. There was vibrancy to the air that seemed to spark a discussion of Timor's economy.

"It's based on coffee, mostly," Senhor Ricardo explained. "Seventy-five to eighty-five percent of Timor's export revenues comes from coffee, about 1,600 tons a year. It brings premium prices, especially from Germany."

"But does this, with the other exports, the rubber, tea, hides, beeswax and all, make Timor a paying proposition for Portugal?"

"Not yet. We manufacture nothing here, and we need petroleum, cloth, machinery and I don't know how many other products. Timor's exports now don't even balance her imports. We get a little revenue from import duties and from taxes, but not much. The Timorese are taxed only a few dollars a year per man, and he may pay this in labor if he wishes. In return we give the people medical aid and improved breeding stock for their animals. We plant coconuts and give them coffee and rubber seedlings so that they can start their own plantations and then we buy the products. Perhaps someday Timor will be self-supporting, but right now it costs Portugal a million and a half dollars a year to support the territory."

"Then why does Portugal want to hold on to Timor?" I asked.

"Because it is part of Portugal," was the proud reply. "You see," Senhor Ricardo continued, "Portugal no longer has colonies as such. Since 1951 all overseas territories are designated provinces with their own government internally and a voice in the central government itself. The people are citizens of Portugal. They may elect their own representatives and anyone may be nominated if he qualifies; that is, if he speaks, writes and reads Portuguese, is of age, and has been a resident at least a year."

An enlightened policy, but even the Portuguese admit that much remains to be done. Though twenty percent of the territory's budget goes for health and education and for the Catholic Missions that have charge of almost all of the elementary education, less than five percent of the children are in school. Of these no more than one percent attend more than three years, and only exceptional students have the opportunity to go to the tiny college in Dili (less than 150 students), and fewer still can pursue advanced studies in Portugal.

The Administration is building more schools, but whether these and other reforms come fast enough to avert an Angola-style revolt, pressured internally or externally, remains to be seen. In the meantime the Portuguese rule with a firm hand and the Timorese soldiers are armed with spears and swords, not guns.

The day that we had allowed to reach Atapupu stretched to a week as the sandy, clay-base soil of Timor turned to a clinging muck with the continuing rains. The already too narrow dirt road, bordered with erosion-creased cliffs on one side and deep ravines on the other, was narrowed even more by slides and washouts.

At one spot the edge of the road dropped sheer for several hundred feet to a river bottom where the water tumbled in a sepia flood along a series of small cataracts. A slide covered part of the road and I wasn't sure Tortuga could make it. I stopped and measured the distance between the slide and the edge of the drop-off. There would be only inches to spare. I started for the Jeep and a crack appeared in the earth in front of me, a fine hair that zigzagged in an arc, spreading under Tortuga from a point at the edge of the drop-off a few feet in front of her to another several yards behind. Tortuga's weight was starting another slide; she, with Helen and Dinah inside, would be carried with it, and there was nothing to stop them between the road and the bottom of the canyon.

I fought the urge to run to Tortuga, to get her out of there. I walked very gently, warning Helen not to move. I climbed in even more slowly, feeling the earth settle beneath me. In front of us the crack was bigger and growing; behind us the mud was already sluffing off. I let the clutch out in the lowest gear. The earth shifted beneath an outside rear wheel, and a slice of dirt separated from the road, the earth tilting as in a fault. I floored the throttle, but the engine was silenced by a roar like that of a piece of glacier breaking off. The wheels scrambled over a low ridge on the far side of the slide and we sped on to a flat spot. We looked back in time to see the road disappear in slow motion; the side of the mountain dropped off in a chunk, disintegrating to a saturated puff that became a blur accelerating toward the river far below.

At each administrative post, no matter how early in the day we arrived, we were invited to spend the night, but, afraid of missing a ship at Atapupu, we hurried on. Often the Administrator or Chief of Post sent men on ahead to help us around other slides or washouts, towing us through mud where there was nothing to winch to or bracing Tortuga when she threatened to topple sideways into a stream or over a ledge. Road crews were working everywhere, digging, chopping trees or weighting planks with boulders so we could cross the swift streams. It was not until we reached the Be Bai River some twenty miles from the Indonesian border that we realized that as much as Portuguese hospitality the invitations were delaying actions. The river, swollen by weeks of rain, was an unfordable brown flood. I estimated the current at better than twenty knots. We camped well away from the edge and all night the sound of the water was a dull throb in our ears.

The next morning three horses, two riderless, sloshed through the marshy grass. We recognized the one rider as Senhor Augusto Castillo, a mestizo Timorese in charge of the small post at Maliana that we had passed a few miles back. He warned that amphibious or not, it would be several days— if the rains let up—before Tortuga could cross the Be Bai.

"My orders are not to let you cross until it's safe," he said, the smile on his round stubbly face erasing the sternness of the words. "Why not ride back and stay with me until the river is lower."

The next morning we returned to the river to try again, but it had risen in a fresh torrent after the all-night rain. We resigned ourselves to a long wait, and spent the rest of the day picking the ticks and leaches that had found Dinah more appetizing than the tall, wet grass.

That evening there was a respite and we saw the stars for the first time in days. We sat on the veranda, the cicadas trilling their song of rain, and the low jungle around the post alive with all the sounds of night. Above the faraway sounds were the persistent pings of flying ants striking the hot glass chimney of the pressure lamp, their wings curling in black crisps, their corpses piling higher and higher on the floor beneath. I looked at Helen; she was restless, as anxious as I was to reach Atapupu and a ship. Her hand was idly stroking Dinah asleep at her feet, but her face was pinched and tired and I realized what a toll, mentally and physically, the last few months had taken. She needed a change from constant moving, a quiet time to reflect. I hoped Djakarta would give it to her. It's strange, but out there on Timor, even Djakarta seemed appealing; the memory of the shooting, the tension, the red tape, had dimmed.

But I knew there was another reason for her restlessness. The same thought had been troubling me too ever since the storm the day we'd arrived on Timor and we'd felt the release that security brings after months of uncertainty. We wanted to know whether our assignment in Indonesia was over. It would be if we could not get clearance to travel in Sumatra, and enervated as we were—a year and a half in the tropics without interruption is too long—I almost hoped that clearance would be refused. But how could we write about Indonesia without a coverage of Sumatra? A story about Indonesia without Sumatra would be like telling of France without Algeria or the United States without the South, the sore spot, the seat of trouble. But with Indonesia this was even more so for without Sumatra's wealth Indonesia could not exist. No, even though it meant weeks of fighting Djakarta's bureaucracy, though we might have to wait there three months for the rainy season to end, I knew that somehow we had to get to Sumatra. And the sooner we reached Djakarta the sooner we would know. Again I questioned Senhor Castillo about the possibility of crossing the Be Bai in the morning.

"The rain has stopped here," he agreed, "but has it stopped in the mountains upstream? That's where the floods start. I've posted a man at the river and as soon as it's safe he'll— Don't move. Stay very still."

His face was hard and I froze, watching him, moving only my eyes. He reached slowly for a stick in the corner beside him. He was a big man, but a cat would have been noisier as he stood up and crept toward me, his arm raised and tense. I heard a growl and scratching toenails on the concrete floor and I knew that Dinah had seen the stick and was trying to protect me and that Helen was holding her back. The stick flashed too fast for me to see but I felt its breeze near my hand and I jumped. A small green snake with a broad head uncoiled itself limply, its back broken, from a rung of the chair about six inches from where my hand had been dangling.

"Very bad," Senhor Castillo remarked casually. "We lose many cattle from these and sometimes a man." He kicked the thin green rope off the porch and the head left a trail of dark heavy venom on the cement. That, except for the python that had frightened Helen on Java, was the only snake we saw, but it takes only one such experience to make you think they are all around, and I was more anxious than ever to reach Atapupu.

It did not rain that night and on the third day word came from the man posted at the river that the water was lower. We rode back to Tortuga, and though Senhor Castillo thought the current still too swift, we felt we had to try before it rained again. The branch that cut along the edge on the near side of the gravel bar was only ankle-deep, but on the far side of the bar the water rushed by in a tight, gray-brown stream a hundred yards wide. Senhor Castillo said that if it was not more than shoulder-deep in the middle we could try. He sent a man to test the depth and I watched astounded as he bounced into the water, not swimming, but hopping, propelling himself from the bottom in leaps that carried him up almost clear of the surface and forward a few feet at a time. He disappeared into a hole, and Helen gripped my arm. I held my breath, waiting for him to appear, but he was still under water long after I started breathing again. When he came to the surface it was far downstream. He signaled that it was all right to cross if we avoided the holes.

A long rope was stretched from bank to bank, a crew of men on the gravel bar holding one end and the other lashed to a tree on the far side. With this to hold to Helen started across to photograph the operation. Timorese were spread along the rope and she was passed from hand to hand, but barely thirty feet from shore she was knocked down by the current. Her feet were being dragged downstream and she was almost horizontal in the opaque water, spluttering and choking and clutching desperately at the rope with one hand while she held the camera above her head with the other. Boots and all I lunged in after her and even with the Timorese holding me it was all I could do to keep my feet. I reached Helen and dragged her back to shore, and still coughing up the silt-filled water, she was carried across by the river-wise Timorese. I was so relieved I was angry with her for not just dropping the camera and hanging to the rope with both hands.

We tied two more ropes to Tortuga, and with fifty men hauling on the bowline and another fifty holding back on the stern to keep us from being washed by the current onto the rocks downstream I eased Tortuga down the bank. As soon as she was afloat I felt the current tug at her; men were bracing the side too and I could use neither the wheels nor the propeller for fear of injuring one if he slipped. The water rose almost to the window on the upstream side, and I felt Tortuga swing sideways as the men lost their footing in the shoulder-deep water. They recovered, lurched on, and with a mighty heave they hauled Tortuga up the steep bank to solid ground. It was Helen's turn to be relieved and she was crying. Her legs and hips were dripping with slimy mud from a backwash she had slipped into trying to get a picture of the crossing. I soothed her and complimented her on her courage and the tears flowed even harder.

"You weren't so nice when you hauled me out of the river," she flared.

Senhor Castillo on the far side waved at us, and I gave him a salute of thanks. Among the men that he had recruited I divided my entire stock of the fine Portuguese cigarettes I had bought before leaving Dili. They were happily puffing a blue cloud, some of them making faces when they lit the unfamiliar cork-tipped filter end, as we headed for the border, still twenty slide-cluttered miles away.

At the frontier we probed through tall grass to find what was left of the swamp-lined road. There was no guardpost on either side, only a pile of rocks, some bags of hardened concrete and foundations, all that was left of the materials supplied by the Portuguese for the good-neighbor arrangement whereby the Indonesians would supply the labor to build a bridge of friendship. We learned later that no vehicle had crossed the border between the two territories in over three years.

At Atapupu, after the familiar checking in with the authorities—which was made somewhat easier by their surprise at seeing us—we were told that no ship had called there in three months, but the *Karawatu* bound for Java was due within the week. The luck that had brought us through a thousand miles of island-hopping was still with us.

Four days later we sailed Tortuga past the reef to where the *Karawatu* was anchored a mile from shore. I circled alongside, tied up to the gangway and clambered aboard. The captain, a rugged-looking Pole under contract to the Indonesian government steamship line, leaned over the side. He was a stranger to me, but he boomed out:

"I never expected to see you again. When they told me where you were headed I said you'd never make it." And then with a scolding grin he added, "You're not very sociable, are you? I ask you aboard for a New Year's Day drink and you keep right on going."

And then I remembered the ship that whistled at us the day we left Larantuka on Flores.

There were no passenger cabins on the *Karawatu*; we had not expected any and planned to take deck passage, living in

Tortuga, back to Java. But one look at the sardine-packed deck was all we needed to make us very generous with two of the junior officers whom we coerced into turning their cabin over to us.

Like a mother cat lifting her kitten the ship's crane plucked Tortuga from the long swells that rolled in along Ombai Strait from the Indian Ocean. Dinah was inside and I was standing on top and there was a moment of panic as a twisted cable spun Tortuga toplike forty feet above the water. Then, ingloriously, we were deposited in the midst of laughing soldiers, startled mothers, crying babies, and a tropical barnyard. In moments Tortuga became barnacled with bundles, an anchor for clotheslines, and a perch for parrots.

Safely aboard after coming unscathed through months of storms, reefs, currents, swollen rivers and broken bridges, Tortuga's crew suffered its only casualty. As Dinah, still dizzy from the uncertain loading, scrambled from Tortuga, she was attacked by a striped blur on a string. In disgust she shook a tiny wild pig from her tail and retreated to the security of our cabin.

Chapter Ten

IT was one of those heat-pregnant evenings in Djakarta when the afternoon rain has stopped and the night rain has not yet begun, when everything seems poised, as if waiting for that first stab of lightning, that first clap of thunder, those daggers of rain that in a few moments flood the streets and sluice off into the old Dutch-built canals. Dinah sniffed the air in apprehension, a drop of nervous moisture hanging suspensefully on her long nose. I watched the drop grow, then splatter to the tile floor to be followed by another. She was a good weather prophet—her one fear was thunder. That and being left behind when we started on another journey.

The electric fan, an archaic model, swung idly back and forth, back and forth, an almost hypnotic movement, rustling the muslin-thin drapes and stirring my disordered pile of notes and travel permits on the table. The fan slowed, then stopped; the lights, a pale yellow at their brightest, flickered and faded to orange to red to darkness as the electricity was cut off. I lit a candle and hurried to the bathroom. It was all right; the mandi, the large cubical tub, was filled with water. Here in the Hotel Duta Indonesia, formerly the Des Indes, Pearl of the Orient, there would be no more water or electricity until morning.

Across the room was the sleeping area, a screened-in cubicle like a cell, with kapok pads over wooden slats and two iron bedsteads painted a sickroom cream. On one, Helen was tossing in her sleep, her form appealingly outlined by the sheet, appearing almost ephemeral in the guttering candlelight, elusive behind the glowing copper screen. I wished it were not so hot.

The drapes were still now, and I stood by the window in my shorts, my body damp with perspiration. How futile to dry after a bath; the exertion of moving the towel over your body made it wet all over again. The wet smell of bougainvillea, canarium, palms and frangipangi drifted from the ground below. Frangipangi, to Indonesians the flower of the dead. I rubbed my stomach. It was still sore from having a Sten gun jammed into it that morning when I tried to get at the soldier who clubbed Helen with a rifle butt. Helen's concept of justice had brought us both very close to death at that moment.

The canal that bisected the street in front of the hotel was several hundred yards away, too far to add its questionable fragrance to the perfume of night outside my window, but I could see the tiny bobbing lights of the *tukang sate* moving along the street. Some of those miniature kabobs, the charcoal-broiled tidbits of chicken or beef skewered on a bamboo sliver and dipped in peanut sauce, would taste good. But I was too lethargic to call the room boy to send for some. He probably would not have come anyway. I knew he was sleeping at the bottom of the stairs, but this was the age of merdeka, free-dom. The cries of the tukang sate, the staccato squeaks, *e, ee, eee,* faded into the night and were gone.

A shot echoed from the direction of the banking district. Someone must have missed the sign; the area was closed by the military after six P.M., but the warning notice was small, the barricade only a coil of barbed wire to one side of the street and the streetlights were dim. I hoped whoever it was had not been killed. The last one had, a European it was, a newcomer who knew not a word of Bahasa Indonesia, who could not have read the sign even if he had seen it. The silence in the streets now was a tension that could be plucked, like a guitar string. The Indonesians had learned to live with that tension and so had we, but we did not cover up so well.

I tried to make some order of the papers on the table. The three months we had been back in Java had been busy ones. There had been more permits to obtain so we could leave for Sumatra; this time there would be no question about Dinah—she was specifically included in our clearance from the mili-tary, still the last word in Indonesia. There had been visas to be extended—with forty-four fingerprints taken and multiple page forms filled out in quadruplicate. More pleasant had been the receptions where we had been given new letters of introduction. And between all these official and semiofficial calls we had finished our article on the trip to Timor. We were packed, we had our tickets and in the morning we would leave, and I was just as anxious to get away from Djakarta now as I had been the first time we arrived there ten months earlier. The glamour that distance had lent to the capital when we were way out on Timor had tarnished quickly under the tension.

I tried to sleep but it was too hot. Dinah panted heavily beside me. The humidity was a damp blanket; in minutes my bed was soggy, a rumpled mess, and the more I tossed the wetter it became. I lay still and watched the house lizards on the ceiling catch mosquitoes. Their little *tjetjak* cries were comforting, and counting mosquitoes was more fun than counting sheep. I must remember to pick up some more antimalarial drug in the morning. There, he got one. . . .

That face, I wish I could forget that face—round, pockmarked, little eyes hiding under heavy overhanging brows, short neck, long arms, stocky body, that green uniform. And the Sten gun, God, how loud that click sounded when he cocked it, like a breech block rammed home on a fieldpiece. It probably wouldn't have happened if Dinah had been with us. I shouldn't have rushed him. But what could I do, Helen crying, holding her breast, I'm so grateful the doctor says she's all right, that the bruise will disappear in a few days. That was as close as I ever want to come to it. Bastard—he was shaking so much he could have pulled the trigger by accident. And then all he would have said was we were resisting arrest and nothing more would have been done. Probably would have given him a medal. Resisting arrest, what a laugh. What right had he to get into the Jeep? And then to slug Helen when she puts out her hand to stop him. Just showing off, a corporal showing three privates how to treat the white foreigners. He didn't even know the name of his commanding officer; there it was right on our pass. He looks at it three times, lets us through the gate three times, in and out, to the customs office at the dock, to the shipping office, back to customs. And when we have only twenty minutes to get to the main office to pay for our tickets, fourth time through the gate, he says our pass is no good, says we have to take him to headquarters and starts to climb in. When Helen said no, that rifle butt came back so fast I didn't even see it. A woman saying no to him, a white woman at that. I guess he lost too much face in front of his privates and he slugged her. And when we take him to headquarters he keeps that gun pointed at us all the time. And the lieutenant won't even let us call the Embassy. Holds us there an hour. We'd still be there if we hadn't been able to call Hari. It's lucky that he's a major and could vouch for us. . . . I wish I could sleep. I'm shaking all over again. I have to forget this. That soldier is probably not all there, probably has combat fatigue or something. Didn't know what he was doing. Maybe he was almost amok; it's happened for less cause than having a woman talk back. What about that man who ran amok just because he lost at gambling. Knifed seventeen people before they killed him. Forget it. You know the Indonesians are gentle people. They've helped you, welcomed you to their homes. Think of all the nice people you've met. What about Chip out there on Lombok? And Lieutenant Basarah—the hobby horse was in Djakarta the next day. And Colonel Supardi and Njoman Oka and Jim Pandy on Bali. Without them you might not have Dinah. And Hari . . . there must be thousands like Hari, kind, understanding, gentle. The look of sadness on his face when he told us about his childhood, how he refused to use the Dutch swimming pools and clubs even though he was invited because his father was one of the high Indonesian officials, one of the few accepted socially. Said if the other kids couldn't use them, he wouldn't use them either. And those signs: NATIVES AND DOGS NOT ALLOWED. You'd think he'd be bitter, but he's not. Wants only to help Indonesia get back on her feet. . . .

I wonder how the people in the villages are making out.

What was that I heard the other day? They can't buy oil for their lamps or cloth or rice between harvests or tobacco, have no place to borrow money now that the Chinese shops have been forced to close. And the Chinese are pretty bad off too. They have to move from the country to the towns, but can't open shops because there are too many already. So they're leaving for China, thousands every week, they say. But who really knows? Correspondents can't cover the sailings. They can't take much with them either. Fifty rupiahs in cash, about a dollar, and only a few possessions. So they convert what they can to gold, smuggle as much as possible and cap their teeth with the rest. Not much to show for generations in the country. After the Chinese and New Guinea I wonder who's next? Portuguese Timor? British Borneo? American and British oil companies? Foreign rubber and palm oil estates? As long as the country is going downhill economically the government will think of something to distract the people from the problems at home. And how Sukarno keeps them hopped up. What a spellbinder. . . .

And yet the officials all say things are better now. Maybe so. We can go to Sumatra. They said no when we arrived ten months ago. The major towns are all controlled by government troops now. And we can drive at least through south Sumatra. There's even talk of a truce with the rebels in central Sumatra and Celebes. But they'll be a long time controlling the Darul Islam. Achmed was pretty badly hit, machine-gunned along the road, dragged from his car and shot again while his wife and child watched. If Noni hadn't been able to get help he'd be dead for sure. . . .

Funny, with problems like these you'd think that Indonesia would be thinking about more important things than spending several million dollars for jet airliners. With Djakarta already tied in with half a dozen lines they want an international airline of their own. And why? All important countries have international airlines. They don't even have regular service to the Lesser Sundas. And look at the activity over the Asian Games; the Russians are building them a stadium, the Japanese are building them a hotel to house the athletes and guests, and all the really important projects are squeezed to the bottom of the priority list just so the stadium and hotel can be finished in time for Indonesia to host the Games. And now Djuanda says Indonesia plans to establish national aerospace power to impress the entire world. . . . I wish I could sleep.

I was heavy-lidded and tired when we arrived at the dock at Tandjung Priok. Sten gun-bearing soldiers patrolled everywhere and tanklike Tortuga drew more than one glance of suspicion as we loaded her aboard the small freighter bound for Sumatra. But Major Nimpuno was with us, and the soldier who had caused the trouble the day before had been transferred. Though nothing was said I had the feeling that he was considered vindictive. A guard had been stationed near us to make sure he did not come back. It was a morning of uncertainty, but Helen and I knew that from then on every morning would be one of uncertainty, that from day to day we would not know how far we could travel through rebellion-ravished Sumatra.

Chapter Eleven

THE haze-blue mountains of Java slipped by in the wake of the small freighter and the post-monsoon wind laced the Java Sea with scudding whitecaps. We got settled for the overnight trip in our little box of a cabin and went topside. Below, Tortuga, too battered after her trip to Timor to risk crossing the Sunda Strait on her own, was already buried under the baskets of chickens, bundles of clothes and sleeping mats of the deck passengers. Government-sponsored transmigrants, they were part of an ambitious program to populate the wilderness of south Sumatra with landless peasants from overcrowded Java and Bali.

To us Sumatra was a name to conjure with, a vast jungle filled with elephants and oil fields, cannibals and rubber estates, rhinoceros and pepper groves, tigers and palm oil, orangutan and fine tobacco. Now the animals were retreating as the jungle fell before giant bulldozers that had been imported to speed the transmigration project. Dragging heavy chains and huge steel balls, they topple yard-thick trees as if they were straw, ripping through age-old forest like a harvester through a wheat field.

I wondered how the transmigrants felt about the island for which they were headed. Surely they knew that their new home would not be like lush, fertile Java. Each family would receive five acres, a vast holding to people from areas where the average landowner has only a quarter acre. They would receive tools, cloth, and enough food to last them until the first harvest. But without fertilizer those five acres of leached Sumatran soil would return less than they could get from a twentieth of that on Java or Bali. Their strength would be sapped by malaria, though the World Health Organization with United States aid is trying to bring the plague under control. Many would be discouraged and return home.

I felt an admiration for these pioneers, for the young couples, many just married, others with infants suckling beneath flowered kebajas or with three-year-olds playing quietly at their feet—contented, well-behaved children who seemed to have already adopted by osmosis their parents' philosophical *insh'Allah*, God's will be done. I felt a special thrill when I saw the old woman to whom we had spoken on the dock. There was a look of real hope in her bleary eyes, a smile on her wrinkled brown face, and a pride in the way she combed her stringy gray hair and straightened her faded kain. "I am going to join my son," she told us. "He has built his house and his first harvest is in. I have not seen him in eight years, and now he has sent for me." And I saw that to her this was worth the heartache of tearing loose from a lifetime in Java. Wandering the world is the way for me, but as I looked at the eager yet sad faces of those eighty families, I felt an empathy with them. To a Javanese there is nothing so difficult as leaving Java, to a Balinese nothing worse than leaving Bali, one reason that though the transmigration project originated more than fifty years ago, to date less than 500,000 people have migrated, barely a third of those born each year on Java alone.

From the bridge the captain called to us. He pointed to a tiny blue-white puff of smoke on the horizon. Through our binoculars we strained to see Krakatoa, the famous volcanic island that in 1883 sent its ashes three times around the world, for months tinted the sunsets with its dust and raised a tidal wave that killed over 36,000 people. Now it lay sleeping in the blue Sunda Strait, but since we had been in Indonesia it had erupted twice and could blast off again at any time.

I swung the binoculars toward Sumatra, nothing but a low haze in the distance. I could not help thinking how similar were these two islands: Krakatoa, a barren pinpoint; and Sumatra, larger than California, one of the richest islands in the world; so different yet both potential destroyers, one of the land, the other of the nation.

"With our rubber, petroleum, palm oil, spices and tobacco," declared a group of Sumatran colonels, in 1956, "Sumatra contributes almost fifty percent of Indonesia's foreign income. Java spends most of it. We want a fair share."

The island erupted into civil war that was quickly crushed by Chief of Staff General Abdul Haris Nasution, a Sumatran himself. The revolt degenerated to disorganized guerrilla actions that still disrupted the economy to the point where exports had fallen to an all-time postwar low and foreign exchange reserves were almost nonexistent.

We disembarked at the quiet south Sumatran port of Pandjang—a pier, a warehouse, a Stanvac Oil depot, a grove of coconut palms and two streets lined with wooden, tin-roofed houses. About ten miles to the north is Telukbetung, where the World Health Organization has its malaria eradication program headquarters. That night our host, Allen Steffen, an American entomologist attached to WHO, had an unexpected visitor. While Dinah's hackles bristled and Helen suppressed a shudder, a grinning Chinese unrolled twenty-four feet of python skin, a gift for Allen.

"It was caught near Ngeriagung, about twenty miles from here," the Chinese explained. "The people were tracking a tiger that was bothering the livestock."

The thought of tigers and pythons so close was too much for me to resist. We headed for Ngeriagung, a village in the heart of south Sumatra's Lampong district. It was not long before we realized why the area had remained so undeveloped. Except that here there were bridges, the roads were if anything worse than on Flores. But the potholes and ruts and boulders were soon ignored when we thought of the romance of the Lampong; the road was lined with pepper groves, each vine like a green column encircling the special shade tree which it must have to thrive. Centuries ago the Lampong was a prime source of this spice, so valued that Alaric the Visigoth demanded—and got—3,000 pounds of it as tribute from Rome. Later, the hunger for this "black gold of the Middle Ages" sparked a wave of exploration that resulted in the discovery of the New World. To satisfy the demand of Asian and European traders, the sultans of west Java sent the first transmigrants to the Lampong no one knows how long ago. They cultivated the wild pepper, prospered, and developed the unique architecture we saw in villages along the way, the elaborately carved wooden houses on stilts. With the wealth from pepper the people of the Lampong built the reputation for being the most elaborately costumed group in the Archi-

pelago. Now with cheaper sources of the black spice elsewhere, their splendor lives only in the jewelry and ceremonial
dress that is handed down in the family through the years.

Proud of their heirlooms, the people of Ngeriagung brought
from each of the score of houses beside the dusty road their
gold brocade kains, ropes of hollow, marble-sized gold beads
and crowns of gold-plated leather with bouncing gold
flowers. In a slow rhythmic dance accompanied by gongs and
drums, xylophones and shrill flutes, a shuffling of bare feet in
the dry red soil, a graceful undulation of arms, faces devoid of
expression but streaming perspiration in the hot Sumatran
sun, young girls told of love, courtship and marriage in the
halls of the kings. It was a dance that dated back to the earliest days of the great Shrividjaja Empire, the powerful Buddhist
dynasty of south Sumatra that in league with a Javanese kingdom built the Borobudur and until the thirteenth century received homage from Madagascar to Japan.

That night after supper of boiled white rice and a cup of
sweet coffee—the regular meal of the Lampong people—we
slept in the house of the headman of the village. There was a
warmth to the bare wood, a simplicity to the hard bunks and
chairs and table with which it was furnished. The thin muslin
that filmed the windows was as still in the damp air as the
carved-wood arabesques and geometrical figures that fringed
the porch and roof. From outside came the steady thump-
thump of the rice blocks and a gay chatter. It seemed quite
late for chores and we peeped out. The same girls who had
danced for us that afternoon had shed their black and red
kains with the golden dragons. Instead they wore batik wrap-
arounds with satin kebajas; their faces were powdered, their
lips bright red, and they looked more ready for a ball than
for pounding rice.

"They're certainly well dressed for such work," Helen
commented to the headman.

"Oh they're not really working," he laughed. "Listen to the rhythm of the pounding. And look at the boys standing around."

Until he mentioned them we had not noticed the teen-agers loitering beyond the circle of light from the hissing pressure lamp. Their dull sarongs and white shirts were pale beside the pinks, lavenders and blues of the girls. Nor had we been aware of the beat of the rice pestles, a one-two-three, one-two, one, repeated with monotonous yet hypnotic regularity.

"When the boys hear that rhythm they know it is time to come calling."

Sort of a mass courtship, I thought. Young people are the same all over, but how restrained were these "dates," with only a shy glance, a meeting of eyes, to fan interest to love, to marriage. The dull pulse of the rice block, its beat rising and falling in the night, continued long after we went to bed, and now that I knew its meaning it seemed as compelling as the call of the Lorelei.

The tiger we had heard of had not been sighted for many weeks, but there was a report of one near the village of Maringai on the east coast of the Lampong. Winding through the forests, dark and green, thick with vines, dank with decaying vegetation, we felt rather than heard the low hooting of black Siamang apes. A large mandrill, like a baboon, outlined itself against the sky and barked hoarsely, showing yellow teeth in its elongated canine mouth. And always the piping of the cicadas.

We twisted and jolted for an hour over little more than a trail. It was low country, with marshes on either side of the way; there were no signs and when we passed an old farmer leading a team of oxen I stopped.

"How far to Maringai, father?" I asked in the Indonesian language.

"Two cigarettes, *tuan*," he replied.

For some reason he seemed surprised when I handed them to him. With an expression of pleasure he put the two cigarettes in his hat.

"Thank you, *tuan*," he said and padded off after his bullocks.

"Hey," I called, "how far to Maringai?"

"Why *tuan*, I told you." He grinned. "The time it takes to smoke two cigarettes."

At Maringai there was no tiger, but the headman was anxious to show us the village pet, a baby hornbill. Only a few months old, it was already as large as a vulture and with its wrinkled bald neck and black feathers it looked like one. Because of the male's habit of walling the female in a hollow tree until the eggs are hatched, the hornbill has long been a symbol of death and resurrection to the animists of the Archipelago.

For several days we crisscrossed the Lampong, winding through tall forests and swamp-studded lowlands. At each village we asked about animals. We learned to address a crocodile as "Grandmother" so that we could safely ford a river, how a tiger addressed as "Grandfather" would not molest us in the jungle, both beliefs common to Moslem and animist alike though they stem from the old ancestor reverence that holds that the spirits of the dead inhabit the bodies of living animals. We learned too that a tiger's claw encased in silver makes a powerful good luck charm, that the whiskers of a tiger when powdered, soaked in alcohol and drunk—in sufficient quantities, I gathered—would make a man strong, and how powdered rhinoceros horn, valued at a thousand U.S. dollars a pound on the Singapore market, makes an irresistible aphrodisiac. We learned much, but saw nothing of animals except the ubiquitous monkeys.

Convinced that the fabled game of south Sumatra was just

that, we headed north for Palembang. Once the center of the Shrividjaja Empire and now south Sumatra's principal port, Palembang was born of pepper, nurtured on tin and weaned on oil. From the Standard Vacuum (Stanvac) and Shell refineries at Palembang and the large Caltex fields of central Sumatra come almost two percent of the world's petroleum. It is a city that lives by and on the river, a hundred miles upstream from the mouth of the sluggish, brown, nipa-swamp-bordered Musi.

But along the Musi, Palembang has a character all its own. With Jim Burrill, a Stanvac engineer who was recommended to us as a man who knew as much about Palembang as anyone in south Sumatra, we hammered along the twisting Musi in a flat-bottomed, outboard-powered "sled."

We pulled in at a floating dock and made our way along boardwalks as Jim led us to a tile-roofed, whitewashed building.

"One of the oldest Chinese temples in Indonesia," Jim announced. The roof was crowned with fire-breathing dragons of gilt and enameled wood. Smaller dragons crouched beside the wide carved door. Jim knew the old Chinese temple-keeper and we were welcomed with low, but not obsequious, bows into the incense-heavy sanctum.

It was dark inside, and after the glare of the Musi it was a while before we could make out more than the glowing star-points of burning joss sticks. Then, as our irises widened, the room spread in reds and greens and golds, raw colors, dragons with benevolent faces, knobby talons and long curling tails, gilt-edged draperies and hanging paper lanterns, all blazing with gold calligraphy that captured the gleam of the ever-burning lamp like water snares a star-filled night.

Against the far wall was the altar, marble-topped, gilt-trimmed, hung with crimson cloth. A small translucently white porcelain image sat with hands folded in meditation, a benign look on the delicately figured face. Was it Confucius? Buddha? I wasn't sure, for Indonesian Chinese profess a kind of Taoist-Buddhist-Confucianist eclecticism.

Jim, with a bow to the temple-keeper,went to the altar, and with practiced hands shook the fortune sticks, eight-inch slivers of polished bamboo, to the floor. He picked one; the temple-keeper interpreted his fortune as good; Jim lit joss sticks and the blue smoke enveloped him in the exotic tang. One by one he burned prayer leaves, squares of paper scratched in black with Chinese characters and coated with a film of silver. His fortune was secure.

For Jim, the ceremony was one of respect, not worship; respect for the customs and rituals of those he called his friends—Indonesian, Chinese, American, Moslem, Hindu, pagan—seemed as much a religion to him as his own faith. Tall, with the build of a roustabout, the energy of a catalytic cracker, and the taste of an art connoisseur, Jim was always ready to laugh—but never at others, and because of this his list of Indonesian and Chinese friends was long.

As we were leaving, we passed a table in one corner near the great wooden door. A blanket of dust, as in a long-hidden tomb, made gray blobs of the figures on it.

"Interesting, these," Jim commented. He picked one up, blew away a sooty cloud, and handed it to Helen.

She held it close to the open door where the light from a Sumatran sunset reflected misty orange from the Musi.

"Exquisite," she breathed.

It was a carved, wooden ancestor statue about a foot high, the folds of cloth so perfectly executed they seemed to move in the warm breeze from the river. There was peace in the face, contentment in the full figure, and a soft sheen on the dark wood overlaid with traces of gold leaf.

"What a tragedy that such treasures should lie here covered with dust," Helen mourned.

A voice behind us agreed. It was the old temple-keeper.

"They were left by families returning to China," he said. "There are many such as these," and he waved his hand resignedly over the table.

"Do you think that . . ." Helen started to say to me. But though the temple-keeper knew no English he knew a woman's mind. Before she could finish he smiled, a sad, lonely smile:

"No, they are not for sale," he said. "But if Njonja will give the ancestor a place of honor in her home she may have it."

So now, in our bedroom in California, on a low lacquered and gold-leafed table, with a Balinese altar bowl and an Indian incense burner at its feet, sits the image of some unknown ancestor of some unnamed Indonesian Chinese who has returned to the land of his fathers.

But there are still many Chinese left in Palembang and Jim seemed to know them all. A few days later he took us to a Chinese wedding reception. Perhaps thirty tables had been set under a canvas shade in the front lawn of the groom's home. On each was a bottle of Cognac that was being emptied rapidly by the white-shirted, black-trousered Chinese sitting around it. The food came, endless courses; shark's-fin and crabspawn soup; *pangsit goreng*, like French-fried ravioli; fried rice; sate; roast pork and pineapple duck; meat and shrimp curries; pickled vegetables; boiled vegetables; tea; mandarin oranges; kumquats; more Cognac.

As usual at the Indonesian affairs we had attended, Helen was the only woman sitting with the men. She seemed to bear up under the "strain" quite well. But that day there was a rather forward Chinese, a rare individual, for Indonesians and

Chinese both are most always courteous to extremes when speaking to women not of their family. But this one was young, handsome, proud of his English and—quite drunk.

"You must drink a toast to the happy couple," he said to Helen as he wobbled over to our table.

The happy couple had not yet put in an appearance, but this was immaterial. Though Helen is not fond of Cognac, or any straight liquor, she raised the tumbler—into which the Chinese had poured three fingers of Cognac—and sipped.

"No, no, you do not toast like that. You toast like this." And he downed an equal quantity in one swallow. "Now, drink."

"With your permission," I said, "I will toast for her." Before he could protest I emptied Helen's glass. But he was not finished. An ugly look entered his eyes.

"She must toast." He poured more Cognac. "Now drink."

The rest of the men, there must have been seventy or eighty, had stopped talking. Chairs had swung around, and if stares were strings we would have looked like the vortex of a spider web.

Helen raised the glass again and touched it to her lips. She smiled that sweet, firm smile of hers that I knew from experience meant that she was not, definitely not, going to do anything she did not want to.

"I drink a toast," she said, "to the bride and groom. But I drink with my heart and not my mouth."

And there was a roar of laughter, a loud applause, our "friend" was shouted back to his seat, and Jim whispered to Helen, "Nice going."

There was another wedding in Palembang—this one a traditional Sumatran affair. It would have been called a society fete in any country, two of the most prominent families in Palembang, the niece of a hero of the revolution and the son of an important official, uniting in a ceremony as old as the Shrividjaja Empire itself.

We joined the hundreds of guests paying their respects to the bride, leaving our shoes at the door of the large Dutch-style house on the outskirts of Palembang. She sat like a statue, an Egyptian queen, on cushions on the floor, her legs tucked under her, her hands folded in her lap, her face a mask

under a gilded leather crown with golden flowers and stream-ers of tiny gold beads. Her lightly powdered skin was shining in the hot humidity, lips full and red, eyebrows precisely arched. The room was packed with friends and relatives, women only, sitting around her on the floor while an old matriarch intoned her duties as a wife. It was stuffy; my white shirt was a wet gray and I felt sorry for her, sweltering under shoulder pieces of black leather and gold, her breasts bound tightly in heavy crimson brocade that seemed more gold than cloth, with her red and gold kain encasing her to the ankles. And yet she sat there so regally, a beautiful girl in any language and by any tastes, that she dominated the room though she never moved an eyelash.

The groom arrived—here tradition was broken, for his conveyance was not the time-honored boat with wheels, but an automobile. He was as resplendent as his bride, a sultan in flowing robes of red and yellow satin rosetted with gold and a gold-encrusted turban. A flap hung like a blinder over the right side of his face and I wondered what it was for.

The bride rose to welcome him, but her face showed no emotion. They were each handed sirih leaves; they threw them at each other, and here again tradition was defied. Custom decreed that he should score a hit and she should miss as a token of her obedience. But they both missed. Since the turn of the century when a little sheltered Javanese princess, named Kartini, stepped from her roll as chattel and launched a lone suffragette movement, equality for women in Indonesia has been advancing and is extending even into marriage.

The rest of the day fled by in a confusion of images: the bride and groom sitting in state, side by side on a white satin, flower-decked couch while little girls fanned them; the couple's faces still expressionless masks; the bride's aunt standing ready to pinch her should she smile or sneak a glance at the groom; the groom unable to see his bride because of that flap about which I had wondered earlier.

The feast: rows of pastel colors, the women guests sitting on the floor in front of the couple, who were not permitted to eat; the men sitting in groups far off under the *pendopo*, the canopy, behind the house; all of us eating in the Indonesian fashion which Helen and I never adjusted to, scooping up with the fingers of the right hand the numberless courses of

curries, vegetables and boiled rice, the peppered strips of buffalo, the drumsticks of fried ground beef molded around
slender rods of wood, the tea and cookies of rice in a dozen
colors, the absence of liquor at this Moslem gathering, the
sedate restraint of the guests.

The rituals: the egg-breaking ceremony, the groom crushing an egg beneath his bare foot, the bride washing his feet in
the liquid, a rite whose origin is lost but which must surely
be associated with fertility; the symbolic bathing, a hilarious
water fight between bride and groom.

The memories: the feeling that when we left that afternoon we had stepped back in time a thousand years to when
Shrividjaja was one of the greatest maritime nations in Southeast Asia, when its monasteries were hosts to pilgrims from
all over the Buddhist world, when the halls of the kings echoed
daily to such pageantry as this.

But we could not think long about the past. It was the
middle of June and our final visa extension, our permits for
Tortuga and all our photographic equipment expired the 19th
of August. We checked on shipping schedules between
Palembang and Singapore. There was a sailing on August 16th.
We wanted to know what chance we had of getting through
by road to Padang in central Sumatra, to Medan in the
north, and back again before that ship sailed. The Army Commandant was the only one who could tell us. We called on
Colonel Harun Sohar.

Colonel Sohar lived in the former Dutch residential district
of Palembang—small square houses with wide lawns and
separate quarters for servants at the back. We drove slowly;
the Army objected, often with shots, to anyone exceeding
ten kilometers an hour when passing military installations.
But most of south Sumatra was now considered secure—
though machine guns still covered the entrances to town—

and the sentries were more curious than wary when Tortuga parked by the lotus-fringed pond in front of Colonel Sohar's home. His aide ushered us into the living room—and we saw our first tiger, one the colonel had shot, a great stuffed snarling beast that sent Dinah into a corner until, realizing it was harmless, she became very brave and showed more teeth than the tiger.

After the usual chitchat, shorter this time since Colonel Sohar is a Sumatran and therefore more direct than the Javanese, we requested clearance to drive north.

"But the monsoon is barely over," he said. The roads are still impassable in places. And you would be leaving my district. I could not guarantee your security."

What he meant, as we were soon to find out, was that the area through which we would have to pass, particularly the Bukit Barisan Mountains, part of Sumatra's volcanic spine, was still controlled by the rebels.

"I suggest that you fly from here. Call at my office tomorrow and my aide will arrange ticket priority for you."

Palembang's airport lies several miles out of town; the plane was leaving early and the morning sun was still only a pale ellipse peeping over the jungle-etched horizon when the Stanvac car called for us at the Company guest house. The airline would not accept Dinah; the Burrills kindly offered to keep her. We left Tortuga with them too and cut our baggage to the barest essentials. We could hardly look back at Dinah's puzzled face in the window, her black wet nose flattened askew against the glass, her head cocked, her mouth opening in a little cry that we could see but not hear except in our hearts.

We felt unencumbered without Tortuga and strangely alone among the crowd milling for tickets in the small waiting room of the airport. With our Army priority there was no problem with tickets; without it there would have been no chance—space was booked long in advance and most of it was allotted to military personnel and their dependents.

Our destination was Padang, 350 airline miles to the northwest. The twin-engine plane of Garuda Indonesian Airways (named after the mythical bird that appears on the official seal of the country) was neat and well maintained. It seemed forever warming up as everything was checked and double-checked. Now wholly Indonesian-operated, Garuda has an enviable safety record, but it is still woefully short of personnel and equipment, despite close to ten million dollars of United States aid and loans. Standby time is high since night flying is not attempted; flights are relatively few, and only between Java, Sumatra, Bali and Borneo could service be called scheduled.

South Sumatra drifted by, peep-sighted through the porthole and the silver circle of the propeller. From the east coast, where only a few miles separate Sumatra from Malaya, flat lowlands extended almost to the rebel-controlled mountains that parallel the wave-pounded shore of the Indian Ocean. We were too low to see the seas, too high to make out details; the world below was a limitless billiard table, its marsh-green cloth cue-ripped by twisting brown rivers, spottily moth-eaten where patches of land had been cleared. It made me think of camping in Alaska, of the thick beds of moss we used to sleep in, soft green moss that seemed to swallow and close over us just as the jungle below would swallow and close over us should we fall from the sky.

How many marvels, how many secrets that jungle kept. Near Bengkulu on the west coast blooms the giant rafflesia whose three-foot blooms exude the perfume of carrion. Scattered from sea to sea live at least eight distinct tribes, some of

Veddoid origin, others of Malay stock that degenerated centuries ago, some numbering hundreds, others thousands; tree-
dwellers who eat mice, snakes, worms and the larvae of wasps;
hunters who know no home, but follow the deer, tapir and
pig, killing with blowpipe and poisoned darts; primitive agri-
culturists who scratch at the poor soil, raise a few yams and
some sago, and move on; people who are so terrified of water,
though they live near rivers, that they are never known to
bathe. And somewhere in the dark hollows of jungle, mountain or valley may live the Orang Pendek, a true Missing
Link, a second cousin to both man and the ape, evidence of
whose existence is at least as well documented as that of the
Abominable Snowman of the Himalayas.

As great a mystery is the Pasemah Plateau, 180 miles west
of Palembang, where more than two millenniums ago lived a
race that carved twelve-foot-high statues of stone in a brutal,
dynamic style, powerful representations of a people who took
heads to absorb the wisdom of their victims, who ate the
flesh to absorb their strength, a people whose bronze kettledrums and daggers relate them to, if not identify them as, the
same Dongson who once moved on their migrations through
Flores and Alor almost 2,000 miles to the east. I closed my
eyes and I saw again that great head from Pasemah, now
mounted hauntingly out of place in front of Colonel Sohar's
headquarters in Palembang, that warrior's face as large as
that of a small elephant, as fierce as a gorilla's, the beretlike
helmet, the protruding brows and jutting jaw, the flat nose
and thick neck, that Athanasian expression, cryptic and fierce,
brooding from out of the past in lichen-blotched stone.

I must have slept, for the attractive Indonesian stewardess
was standing over us asking that we fasten our seat belts. The
plane was climbing, quaking in the unsettled air, into a layer
of cotton clouds to clear the 10,000-foot-high peaks of the

Bukit Barisan. A few minutes later we were circling Padang, a small coffee and copra port on the Indian Ocean.

Padang is the center of the Minangkabau, paradoxically a matriarchal and at the same time a devoutly Moslem society. Among the most enterprising people of Indonesia, Minangkabau has contributed many of the country's greatest statesmen, among them former Vice-President Mohammed Hatta and the late Hadji Agus Salim, both revered leaders of the independence movement. And most of the tukangs, the vendors, that roam the Archipelago are from Minangkabau. But the independent spirit of the Minangkabau had become a problem for the government; the area was one of the most actively rebellious in the island.

We could feel the tension the moment the plane landed. We could sense it in the over-thorough examination of our baggage, in the reading and rereading of our documents, and in the Army Information Officer who met us at the airport.

"When will you be leaving?" was Lieutenant Wardjono's first question.

We felt like the guest who has just been handed his hat. I attempted a smile. "But we've just arrived."

At the small hotel, we were assigned the one room not permanently occupied by military or government personnel, and we spent the rest of the day, restricted to the grounds, waiting for word from the Military Commander of the area as to what we could see and where we could go.

For the first time we realized how dependent we were on the local military commanders. True, during the year we had spent in Indonesia, we had always reported to the officials wherever we went. But up to now we had been in relatively quiet areas; though the calls had been required we had always thought of them as courtesy calls and the military commanders had received them with corresponding good will. Now, without Tortuga, without our rolling home, we were dependent on the military for transportation—there were no cars for hire; for a place to sleep—the room we were in was reserved for visiting officials; even for space on the over-crowded plane to take us away from Padang. And, in Sumatra, the military commander of each area was nearly autonomous; he could honor or revoke our travel permits and clearances issued in Djakarta as he saw fit; he could offer or refuse the cooperation requested in our letters as the mood struck him. We felt frustrated, helpless, and yet I knew that anything the officials did for us, no matter how little, would be a generous concession, time out from the pressing business of quelling a rebellion, rounding up guerrillas and restoring a nation to peace.

What's more, in the Padang area at least we had no reason to expect any consideration. The rebels, in addition to their demands to keep more of Sumatra's wealth in Sumatra, claimed also to be fighting Communism. They demanded the ouster of all Red-leaning officials in the government and the replacement of President Sukarno. To the annoyance of the Indonesian government the American press had been highly sympathetic to the rebels. Two American adventurers were in jail in Djakarta for allegedly trying to negotiate an arms deal with the rebels. Another American, a soldier of fortune, a pilot in the hire of the rebels, had been shot down during a bombing raid and captured. And to climax all this ill will, a paradrop of U.S.-made arms intended for the rebels had been intercepted. The shipment was labeled Formosa and our government denied any complicity, but it seemed that any American, no matter how good his credentials, who came anywhere near rebel territory was suspect. In Padang we were about as close to the center of it as it is possible to get. We expected to hear any minute that we would be escorted aboard the next plane back to Palembang.

Late in the afternoon Lieutenant Wardjono returned.

"We have arranged a military convoy to take you to Bukittinggi," he said.

In Asian fashion I muted my gratitude. It would be unseemly to appear too excited—and suspicious as well—even though Bukittinggi in the Padang Highlands was the place we wanted most to see in central Sumatra. That evening, carrying a pass allowing us to leave the hotel, we relaxed over supper at a Chinese restaurant, a welcome change from the cold spicy-hot rice of the hotel dining room. That is we *were* relaxed until three soldiers in jungle-camouflage uniforms sauntered in. With the respect a child gives to a cap pistol they slammed their Sten guns on a table. It was only coincidental, but those powder-flashed muzzles were pointing in our direction; they looked as big as three well-pipes and our appetites were suddenly gone.

The next morning a Russian-made Jeep with two rifle-equipped Indonesian soldiers and an officer picked us up. Preceded by another Jeep bearing a .50-caliber machine gun and crew we raced through the narrow streets of Padang, the sparse traffic scattering before the harsh blast of the horn. Along the slightly wider shop-lined way that was the business district we slowed; the street was packed. The driver leaned on the horn; we ducked instinctively as the sound was suddenly smothered by a rapid-fire burst of . . . firecrackers. Sheepishly we raised our heads when the firecrackers were followed by drums and a discord of gongs emanating from one of the shops. It was a Chinese funeral.

Along one side of the street a table was laid with the ceremonial feast honoring the dead. Whole chickens were spread-eagled flat on platters; heads of pigs lay with bits of fruit staring from empty eyesockets. There were roasts of buffalo, bottles of Cognac, colored rice cakes; the table was showered with sprays of bright paper flowers. Sweet, heavy incense clouded the still air.

At one end of the table stood two men in white skullcaps, loose white blouses and trousers. One was hammering a gong; the other chanted as the mourners, dressed in sackcloth, came one by one to the table, bowed, kneeled, moved lips in silent prayer, holding lighted candles at their chests.

A member of the family saw us and signaled us to come closer. We felt we should not intrude, but there was no mistaking the welcome. Here was none of the pathos of a Western funeral; here was the stark acceptance of the Asian.

There was another ringing of gongs, and the coffin, an immense carved and enameled teak sarcophagus, was carried from the shop, twelve men straining under its weight. Flowers smothered its shiny green surface, and from the top a white chicken, destined for sacrifice, fluttered in tight, nervous movements.

I could see that our escort was nervous too, anxious to be underway for Bukittinggi. But a son of the dead man, a stocky Chinese in white mourning clothes, had made us his guests. The officer, who we surmised was attached to Intelligence, tagged glumly along as we joined the funeral procession: the sarcophagus, mourners, the long streaming banners of scarlet, yellow and turquoise satin, the platoon of gongs and the firecrackers.

A river, oily green and slick, flowed on the outskirts of town. There was a bridge over it, but a small raft was waiting to float the sarcophagus across as a symbol of leaving life. The tempo of the gongs and the wailing of the mourners rose to a bedlam to frighten away any spirits who might be after the soul. On the far side, the sarcophagus was raised again. We wound up a steep brown path to the Chinese cemetery, a medieval procession in white snaking along a hillside of grass and acacias, through a profusion of horseshoe-shaped concrete cenotaphs that watched over an expanse of sun-streaked

Indian Ocean as blue and smooth as a piece of Ming porcelain.

At the family plot, the smell of the fresh wet earth heaped beside the grave was melded with more incense; the tree-murmur of a welcome breeze was drowned by more chants and gongs as the coffin was aligned with plumb bob and compass precisely toward China. Grandchildren threw the first clods; the older sons scooped earth into the grave. A photograph, a sepia image of a dignified, gray-haired man, the deceased, was propped on the mound beside a garlanded white image. The eldest son burned a green crepe-paper dragon, feeding the flames with silver-coated prayer leaves. A baked chicken and platters of rice and sweet cakes were left to provide for the soul on its long journey across Sumatra, Malaya, the China Sea, Thailand, Laos, Vietnam, to the village of his ancestors in a land he had never seen. The white chicken, tethered nearby, clucked weakly as though knowing that its time too had run out.

The road to Bukittinggi skirted the shore for a while, the sun on the Indian Ocean throwing bright spears of light through the fanning branches of nipa palm. In places, coconut palm slanted skyward in long swoops; sandy-red monkeys, almost as large as Dinah, with bristling collars of fur and no tails, were tethered to their masters with long ropes. The officer escorting us agreed to stop for a moment while we photographed them as they ran up the smooth trunks to twist and drop only the nuts that were ripe. One, annoyed by our presence, jibbered and threw a large coconut at us. We dodged and with a head-crushing clunk it dented the ground where we had been standing.

As we climbed higher toward Bukittinggi in the Padang Highlands, the palms gave way to casuarinas and evergreens much like our pines. We passed through coffee and nutmeg country; the air cooled, and villages became more substantial-looking. Thatch gave way to wood, and the architecture of the Minangkabau, unique to this part of Sumatra, was more evident. I recalled the Minangkabau official in Djakarta who told us the legend of how it originated.

Long ago a Javanese king made war on Sumatra. But instead of men fighting men he challenged the Sumatrans to pit their best buffalo against his champion animal, the outcome of the contest thus deciding the outcome of the war. When the Sumatrans saw the huge beast, the powerful legs and shoulders, the thick neck and the horns, long and sharp and curved like the arc of a circle, they pleaded for time to find a worthy adversary. But they knew that in all their land there was none that could defeat it. The Javanese was confident of victory, for his buffalo had never been bested.

The day set for the contest arrived, and the Javanese king and his followers roared with laughter when the Sumatrans led their protagonist into the arena. It was only a little buffalo calf. But the Javanese did not know that the wily Sumatrans had kept the unweaned calf from nursing for ten days. And secretly they had fashioned sharp horns of iron. Now they strapped the horns to the calf's head and released it. The starved little creature thought it saw its mother and, in its eagerness to nurse, it rammed its iron horns up into the soft underbelly of the Javanese beast, killing it.

The Javanese king withdrew, and ever since, the people of central Sumatra commemorate the great Battle of the Buffaloes. They took the name Minangkabau, meaning victorious buffalo. They adopted a ceremonial headdress of cones of cloth worn on the head like buffalo horns. And they built their houses with roofs that dip in the middle and sweep gracefully skyward to sharp points at the ends.

But like all things traditional in progress-hungry Indonesia, this lovely architecture is fast disappearing. We saw few examples of it that day, and these were roofed with gray corrugated iron.

In Bukittinggi we were taken first to the Military Commander, Colonel Soetanto, and then to the hotel. Ironically, here where only those with special clearance could travel, we

found the cleanest, best-managed and best-catered inn we had encountered in Indonesia, an almost empty, homey little place with less than a dozen rooms. We were shown to ours and advised by the clerk that a plainclothes agent was stationed in the street and that it would not be wise to leave the hotel.

A dinner had been arranged that night at Colonel Soetanto's home, and all the officials were there. Most were military and all but two were Javanese. The entertainment was a dance performed by a group of seven exquisite Minangkabau girls in their teens. The leader, with her tiara-like golden crown, could have been a princess and the others her maids-in-waiting. Their faces were lightly powdered, their lips alluringly shaped and tinted. They wore knee-length overblouses of purple or maroon velvet, long kains, and sashes of silver-thread handloom slanted across their breasts. They were weighted with golden bracelets, necklaces and ear pendants. But though regal they looked, their dance was of the people.

To the plaintive music of violin, accordion and subtle drum, they pantomimed a woman's day. We saw her greet the rising sun and respond to the waking cry of her child; she pounds rice and digs in the soil; her child cries again, she raises her head to listen and runs from the field to give comfort; she spins and weaves; and at day's end she stoops by the hearth to fan the flames and prepare the evening meal. The movements were fluid, the mood gentle, a contemporary dance originated as part of President Sukarno's nationwide campaign to stimulate rice and home-textile production.

The next day the girls repeated the dance so we could photograph them in their village about twenty miles from Bukittinggi. They performed in front of a fine old Minangkabau house. The plaque in front bore the name of the matriarchate, and many wings had been added as each daughter married and brought her husband home to live with her family. The roof over the main rooms had the high swooping points of the buffalo horns, and each wing projecting from the house proper its own horn, the whole giving somewhat the effect of a pagoda. The wooden outside walls were carved in delicate flowers and scrolls; a fine brush had colored each motif a lavender or pale orange, and if I squinted my eyes the patterns, tints and panels became a suffused texture like a garden at dawn as seen from a high window.

Before the dance the local C.O., a Javanese captain, made a welcoming speech, assuring us that "as you can see, the area is secure." Helen and I glanced at the soldiers on the alert behind every tree and wall within sight. The clicks as those near us checked their rifles was dramatic refutation of his statement.

Everywhere we went there were reminders that this was a troubled region. At the dinner the night before, the guests had worn side arms at the table. When a convoy took us to Lake Manindjau, soldiers were posted at every curve; at the lake, an amethyst set deep among hills of nutmeg and clove, the newly built government rest house lay gutted, and empty cartridge shells littered the grounds. The Minangkabau area is one of the few places left in Indonesia where silver-thread weaving is still done, but for a walk to a village specializing in it, only 300 yards from a main road, we were escorted by twenty-three soldiers. We felt a continual undercurrent of suspense, and though we were grateful for all the Army had done for us in central Sumatra, particularly Colonel Soetanto who could not have been more helpful, it was with some relief that we received a message from Padang that a nonscheduled flight was leaving for Medan the next day and could we please be on it.

At Medan, a neat bustling city near Sumatra's northeast coast, we called on Colonel Djamin Gintings, Supreme Commander of North Sumatra. A stalwart, impressive Sumatran, he listened quietly as we presented for his approval our list of objectives in the area: Lake Toba; the Karo and Toba Bataks; some of the tobacco, palm oil and rubber estates. Colonel Gintings nodded at each item. Then he introduced a young officer.

"This is Lieutenant Ibrahim Nachi," he said. "He will accompany you on your travels in my territory. If you want anything, tell him. He'll take care of you."

There was one place we wanted to see more than any other, but discouraged by the restrictions we had encountered in the Padang area, I had not mentioned it. Now, I felt that old optimism rising again. Helen signaled me with a nudge that said unmistakingly No, but I gambled anyway.

"Is there any chance of getting to Nias?" I asked.

I knew that few, if any, travelers had visited this island of megalithic culture since before World War II. There was no landing strip there, and it was not on any regular shipping schedule. To reach Nias we would have to drive through two hundred miles of guerrilla-plagued mountains and then hope to find a small coaster to take us across another ninety miles of Indian Ocean. It was a sizable request, and judging by our experience with Javanese officialdom, I did not expect an answer for at least several days. But Colonel Gintings was Sumatran; what's more, he had the reputation for making quick decisions. He looked at Lieutenant Nachi.

"Arrange that, Lieutenant," he said.

And this time we made no effort to conceal our enthusiasm, though we had no idea of the extent of the arrangements he would have to make.

Ibrahim—with that wonderful Indonesian informality, we soon reached the first-name stage—was a thoroughly likable young Minangkabau who was serving his obligatory national service. Slim, of medium height, he had a boyish face and an exuberance to match. He had majored in economics at Sumatra's Islamic University, followed by two years in the United States on graduate scholarships, and he spoke English well. All this we learned the first day. That Ibrahim had also a talent for organization and a rare depth and emotional intensity we were to learn soon.

We had been invited to a reburial ceremony at the town of Kuta Buluh, near Brastagi, and Ibrahim called for us with a car and driver which were to be at our disposal during the rest of our stay in north Sumatra.

Brastagi, a popular mountain resort about forty miles from Medan, lies in the territory of the Karo Bataks, who, together with the Toba Bataks to the south, make up the dominant racial group in north Sumatra. All the way to Kuta Buluh, Ibrahim was musing anxiously.

"*Aduh*," he said, "you know, the Bataks eat dog meat. I don't know what we'll do if they serve it to us at the feast. I can tell them I'm Moslem, that it is forbidden by the Koran. They'll understand. But what can you say?"

We began to worry too. We knew we could not offend our hosts at Kutah Buluh, but, thinking of Dinah, the idea of eating dog was horrifying. I told Ibrahim what had happened to us the day before when we were coming back to Medan from Goodyear's rubber estate.

"They sent us back in a car with one of their accountants. He was a Batak. About twenty-five, I guess. The driver was a Batak too, but he drove like a race driver. We were about halfway to Medan when a dog ran in front of us. Well, Helen was petrified. 'Look out, look out, you'll hit it!' she cried. We missed it, but when Helen begged the driver to be careful, the accountant just told her, 'Don't worry. If we hit one, we'll just take it home for dinner. Dogs are very good to eat. Especially the black ones.' Well, this was too much for Helen. She said as far as she was concerned eating dogs would be just like eating people. And do you know what he said? He said, 'Why, people are good too.'

"You know, Helen and I just looked at him. We didn't know whether to believe him or not. He was a real nice-looking young fellow. He had on a crisp white shirt and a tie. His hair was combed. Why, he could have been any young accountant anywhere. And here he was telling us that people were good to eat. I laughed. I was sure he was joking."

"Maybe so," Helen interrupted, "but I certainly couldn't tell from the expression on his face."

"*Aduh*," said Ibrahim.

"Anyway," I continued, "I think Helen was embarrassed for him. Wanted to give him an out."

"Well, I was," Helen said. "I told him that I knew that the Bataks used to practice cannibalism, but that I always understood that it was more of a spiritual thing with them—you know, so they could acquire the strength of the enemies killed in battle."

"That's the way I understood it too. But do you know what he said then? Just like he was talking about chicken. 'No,' he said. 'Just good meat.'"

"*Aduh*," Ibrahim repeated when I had finished. "*Aduh*."

Much later we realized that this particular young Batak was just pulling our leg. But all we knew at the time was that cannibalism among the Bataks was a fact. Herodotus first mentioned it, and in 1292 when Marco Polo visited "Little Java," as he called Sumatra, he reported that the people ate their elders when they were too old to enjoy life. What's more, cannibalism was not, as we had thought, for the purpose of gaining spiritual or physical strength. According to one scholar, Edwin M. Loeb: "While the Bataks enjoyed human flesh, preferring it to pork, the habit was practiced merely as a severe form of capital punishment" meted out to adulterers, spies, traitors and enemies captured in battle. Another scholar, Junghuhn, witnessed the official practice of cannibalism during his stay among the Toba Bataks during the early part of the nineteenth century:

> When an enemy is captured the day is set upon which he should be eaten. Then messengers are sent to all allied chiefs and their subjects inviting them to be present at the feast. Hundreds of people stream to the village. . . . The captive is now bound to a stake in an upright position. A number of fires

are lighted in the vicinity, the musical instruments are struck
. . . Then the chief . . . draws his knife, steps forward and
addresses the people. . . . It is explained that the victim is an
utter scoundrel, and in fact not a human being at all, but a
ghost in human form, and that the time has come for him to
atone for his misdeeds. At this address the people water at the
mouth and feel an irresistible impulse to have a piece of the
criminal in their stomachs, as they will then rest assured that
he will do them no further harm. This is the expression they
themselves use to explain their cannibalism. According to their
description, the pleasure they feel in satisfying their revenge
in this manner, and the consoling quiet which it gives them, is
not to be compared to anything else. All draw their knives.
The radja cuts off the first piece, which varies according to
his taste, being either a slice of the forearm or a cheek, if this
be fat enough. He holds up the flesh and drinks with gusto
some of the blood streaming from it. Then he hastens to the
fire to roast the meat a bit before devouring it.

Now all the remaining men fall upon the bloody sacrifice,
tear the flesh from the bones and roast and eat it. Some eat the
meat raw, or half raw in order to show off their bravery. The
cries of the victim do not spoil their appetites. It is usually eight
or ten minutes before the wounded man becomes unconscious,
and a quarter of an hour before he dies. The remainder of the
flesh then is cut from the bones (and eaten that same day) and
the skeleton buried outside the village.

The first acceptedly accurate account of this custom among
the Bataks was by Marsden in 1783, a report which when
published amazed the so-called civilized world of those days
with the paradox of a people who practiced cannibalism and
yet had a highly developed culture and an efficient system of
writing. Cannibalism persisted among the Bataks into the
twentieth century, and as late as 1935 a family was tried and
convicted of it, and even today isolated cases of its occurrence

are reported. Generally, however, the Bataks are Christian-
ized and their taste runs to dogs, which accounts for Ibrahim's
concern and our squeamishness at the prospect of the feast at
the reburial ceremony in Kuta Buluh.

Kuta Buluh seemed actually to be two villages. The old,
stylized one about a quarter of a mile away looked more interesting, but it was in the new part, a scattering of cor-
rugated-iron and wooden houses, that the festivities were taking place. In front of the large communal hall hundreds of
Karo Bataks in silver-thread kains and dark velvets draped
like togas across their shoulders moved in a weaving dance.
We heard a wailing from the center of the group where a
woman was posturing and beating her breast. A yellowed
human skull wearing a new black pitji and red kerchief lay on
a small table near her. The wailing rose and fell out of phase
with the clanging and whining of gongs and flutes. Beside the
skull were a few smaller bones and some teeth, all that remained of a village dignitary who, some ten years earlier, had
died and been buried. Now he was brought back among the
living, and I felt those blank black eyes staring into the crowd.

The *kepala*, the village headman, a broad Batak with a pitji
squared on his head and a kain over his Western-style trousers,
welcomed us. A woman dressed Helen in Batak costume, and
as required by custom we joined the dancers around the skull.
Helen had trouble keeping the heavy three-cornered pillow
of a headdress in place; under the thick velvet and kain she began to fade in the heat; I could not get the knack of the dance
which to me seemed a combination of a twist in slow-motion
combined with deep-knee bends. But aside from our own dis-
comfort and awkwardness there was a stately grace to the
other dancers, a dignity appropriate to the occasion, the last

honor paid to the deceased before the remains were interred finally in the family sarcophagus.

During a recess—the dancing, we were told, would continue until late that night when the actual reburial took place —I asked the kepala when the buffalo would be sacrificed. I knew that Bataks, like many groups in Indonesia, traditionally beheaded a buffalo on any important occasion (a carry-over from their animist forefathers), be it the opening of a new home, cement plant, oil refinery or bank. But for the reburial ceremony my question was a shot in the dark. The kepala seemed shocked that I should even ask.

"Why," he exclaimed, "we don't do that anymore."

The gongs sounded for the feast, and as we filed into the communal hall and sat on the floor with the rest of the guests Ibrahim resumed the morning theme:

"*Aduh*, I do hope they don't serve us dog."

"Me too," Helen whispered back, "and I haven't seen a single dog all day, have you?"

A bowl of water to rinse our hands was passed first to us and then down the line of other guests. We rinsed only our right hands; to eat with the left is taboo since by custom it is used for other functions. The food was passed, a meat curry over rice. Ibrahim, Helen and I exchanged glances. We had no idea what dog meat looked like, but this was certainly dark. We hesitated, but everyone was watching us, waiting for us to begin for as foreigners we were special guests and must eat first. The kepala leaned over solicitously.

"*Selaken*," he said. "Please eat. . . . I do hope you like buffalo curry."

"*Aduuuuuuh*." Ibrahim grinned.

The feast over, the guests resumed their dancing around the skull. I detected a slightly different beat to the rhythm and headed toward them, but the kepala suggested that we see the old village, a little *too* solicitously, I realized later.

The houses, raised on thick stilts, were not in the best of repair, but like those of Minangkabau there was an ageless beauty about them. The thatch roofs rose in steep, concave, rectangular pyramids from low windowless walls. On many there was a double roof, the top one sitting like a four-cornered cocked hat that extended a third of the way down the lower one. On some were carved wooden buffalo heads, painted white and red and facing the four points of the compass. Smaller versions, the rice barns, were beside each house.

Back at the reburial I saw that the dancers were clustered in a tighter group. I wanted to see what was going on, but the kepala maneuvered us to his home to show us the family heirlooms, eight-inch-long ear pendants of silver rod that was coiled in a flat double spiral. They were almost identical to the breast ornaments found in Croatia. They weighed over two pounds apiece and the earlobes of his mother who modeled them were stretched to loops that could have encircled a small orange. An hour passed with tea and conversation, and it was time to leave if we were to get back to Medan that night and pack for our trip to Nias. As we drove onto the road, we saw a still-dripping buffalo head hanging from a post—so much for abandoned customs!

Chapter Twelve

WE'LL pick up our first convoy at Pematang Siantar." Ibrahim penciled a circle on the map about seventy-five miles from Medan. "They will escort us to Prapat at Lake Toba. Other convoys will be standing by at Prapat, Balige, and Tarutung to take us in stages to Sibolga." He marked four more places on the map more or less equally spaced along the two-hundred-mile route to Sibolga on the Indian Ocean.

"At Sibolga," he continued, "there will be a government ship to take us to Nias."

Helen and I were incredulous. We knew that the trip to

Nias would be no simple excursion, but this sounded like a campaign.

"How often do these convoys run?" I asked. "And what time of day do they leave?"

Ibrahim shrugged. "No schedule. Whenever we get there."

"You don't mean that these are special convoys, just for us?" Helen said.

"That's right. Colonel Gintings' orders."

It was barely light when the black Chevrolet sedan stopped in front of Vice-Consul Paul Miller's home where we were staying in Medan. It was fifteen minutes early and we were just finishing our coffee. For a moment we did not recognize Ibrahim. He was in civvies, and he looked even more boyish with his too large sport shirt hanging out and his hair tousled. Nurdjali, the driver, helped us with our bags and equipment. He was Minangkabau, like Ibrahim, and he was just as good-natured.

About two-thirds of the distance from Medan to Lake Toba was considered secure, at least by day. The road ran through tobacco land, the plants shaded by white squares of cloth; through palm oil estates where the oil-bearing nuts clustered like red grapes in the shade of green fronds; through rubber groves, rows of majestic green arches that shut out the light, spirals of white latex on the trunks, dark figures drifting from tree to tree, draining the little cups. "He who would bring back the wealth of the Indies must carry the wealth of the Indies with him." Here was the wealth of the Indies.

In front of Military Headquarters in Pematang Siantar, fatigue-suited troops stood at ease as though waiting for some maneuver or operation to commence. But it was us they were waiting for, and as soon as we drove up they hopped into an armored truck and a Jeep. There were eighteen of them, some

with Sten guns, others with Browning Automatic Rifles or
Garands. They wore the Tiger Head shoulder patch of the
crack Siliwangi division, and they were scrubbed, pressed and
polished. Their weapons were clean and oiled, and I began to
see why they were considered one of the Indonesian Army's
best outfits. Their history went back to the revolution when,
poorly equipped, without provisions, and outflanked by
Dutch infantry and paratroops, they made a heroic march
across Java, close to three hundred miles over mountains, and
through jungles and swamps. The Siliwangi took part in most
every campaign after that, and so impressive was their reputation that their very presence in the area discouraged rebel
activity.

With the sedan sandwiched between the Jeep and the truck,
we climbed into the mountains. It was dark forest land, acacias, casuarinas, evergreens, high-hanging webs of Spanish
moss, low-creeping gardens of ferns. It was a hairpinned asphalt road with picket posts and tripod-mounted machine
guns spaced at one- to two-mile intervals. At each one there
was a shouted exchange of greetings and a waving of hands.

Of all the scenic beauties, and in much of Indonesia they
are everywhere you turn, I remember best that view as we
topped the last rise and descended into the green-fringed basin
of Toba. The lake, stretching more than fifty miles long and
twenty-five wide, was an oval crater of some forgotten volcano. Its water was a ring of cobalt around Samosir Island,
rising in the middle like some great, humpbacked whale.
There have been times when I lamented that I was born too
late, when I wished I had lived a hundred years ago, when
international politics had not so narrowed the world, when
one could travel anywhere on only courage and a passport.
But that day on the ridge was not one of those times, for a
hundred years ago no stranger could look upon Toba and

live. So sacred was it to the Bataks that all who approached it were slain.

Samosir was only partially secure and a group of soldiers from the garrison at Prapat accompanied us to the island. It was midafternoon and we could not stay long. Ibrahim cautioned us that it would be wise to be back at the pasangrahan, the government rest house, before dusk.

A month on Samosir would be too short a time; to spend an hour was like glimpsing the stage through a rustling curtain and then leaving before the play begins—tantalizing, frustrating, mysterious.

Who were these people who built forts and towers on the cliffs of Samosir, who carved thrones, tables, and benches of stone, who interred their dead in stone urns and ten-foot-long stone sarcophagi shaped like crouching beasts with faces that could be twins to those of Easter Island? Why, as on Easter Island, were some left unfinished? Who or what interrupted the work?

Some of the megaliths are of comparatively recent origin, carved during the ten generations or so, approximately five hundred years, that the Bataks can trace their lineage. But the coppery-skinned, round-faced Bataks—who are related to the Dyaks of Borneo, Toradjas of Celebes, and Igorots of the Philippines—could tell us nothing about the origin of the older megaliths.

Nor, for certain, do the scholars know. They can only point to the Batak art and say that here are remnants of the Dongson culture, that between two and three thousand years ago, this migration that started in the Caucasus (Heine-Geldern's Pontian Migration) left its stamp on Samosir, as it did at Pasemah in south Sumatra, in Java, Bali, and in varying degrees all the way east to Alor.

But even were all questions answered, Samosir would have

held us. We wanted to climb the ladder to one of the great houses that parade on stilts across the villages in twin rows as evenly spaced as if planned by a subdivider. We were sure that the inborn hospitality of the people would overcome their initial distrust of us, even though we arrived escorted by soldiers who hunted their brothers hiding in the hills. We wanted to sit on the ledgelike porch under the thatch roof that angles out and up from the eave-corners to a high sharp peak at the ends, then dips back to a saddle in the middle.

Even though we stayed a long time we would need no books, for unlimited reading is carved on every foot of the outward-spreading wooden walls. There is the story of a wild pig hunt: men with spears surround a ragged creature with a long snout and an oversized crooked tail. The sun rises behind it and a rooster rides on its back. Or perhaps that stylized figure is not a pig at all, nor the men hunters. Perhaps they are warriors, and the animal the Horse of the Soul, carrying in the form of a bird the spirit of a man killed in battle. The Dongson people had such a symbol; so did the people of west Russia and of Sumba in the Lesser Sundas.

There are other books: in the larger-than-life-sized head of Singa, the man-lion, we read the story of another hunt, for in days past only he who had taken a head might carve Singa on his lintel. And if we tire of reading we still enjoy the books, for the margins are illuminated like an old manuscript with scrolls and spirals and curlicues and even a bit of whimsy in a grinning face that I fancied as Kilroy.

We unroll our sleeping mats on the floor. The stench of livestock seeping through the cracks from their pens beneath, the smoke and all the odors, soon numb our olfactory nerves. Samosir is almost five thousand feet above sea level; the nights are cool, there are few insects and we sleep behind our woven partitions.

We do not hear the unmarried girls and their callers competing to compose little rhymes. If the girl wins we might waken, for the boy gives her a present, perhaps a bit of jewelry or clothing or a knife, and she claps her hands in pleasure. But if the boy wins there would be silence and we would sleep on, for then the girl gives herself. In contrast to the guarded customs of Indonesia's Islamic population, among the Bataks premarital virginity is less important in a wife than diligence. As the old Batak saying goes: "There is no dainty cake on which a fly fails to sit."

At dawn the thump of rice blocks wakens us. We watch over the ledge at the long rice block of stone with the carvings of lizards on the side. We are hungry and the plain boiled rice does not satisfy us, but this is the normal fare and we are guests. We hope that someone will catch a fish for supper. We do not expect meat for it is rarely eaten except at special feasts. Helen and I bathe in the lake and take separate walks in the forest for there are no sanitary facilities.

A man is ill and the *datu* is called. He brings his accordion-folded divination book and from its alim-leaf pages he reads the causes; the patient has been disrespectful to the ancestors and an evil spirit has entered him. The datu stretches forth his magic staff of black wood with its carved animals and lizards writhing along the shank toward the seated, hair-tufted human figure on the crown. If the *pupuk* that fills the hollow staff was properly prepared, if the flesh and body fluids of the little boy from which it was brewed were mixed with the auspicious herbs and accompanied by the right prayers, the magic of the staff is strong. The patient will heal, often quickly, for the datu works more on the mind than the body. The staff can also kill, bless a marriage, and, the Bataks believe, bring rain.

A woman is ill too, but the datu diagnoses her case as fever from natural causes. He prescribes a tea of herbs and a sweat bath in the steam from certain leaves boiled in water. He does not tell us what herbs or what leaves.

One of the village elders has died childless, and that night the *si galegale* dances to appease his spirit; otherwise, having left no heirs to comfort it, his ghost will continue to wander.

A wooden doll in the dead man's image, almost life-sized, is brought forth. It is a puppet with jointed arms and legs, a head that turns and nods, eyes and jaws and tongue that move, each action controlled by a web of strings. Sponges are behind the metal eyes so that the si galegale can weep. The image is mounted on a long box with small wheels. We do not see the strings, for the puppet is robed in the dead man's clothes; a checked kain is around its waist, a black jacket and gray shawl over its shoulders, a red turban on its head. The strings disappear into the box, leading to a man who sits at the other end, his hands concealed inside, his fingers bringing the si galegale to life.

An old woman sings of the virtue and bravery of the departed, but we do not understand the words. A flute whines a dirge and a gong clamors as the si galegale is wheeled from person to person, embracing relatives and friends in its hard wooden arms. Tears stream down its cheeks and its eyes roll skyward as the dead man's soul—

"Helen," Ibrahim called, "Frank, we must go. It's getting dark."

Our mental interlude among the Bataks was over; a day, a week, a month compressed to an hour. Yet we saw and ran our hands over the sarcophagi, the houses, the incised walls, the magic staff. If we could have stayed we might have lived the whole play as the scholars Loeb and Schnitger did in the thirties. But now the magic staff, unless it were very old, would be filled with pupuk made of chickens instead of a little boy. The datu would probably be a male nurse or a doctor and there would be few who could read the divination book. The girls would still recite rhymes with their callers and occasionally one might gamble away her maidenhead, but she would no longer be excused, for much of Batakland is Christian.

In that hour on Samosir we saw the si galegale, but it was a sad broken thing, and when it was dragged disrespectfully from beneath a house, children's eyes widened in wonder for it was as new to them as to us. Later, at Balige on the other side of the lake, a new si galegale danced for us, but the sun was hot, the mood wrong. We wanted to see the si galegale as Schnitger did when he wrote:

> No one who has seen it dancing and weeping in the green mists of Samosir, in a night filled with silence and stars, will ever forget it.

The pasangrahan perched on a high point with a commanding view of Lake Toba. Helen, Ibrahim and I were taking tea together on the semicircular veranda. Ibrahim reached under his ample sport shirt.

"I hope you don't mind," he said, "but this is most uncomfortable."

He withdrew from his belt a large revolver and placed it carefully on the table. We had not known that he was armed; we had forgotten even that he was Lieutenant Nachi, our escort. To us he was Ibrahim, our friend.

The lake was fading. High Grecian columns rose from the veranda to either side of us, and the wooden walls behind us were weathered black. Just inside the door was our room. In that same room Sukarno had been held under house arrest after he was abducted by the Dutch during the revolution. There were two narrow cots, a high wardrobe, a dressing stand, an alcove with W.C. and mandi, all the essentials and everything spotless, but how bland beside the great swooping houses of Samosir.

The rolled-lead surface of Toba was amalgamed with streaks of silver from the wake of a canoe; smaller flashes dripped from the paddles. It was too far away to see clearly, but more than likely a wooden horse, buffalo or bird figure-headed its prow.

Twenty-five hundred years ago, near what is now Tonkin in north Vietnam, lived a branch of the Dongson culture, a people who sailed boats such as those we saw on Toba, who lived in houses such as we saw on Samosir. At least these are the boats and houses that the people of Tonkin depicted on their bronze drums.

I knew that many historians and anthropologists had pondered, theorized, and written of these mysteries, that my thoughts were perhaps elementary. But as I sat there looking out on the gray lake that was so blue, I thought of the year we had spent in Indonesia and of the people we had met. I looked at Ibrahim, at the revolver on the table. The nearby hotel and weekend bungalows were seldom used now. They were dark and empty. I probed beneath today's nationalism and hunger for progress, and through the layers of Dutch, Christian, Islamic and Hindu influences, all of which vary in strength from island to island and even to locale. It seemed to me that in all that diversity there was still one underlying unity in Indonesia that appeared on every island we had seen, the cultural continuity brought by the Dongson. I thought of stone altars and animism, rice and rituals, buffaloes and bronze, motifs and music. Suddenly, the thousand unrelated images and emotions that had so jumbled my mind became links in a giant chain that stretched far back into time to those enigmatic people who fashioned the drums of Tonkin.

For much of the distance from Prapat to Sibolga we were in Batak country. For a while the road—damaged in places by military action—skirted the shores of Lake Toba before it climbed into the mountains on the far side. At each garrison we were passed from convoy to convoy, the change-over impressively smooth and efficient. Consisting of as many as forty soldiers with four armored, machine gun-bearing trucks and sometimes wheeled, two-man tanks deployed well out in front, the size of the convoy varied with the wildness of the terrain and the likelihood in each area of rebel action. Many houses along the way were shattered or pocked with holes. We saw few people.

The convoys were comforting, yet as we passed under cliffs, through deep cuts and around curves, one thought kept recurring to me: if I were a guerrilla leader and I saw the convoy, which judging by its size could well be escorting someone of much more importance than a pair of journalists, my first target would be that unarmored black sedan with the official license plates.

We arrived in Sibolga late in the afternoon, and at the one hotel Ibrahim arranged for us to have the only room not permanently occupied, the one reserved for visiting officials.

Ibrahim and Nurdjali were quartered at the garrison; since Medan we had traveled and eaten together and slept in the same building. Our relationship was no longer that of escort, driver, journalists, nor even of two Indonesians and two Americans; we were four companions. They were always joking with each other and with us. We enjoyed their company and now we missed them.

That evening Ibrahim showed up with a long face. It was

an expression very foreign to his happy nature, so much so that it seemed almost a look of pain, as though his face were hurting from the unaccustomed contortion of frowning.

"The government ship cannot take us to Nias," he said. "It's been ordered on a special mission."

"For how long?" I asked, thinking of that August 16th sailing from Palembang and the August 19th expiration of our permits. In Djakarta we had been told we must allow at least nine days to get an exit permit and judging by past experience this would almost certainly prove to be an underestimate. It was almost the middle of July; allowing for time to return to Medan, then to Palembang, to Djakarta and back, even with no delays we would not have long on Nias.

"It will be tied up indefinitely," Ibrahim answered. "Something to do with a military operation. Secret. But there's another ship in port that's leaving for Nias in a few days. Maybe we can persuade the captain to leave earlier."

It was a ninety-mile journey to Nias, and though it was Sumatra's dry season the Indian Ocean was still unpredictable. At the dock, Ibrahim passed judgment on the ship with one word.

"*Aduh*," he said.

We looked at the seventy-foot *Utama*, a wooden craft of very dubious vintage. Her gunwales were drooping almost to the water, and she was only half loaded. The rest of her cargo was stacked on the pier, enough timber, corrugated iron and drums of fuel oil to fill a ship twice as large as *Utama*. I looked at Helen, Helen looked at Ibrahim who looked at Nurdjali who looked at me, and the word chorused out:

"*Aduh*."

The next morning Ibrahim announced that Sibolga's Army Transportation Officer—who, in those times of martial law, had absolute authority over all shipping—had "persuaded" the *Utama's* captain to leave on the evening tide. I doubt that any ship at Sibolga had ever been loaded as fast as was the *Utama* that day.

It was a glum captain that greeted us when we boarded. It seems that he had also been persuaded to reverse his itinerary. Instead of heading for Gunungsitoli, the main port at the north of Nias, he would call first at Telukdalem in the south, the area which we had casually mentioned was the part of the island in which we were most interested. We felt sorry for the captain, but by the time we learned of his forced change the sailing orders had already been written. After that we were more careful; with Ibrahim, expressing a preference was like waving a magic wand.

The *Utama's* decks were already jammed with passengers bound for Nias with their goats, chickens and baskets of evil-smelling durian, a slightly oval fruit about the size of a large coconut, green, covered with spines, with a thick tough rind and a cream-colored, pulpy center. I have heard durian described as tasting like "butter custard flavored with almonds, with flavors of cream cheese, onion sauce, and brown sherry, neither acid nor sweet nor juicy nor dry." We had tried durian, and our analysis of its flavor differs somewhat, influenced, admittedly, by its odor, which to me compares unfavorably with a barnyard on a hot day with the wind blowing from the direction of an outhouse. Yet some people actually become addicted to it, and it is said that the Dyaks of Borneo will kill for a mere taste of this fruit. Before that voyage was over I was ready to do the same just to get rid of it.

There were no cabins on the *Utama*—nor facilities, except for a platform extending over the stern uncomfortably close to the water and in full view of the galley—but if the other deck passengers could stand it for the twelve-hour trip, so could we. If we had known that we would spend four days on the *Utama* we might not have been so confident. We sailed as the sun dropped crimson into the Indian Ocean, and lulled by the creaking of the ship's timbers, we dozed.

About midnight the creaking grew to a groan, a chorus of groans. Everyone was seasick. Of all ages, they were so packed on the deck they could not get to the rail and they were too weak to move even if they could. Toughened by Tortuga's agitated pitching, we were unaffected. Ibrahim had no trouble either, but poor Nurdjali's golden skin was the color of damp parchment. The *Utama* was moving in every plane, all at the same time, her gunwales scooping up water and sluicing the deck—happily, for the sea was preferable to what was already slopping around. The sound of retching seems to induce a sympathetic reaction especially when you can't get away from it; we stoppered our ears with cloth; we were fluttery in the stomach, but held out—until the wind shifted and that vile stench of durian attacked us.

Though still dark it was nearing morning and we should have been over halfway to Nias when a violent thud jarred the *Utama*. Water poured over the bow and the whole ship shuddered. Then, strangely, the waves were at her stern and she sailed more smoothly. When dawn came we understood why. The captain had changed course 180 degrees and we were heading back for Sibolga. "For nothing, all this for nothing," Helen lamented, still holding her hands tight against her ears.

It was two days before the captain decided it was calm enough to try again. Nurdjali came to us and with a meaningful tap on his midsection, he intimated that perhaps he had better wait for us in Sibolga.

"Of course, Nurdjali. We understand. But we'll miss you."

When the ship sailed that afternoon Nurdjali was aboard;

greater love hath no man but that he suffer seasickness for a friend.

For Nurdjali—and for us—I was grateful it was an easier crossing. Early in the morning we anchored in the palm-ringed bay of Telukdalem. The *Utama*, her captain promising to return for us in a week, headed for Gunungsitoli.

With Ibrahim I checked in with the police, leaving Helen to pursue her favorite occupation—next to painting—window-shopping, hampered somewhat since the dozen or so shops on the village's one street had no windows. Suddenly a fierce rattling and a sharp exclamation came from outside. We found Helen retreating before a Nias warrior brandishing spear, shield and sword in a jerky dance. At her startled expression he stopped.

"*Minta maaf, njonja,* I'm sorry," he said. "You like to buy my weapons. I don't need them now. I'm Christian."

A most effective approach. The foot-in-the-door vacuum cleaner demonstrator was a shrinking violet by comparison. But the reformed warrior's efforts were not unrewarded; before leaving Nias we bought his whole outfit.

In the one Jeep in south Nias we bounced over a slide-littered trail with Dr. Gottfried Hartman, a German under contract to the Indonesian government. It was hilly, rugged country, heavily forested, with streams cutting through rocky ravines and spreading into marshland. As we crossed one swamp-bordered brown river, Dr. Hartman remarked, "a girl was killed by a crocodile here last week."

"And now it will rain for nine days," added a Nias youth riding in back.

"This is the dry season," I reminded him, eying the brilliant hot sun and the clear skies. But crocodile magic is strong. Soon the clouds gathered, the sky darkened and the rains came down.

Fortunately, Dr. Hartman offered his spare bedroom, where we waited for the skies to clear. It was dry and sociable and lively in the cream-colored wooden house where he, his wife and five blond youngsters lived near his small hospital. But we were frustrated as we watched our too-few days on Nias wash away. Then after three days, crocodile magic weakened and allowed us a few hours of sun—though we feared constantly the guilty crocodile would be killed by the villagers hunting him. Then it would rain for nine days more.

On the first clear morning we set out afoot for some of the nearby villages. Narrow stone paths, some made of mere rocks set in the wet soil, others of worked blocks laid with a mason's care, angled along hillsides and across fields that were deserted in this, the period between plantings. The trails, many of them estimated at more than eight hundred years old, twisted through tall, heavy jungle where razor grass, elephant ears, and ferns still sparkled with drops of silver moisture. But as the sun rose higher the moisture turned to steam and we began to wilt. I stripped off my shirt and then my T-shirt, and Helen wished she could do the same, but each time we approached a village our young Nias guide cautioned me to put them back on again. The people of Nias, it seemed, no longer favored nature's dress.

The villages crouched atop sheer hills notched by stone steps. Their very location seemed impregnable, but until relatively few years ago intervillage warfare was a constant threat, and fortifications were carried to extremes. The paths leading to the villages were purposely narrow, the stairways sliced into the steepest side of the hills, the stairs switched back and forth and the landings were easily defensible. By the time we reached the first village, I was convinced that such precautions were superfluous; anyone who had climbed those hundreds of slippery steps would have little fight left in him.

But the people of Nias were of a different mind—or had more energy—for the villages were veritable fortresses. They were surrounded by stone walls, and the houses, raised on eight-foot-high piles, almost touched each other in two long rows that flanked a stone-flagged strip between. They were immense, some towering over fifty feet, with concave wedge-shaped roofs that sloped steeply, dropping almost vertically from the ridge, then flattening toward the bottom like a Goliath's playground slide. Each house had a trapdoor in the roof and barred windows. The main entrance was a trapdoor in the floor, accessible only from beneath through a forest of foundation timbers. There were no other entrances either in front or back, but adjoining houses were connected by passages so that in emergencies the people and warriors could run from one end of the village to the other without stepping outside. The walls of the older houses were of polished hand-cut timbers, ingeniously interlocked without pegs or nails.

At each village the men welcomed us with tea or sirih or a bowl of rice. They were small and well built, their skins bronze, their features angular, with little trace of the Malay that gives softness to the faces of most Indonesians.

The women, however, ran at our approach, then peeked from behind the bars at the windows. Perhaps it was just shyness or perhaps some inborn fear of strangers, dating from the time the girls of Nias were prized as slaves all over Indonesia. I could see why; they were lovely, their figures supple and full-curved, their features delicate. Until the practice was stopped by the Dutch in 1904, Nias's main export was slaves, as many as fifteen hundred a year.

After several hours of climbing up to villages and stumbling down again I was convinced that the climate of Nias was the most oppressive in Indonesia. It was probably no worse than the other coastal regions we had visited but I seemed to feel the heat more. With the time we spent in India, we had been in the tropics twenty-one months without a break. A walk of a few miles tired me more now than did the all-day hikes and volcano climbs that so exhilarated us when we first arrived on Java. Helen was less affected than I, and she teased me when I stopped often to rest. One by one, the tripod, motion picture camera, still cameras and lights were transferred to willing Nurdjali and Ibrahim, neither of whom had ever been to Nias and were just as interested as we were. We hiked fourteen miles that day, as much up and down as forward, and when we returned at dusk to Dr. Hartman's home I fell into bed, completely done in and confused at my lack of energy. I was sticky damp with perspiration, I was nauseated and cold despite the heat. I began to shiver, little crawling sensations on my skin that spread until I was shaking all over.

"Malaria," Dr. Hartman diagnosed after checking my temperature and pulse. He put me on a course of medication, warning that I must not place too much confidence in the antimalarial drugs we had been taking faithfully for almost two years; the body, he said, sometimes develops a resistance to them after a while. I thought of Alor with its 100 percent incidence of malaria and all the other places we had slept, all the mosquito bites we'd scratched, and I realized how lucky we'd been to remain well so long. But Dr. Hartman's treatment worked fast, and the next afternoon I was up and ready to hike some more—considerably slower, but just as eager.

Nias is known as a megalithic culture, a society where large stones play an important part in the rituals of the people. This is particularly true of south Nias, and there were megaliths in all of the villages we visited.

In Hilisimaetano there were scores of them. They lined both sides of the broad, stone-paved area between the houses: benches like dolmens made of slabs of smooth gray stone straddling low blocks; a form-fitting chair chiseled from a massive cube of granite; tapering flat-topped obelisks as symmetrical as a square of mill-rolled steel; blocks in the shape of treasure chests with designs of pistols and keys on the sides; a throne with armrests and a crocodile embracing the back; another throne with a back like the top of a flattened Ionic column.

These megaliths were not the roughly chipped slabs and wedges such as we had seen on Flores; they were smooth, and decorated with an unrelated array of bas-relief symbols: lotus blossoms, spirals, swords, monkeys, lizards, hornbills, triangles and squares and a few crescents like the golden, buffalo-horn headdresses of the Timorese soldiers.

On one large flat slab were the patterns of two feet with lotus blossoms on the heels. We had seen similar representations on Buddhist shrines in India. When we asked the chief of Hilisimaetano what these symbols meant, though he had never heard of Buddha he answered, "They are the feet of God."

There seems to be no question among scholars that Nias has been influenced by many cultures. There are strong traces of the Dongson. Suleiman, the well-traveled Persian merchant, wrote of Nias in the ninth century. The British occupied parts of the island for a few years and then the Dutch. Nias had contact with the Hindu and Buddhist cultures of Java and Sumatra, but when and for how long is moot. The people themselves, like the Polynesians, trace their ancestry back to the gods. Perhaps it is only coincidental, but their dialect is related to the Polynesian language. It is their refinement of the megalithic cult, however, that distinguishes the people of Nias.

Each of the great megaliths we saw in Hilisimaetano had been hauled from riverbeds miles away, the largest requiring hundreds of slaves to drag them up the steep hills. Each is a memorial to some chief or important person in the village, but only a few were dedicated after the person died. Accompanied by the ritual sacrifice of as many as five hundred pigs, most were erected by the living as a memorial to himself so that he might merit greater respect from his people, immortalize his name, and attain a higher station in this life or the next. For all but the most recent, at least one head and often several had been required to complete the ceremony.

There was one megalith that was different from the rest. About six feet high and four feet wide, it was like a thin truncated pyramid formed of individual stones as precisely mated as those we had seen in the walls of Cuzco, Peru. I asked the chief what it was for.

"We call it a jumping stone," he said. "It represents a wall."

He spoke a few words to a group of Nias youths standing nearby. In turn, each made a running leap at the wall, clearing it with at least a foot to spare. My first thought was of the Olympics. These boys, without any formal training, were making close to record high jumps—even allowing for the small stone at the base of the wall from which they started their leaps.

"Now, this is a sport," the chief continued. "But when I was young it was a test of manhood. I could clear that wall with a burning torch in one hand, and while still in the air I could draw my sword with the other, ready to take a head, fire a village and get away before the alarm could be given.

He went on to tell us that wars used to be an everyday thing, wars to avenge a killing or the rape of a woman, wars over territory, wars to capture slaves and wars just to get heads.

"Before a man could marry he had to take at least one head. Boys were trained in war from childhood."

Later, the older men, the only ones who remembered them,

performed their traditional war dances. They wore armor of blackened metal, buffalo or crocodile hide, like flaring hip-length jackets with shoulder plates that made them look twice as broad. Their helmets were black metal skullcaps with wide horns and frilly bits of metal that wiggled when they moved. They wore masks with two long tusks like a wild boar and hung with beards of black hair. Their shields were long and leaf-shaped, carved of wood and reinforced with strips of brass. They carried swords in wooden sheaths and spears with double-edged, tapering blades or with a barb like a harpoon. The whole outfit was designed to frighten the enemy.

They deployed in battle formation, perhaps twenty of them, grunting and moving from foot to foot with short choppy steps. With a quick snap of their wrists they slapped the shields against their forearms, making a loud, sharp crack almost like a whiplash. They worked themselves to a high pitch, their grunting and clacking coming faster and faster. The tempo changed, they became silent, crouching in a line, shuffling toward their unsuspecting victim. The leader drew his sword and with one slash severed the head, symbolized by a banana trunk. He snatched the head from the ground; they retreated and took a stand to repel the invaders.

When the dance was over, one man approached me with drawn sword. It was a handsome weapon, its hilt carved in the shape of a hornbill, symbol of death. The wooden sheath was bound with strips of silver. Near the top was an awkward-looking ball woven of rattan, about the size of a grapefruit; it was covered with crocodile teeth, symbol of supernatural power, and tufted with bits of hair and cloth from its victims. Inside the rattan ball was a white porcelain doorknob; he couldn't tell me what that was for, said the sword had been in his family over a hundred years. He was Christian, but he knew the vital statistics. He showed me the keen, still-bright blade with the curve shaped to fit the neck. Proudly he told me it had taken thirty-four heads.

We had only two days before the *Utama* was to call for us, and there was still one village we wanted very much to see— Bawomataluo, whose chief has the largest and finest house on Nias. I was still weak, and there were over seven hundred steps, by actual count, to climb. But when we saw that great house, its spike-topped roof soaring over seventy-five feet high, its walls carved and fitted with a cabinetmaker's care, its massive foundation of timbers, some so large I could not encircle them in my two arms, we felt it was worth the climb.

Bawomataluo was about half pagan, the rest only recently converted to Catholicism by Father deVet, a Franciscan priest who had been on Nias but a few years. After the war dances and the stories of headhunting, the gentleness of the people seemed incongruous. Children ran to greet us, leading Helen through the dark passage beneath the house where the pigs were kept and taking her hand as she climbed the steep ten-foot ladder to the trapdoor in the floor. They were quiet, well-behaved children and they lined themselves along the carved walls when we entered the main room, a great chamber at least forty feet long and thirty-five wide. Overhead the beams faded off into the blackness.

We were welcomed with sirih, the kepala's wife folding the green, lime-smeared leaves and presenting them to us with both hands outstretched. Many of the village elders were there, their pitjis and white shirts looking plain beside the loincloths, short jackets and turbans of red and yellow striped cloth, the ceremonial costume of the seven warriors present. Each of the latter carried his weapons, and around his neck he wore the "ring of bravery," disks of polished brown coconut shell strung on a circle of brass, in former times allowed only to those who had taken heads.

Father deVet had notified the village of our coming and a pig had been sacrificed. We realized that this was an honor, for meat is eaten only on special occasions. But Ibrahim had that worried look again that said plainly, "What can I do?" By this time we knew how devout a Moslem he is. He never failed to pray five times each day, excusing himself no matter where he was or who the company. And all the way to Sibolga he had steered us straight to the orthodox Indonesian restaurants with their peppery-hot food while we longed for the Chinese food next door or down the street. Now, when the food was served, first to us since we were the foreign guests, Helen's look was as concerned as Ibrahim's and I'm sure mine was not much more enthusiastic.

One by one the others, the elders, the warriors, the chief, were served by the women, the selection of each piece of meat, as prescribed by custom, a matter of great import. In former times it was the gravest of insults when a guest or chief received part of the animal that was beneath his rank— and murders and wars ensued. Ibrahim and Nurdjali barely concealed their relief when, out of respect for their religion, they were given their special plates—chicken. Everyone was waiting for us to begin, for we were honored with the portion of the pig reserved for the highest chiefs. Ibrahim's eyes were laughing mischievously as we tried to look as though we enjoyed our cold boiled pig's brain served in the half skull, cushioned on a bed of cold rice.

It rained that afternoon, and we sat by the windows watching the gray megaliths below darken and brighten with the sheen of wet polished stone. A slender obelisk twenty feet high stood at one end of a truck-sized slab. At the other end a disk of stone a foot thick and as large and round as a cartwheel rested on four low columns. Smaller obelisks and menhirs were in between, all glistening in the spray of raindrops. A little boy belly-whopped and slid along the slippery stone slab, his bare bottom shining like twin apples.

That night, Helen and I were alone in the high vaulted chamber of this house that was built by slave labor 150 years ago. The kepala and his family were in their sleeping quarters at the back of the house; Ibrahim and Nurdjali were in Fa-

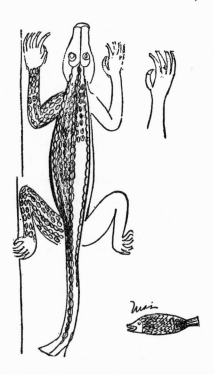

ther deVet's spare room far down the mountain. Clean embroidered sheets had been spread for us by the barred windows, on the bench where warriors once slept. Outside, the megaliths and the flagstones were etched by the moon. Far down the row of houses a fireguard whistled his "All's well"; it was repeated from house to house, answered by the shrill yap-yap of dogs, then silence.

In the polished dark wood over our heads was carved a life-size crocodile; it seemed to live, each scale and tooth delineated by the moon streaming through the open trapdoor in the roof. In a dark corner hung a war drum, round and tapered like a cannon and over ten feet long.

Pillars of wood, gleaming and as perfect as any Greek columns, supported the rafters. The crown of one spread into an opened flower, the long slender petals unsurpassingly carved. We had seen a similar support in Akbar's deserted city of Fatehpur Sikri in India.

Another column was circled with phallic pegs where human heads may once have hung. The rafters were studded with other pegs like the heads of long-necked birds. Across the room a mammoth stone fireplace was soot-blackened and dead; overhead and all along the walls gleamed the spiral-tusked jawbones of nearly a thousand sacrificial pigs, reminders of generations of feasts and dedications of megaliths that keep the people always aware of the greatness of their chiefs.

A rusted chain looped from the beams, looted from a European ship that was captured by the fierce Nias warriors. The story of the battle was carved in relief on the wall: a shoal of fish and a lizard swam round a craft like those of Columbus; a monkey climbed above it as though mounting the nonexistent mast; men aimed a small cannon at nothing.

On every panel were other reliefs: a pair of woman's breasts, round and widely spaced; oversize phallic symbols. There was a carved model of a set of chieftain's jewelry, ear pendants, necklaces, breastplate, the fashioning of each piece a ritual accompanied by feasts and sacrifice and slaughter; a slave was required to wear the ornaments first to absorb the curse of the gold; he was beheaded, and then it was safe for the chief to wear them.

The moon was higher; its shafts sent shadows of sprawling giants across the walls, lighting, shading, coating with nebulous silver these remains of a culture that is nearing its close. Now children use the memorials of chiefs for slides; the wall niches where once sat the images of ancestors are empty; the great war drum is broken.

Back in Telukdalem we looked for the *Utama*, but the deep bay was empty. There was no radio, telephone or telegraph, and we had no way of knowing where she was or when she would arrive. We could only wait—and worry. Our deadline for the ship in Palembang was too close.

Two families of German Protestant missionaries lived in Telukdalem. One, a young couple lonely and fresh from Germany, invited us to take our meals with them. The other offered their spare bedroom. We accepted both—and gratefully, for there was no place to stay. Ibrahim and Nurdjali were quartered with the military.

As we talked to these families and to Father deVet, we found ourselves trying to analyze the impact of the missions on the people, to correlate what we had seen of Nias and what we had read it was like a few years ago.

For twenty-five years the people of Nias have been exposed to Christianity, beginning with the old school of German Lutherans. Now, instead of hunting heads they sing hymns; instead of keeping slaves, they barter copra and pigs for bicycles and gold teeth. But in the north of Nias the dances and music have been wiped out. In the south these remain, but we searched in vain for examples of the strong, artfully carved wooden images through which the people expressed their reverence for their ancestors. They have been burned, and with them much of the creative drive of the people, destroyed by a missionary zeal that believed that only by the complete repression of the old culture could the new one be imposed.

The Protestant and Catholic mission groups now on Nias, however, are of the new school. They believe in the opening wedge of medicine and the education of the children. Instead of destroying, they try to adapt to the work of conversion as much as possible of the old culture, rejecting only that which is incompatible to the new.

We found both groups kind and extremely hospitable. Each was patient, self-sacrificing and dedicated; each was convinced that his way was right. And yet Helen and I could not help thinking: If interdenominational rivalry is confusing to us, how much more confusing it must be to the people. How wise seemed the Indian poet, Rabindranath Tagore: "The sectarian thinks that he has the sea ladled into his private pond."

During those days that we waited for the *Utama*, I asked myself many times why it is that men have always felt they must impose their own culture, religion, and politics on others. And why it is that one culture looks upon another and, because it is different, judges it primitive.

Any people that could design and build such magnificent and functional houses as on Nias and work stone with the precision and imagination of a sculptor, I can hardly call primitive—even though hunting heads was their favorite pastime and slaves their principal wealth. There have been many societies who kept slaves—ours among them—and yet they were considered civilized. And I wondered, is taking heads with a sword any worse than blasting them off with bombs?

Chapter Thirteen

FIVE days overdue the *Utama* arrived. The captain pleaded bad weather, but a passenger refuted this; the *Utama* had just been sitting at Gunungsitoli, and Ibrahim was furious —as furious as his easygoing nature allowed him to be.

"Let me shoot him," he fumed, patting the revolver under his shirt.

"Ibrahim, what are you saying?" Helen exclaimed.

"Well, just in the leg." He grinned.

That night, with a dozen Nias boys bound for mission school in Sumatra and one soldier on leave, we sailed for Sibolga. As on the trip over, in the evening the sea was calm and glassy. As before we were awakened by a rending crash. The ship rolled and tossed and we longed for Tortuga. We would have felt safer.

When dawn broke we saw the low hazy coast of Sumatra and the mountains beyond. But there was something wrong; a buzz ran through the passengers; Sumatra was to portside. It should have been on our starboard.

"We're going the wrong way," Helen blurted.

The captain had changed course again. He was running from the waves, and by morning we were eighty miles south of Sibolga, paralleling the rebel-held coast of Sumatra.

Ibrahim brought a message from the captain: "He says the ship can't buck these waves and this blow might last two days. He wants to wait in port. But he's not sure which ports are in government hands. Possibly Air Bangis—that's halfway to Padang—is all right, but he's not sure he has enough fuel to get there."

For the rest of the day *Utama* wallowed before a following sea at a fuel-saving four knots. We were all tense; we kept watching the shore. Ibrahim tried to joke: "I really don't know what I'd do if we met a rebel. Just shake hands, I guess." But when the captain reported a large speedboat coming to intercept us, Ibrahim was at the bow, his revolver out. But we all knew that his stand would be futile; no rebel boat would try to stop us unless it was well armed.

The gay chatter of the Nias boys had stopped; the throb of the engine was like a drumbeat over the silence. Ibrahim and the soldier were behind empty oil drums, waiting. We were too low in the water and the waves too high to see how close the boat was. A few minutes later the captain, with a relieved and very red face, reported that the speedboat was a drifting log.

At dusk we anchored behind an island opposite Air Bangis.

We still did not know whether the port was secure. We waited, bobbing in the swells, melting in the hot air. A fisherman from the island paddled alongside and assured us that Air Bangis was in government hands; the captain said we would raise anchor and enter in the morning. But morning came and we were still bobbing behind the island. We were counting days now until our visas and permits expired and the ship left Palembang. The captain said we would sail in another hour; it was another hour all that day and all the next night, and no amount of cajoling by Ibrahim could move him.

"He's a Minangkabau," Ibrahim stated flatly, "and that means he's contrary. He won't sail until he's ready. I know. I'm Minangkabau too."

"But what can we do?" Helen frowned.

"Let me shoot him, just in the leg. So he can still handle the ship," Ibrahim teased.

It was not until the morning of the third day after leaving Nias that the captain would enter port. Helen and I no longer had any sympathy for him.

Air Bangis is one of the northernmost of Minangkabau towns. It had only recently been retaken, and while we were waiting for the *Utama* to refuel, a meeting of the women was called. The women, their head scarves and kains a sea of pastel pinks, yellows and greens, were reserved and expressionless as the Indonesian Army officer, still in jungle camouflage, spoke to them in the Minangkabau dialect. Minangkabau is called the birthplace of the Indonesian language, but it was different enough so that we had difficulty understanding. Ibrahim translated the words, but the sincerity and urgency in the officer's voice needed no interpretation.

"Women of Air Bangis," he pleaded, "call back your men from the mountains. Beg them to rejoin the republic."

All during the twenty-hour cruise to Sibolga, Ibrahim was

silent, depressed. It was so unlike him. Cheerful when times were trying, ably forceful when necessary, he was a good soldier. And yet he was a gentle man. It was no surprise to hear him lament: "We have so much to build. Why must we fight each other?"

With the same smooth efficiency, convoys escorted us from Sibolga northeast across Sumatra. But when we arrived at Lake Toba, we learned that the Siliwangi division had been transferred to another theater of operations. The rebels had lost no time in taking advantage of the change. At 2:30 that same afternoon, they had attacked and burned a truck less than a half mile from a machine-gun picket post.

It was close to four in the afternoon when we learned this. After four no traffic was allowed over the road to Medan; the picket posts were not even manned. But there was a plane leaving Medan for Palembang the next day. Ibrahim knew we should be on it, but the garrison commander at Prapat could spare no men or armored trucks for a convoy.

Ibrahim left the decision to us. We had lost eight days with the *Utama*; if we missed that plane we would lose several days more; already we would have to rush the officials in Djakarta to get our exit permits in time to leave with the ship. The officials did not like to be rushed, and if we missed the ship all our papers would expire before the next one sailed. When it came to a choice between the rebels or Djakarta's officialdom, I preferred to face the rebels. And there was one important thing in our favor—the rebels knew that no traffic was supposed to be on the road. They would not be expecting anyone. I asked Nurdjali what he thought.

"I'll drive," he said without hesitation.

"Ibrahim?"

"If you're willing to risk it, so am I."

When the garrison commander realized we were going

anyway, he assigned us a Jeep and six soldiers, all he could spare, a popgun convoy compared to the armored trucks that had escorted us over the same stretch almost four weeks before.

It was dark when we left Prapat and headed over the mountains. When we had traveled the road the first time, each strategic place had been carefully pointed out to us. We passed under overhanging rocks, through dark forest, past roadside ditches, the Jeep's spotlight cutting a white streak through the night, sweeping, catching glints like sun on a rifle barrel, the white circle passing, returning to startle a deer, flicking from side to side as the road twisted toward Medan. We saw movements where there were none, heard signals where there was silence. We felt like a little boy whistling in the woods.

The rest, of course, is anticlimactic: our arrival at dawn in Medan; our thanks to the six soldiers who had so cheerfully stuck their necks out for us; Ibrahim's miracle—the nine or more days in Djakarta that he saved us by getting our exit permits in Medan in twenty minutes and the sudden collapse of time pressure that resulted.

And there was the flight to Palembang by Garuda, to Djakarta and back by Stanvac plane to get the baggage we had left there; the preparing of Tortuga and the crating of equipment and souvenirs for the trans-Pacific voyage from Singapore to California; the anticipation of our own voyage the other way for a holiday in Europe.

There was the face-licking, tail-wagging reunion with a much fatter and sleeker Dinah; the good-byes and thanks to friends in Djakarta; the warm companionship we had with the Burrills those last days in Palembang.

And finally, there was the little *Matang*, a gaslight and brightwork ship with all the romance of a Conrad novel. There was the trip down the Musi and across to Singapore.

But there was one brief moment in all that confusion that was not anticlimactic. I recall that last moment as we left the airport in Medan, that last image of Ibrahim and Nurdjali, two waving hands and two smiling faces—smiling but a little sad as ours were. That moment became a symbol of what our thirteen months in Indonesia meant to us.

Ibrahim and Nurdjali were still waving as the plane taxied down the runway, and somehow my thoughts flew halfway around the world to Callao. Though we had not seen Borneo, Celebes or the Spice Islands, we had experienced much of the old Dutchman's "paradise on earth." But we had found so much more.

We had found Ibrahim and Nurdjali, Hari and Chip, Humardani and Basarah, Njoman and Jim and dozens of others. Even if we had never left Java and could still have met these Indonesians and their families, the trip and the time would have been worthwhile.

And we were certain that for every one of these men there are thousands more like them throughout Indonesia. These are the men who can make of Indonesia a strong, stable country. And perhaps they can also make of it a paradise. But then paradise might be a very dull place indeed.

Postscript

ON August 16th, when the *Matang* was about to sail for Singapore, the word in Palembang was that something momentous was stirring for the 17th, Indonesia's Independence Day: there would be a revolution; Sukarno would be assassinated; the Indonesian Army would invade New Guinea; British Borneo would be annexed; the Communists would take over; the American and British oil and rubber companies would be expropriated; all foreigners would be in danger. The rumors were as rife as the doomcriers.

All day on the 17th, ignoring the beauty of the Riau Islands, the Strait of Malacca and the approach to Singapore, we stayed close to the radio. Sukarno's usual Independence Day tirade announced the banning of two anti-Sukarno political parties and the breaking off of diplomatic relations with Holland—which *ipso facto* had already been the case for several years. But except for this, all was quiet in Indonesia.

Since that time there *have* been more attempts on Sukarno's life; Indonesia *did* attempt to land troops on New Guinea; the Communists *are* more influential since the negotiation of a multimillion-dollar arms deal with Russia. And Indonesia *is* eying British Borneo with new interest since the latter's proposed federation into the state of Malaysia will challenge Indonesia's supremacy in Southeast Asia.

But there is a brighter side. Except for a few holdouts, the major rebellions in Indonesia have been settled. And New Guinea, for almost two decades Sukarno's rallying cry, the red herring with which he diverted his people's attention from their troubles at home, is now West Irian. In May of 1963, as a result of long negotiation with Holland, New Guinea was turned over to Indonesia, pending a plebiscite—scheduled for 1969—at which time the people will opt to remain part of Indonesia or become an independent state. In the meantime, Sukarno's dream of a united Indonesia from "Sabang to Merauke" has come true.

With the easing of these problems, which have long been used as excuses for the country's stagnation—and barring the creation of another diverting crisis such as Malaysia—Indonesia has the opportunity to realize her potential as one of the world's richest nations. She can be an influential and worthy voice in the Afro-Asian bloc. She can be a land where a warm, friendly, intelligent and sensitive people can live in peace and prosperity, enjoying their music and dancing, their plays and feasts, where laughter instead of shots fills the night. This is our fervent wish for Indonesia.